MAKING SENSE

Robert R. Potter

MAKING SENSE

exploring semantics and critical thinking

GLOBE BOOK COMPANY, INC.

New York—Chicago—Dallas

Robert R. Potter received his B.S. from the Columbia University School of General Studies and his M.A. and Ed.D. from Teachers College, Columbia University.

Dr. Potter has been a teacher of English in the New York City School System, a research associate for Project English at Hunter College, and a teacher of English at the Litchfield (Conn.) High School. He has held professorships at both the State University of New York and the University of Connecticut.

Dr. Potter is author of Globe's *Myths and Folk Tales Around the World,* *English Everywhere,* and *Americans Meet the Challenge* and the consulting editor of *American Folklore and Legends,* and the *Pathways to the World of English* series.

Edited by Thomas Maksym

Illustrations: Mel Erikson Sandy Huffaker Dana Rasmussen

Cover and text design: Art Ritter

Photo Acquisition: Adelaide Garvin Ungerland

Photo Credits

Biofeedback Instruments, Inc.: 39 Harry Lebelson: 51, 52
Cliche des Musees Nationaux: 34 Ron Partridge: 13
Rapho Guillumette Pictures: 101 San Diego Zoo: 46
Institute of General Semantics: 18 Sears, Roebuck, and Co.: 147
Mark Kane: cover; 30, 31, 70, 72 The New York Times: 187
Alfred Korzybski Estate: 141, 144

ISBN: 0-87065-263-X

41,879

CONTENTS

UNIT I

GENERAL SEMANTICS: MAPPING
THE TERRITORY

UNIT 2
LOOKING AND LABELING: EXAMINING OUR MENTAL MAPS

UNIT 3
A MENTAL TRAP: THE ALLNESS ATTITUDE

UNIT 4
TIME OUT FOR SILENCE: BODY ENGLISH, ETC.

UNIT 5
ANOTHER MENTAL TRAP: THE TWO-VALUED ORIENTATION

UNIT 6
LEVELS OF KNOWLEDGE: TWO KEY UNDERSTANDINGS

UNIT 7
LOOKING OUTWARD, LOOKING IN: PROPAGANDA AND PERSONALITY

UNIT 8
CRITICAL THINKING: SOME THOUGHTS ABOUT THOUGHT

The First Word:
Impressions and
Expectations

Making Sense is a book about words. It is about how we use words, and how words use us.

Look at that last sentence again. The first idea—how we use words—should cause no trouble. In English class, after all, we expect to study the effective use of our language. We learn to write clearly and correctly. We learn to speak smoothly and easily. We learn to read with comprehension and understanding. Most of us have been learning these skills for years.

The second idea—how words use us—may be a new one. But wait. Have you ever agreed with someone that "there are two sides to every question"? Have you ever tensed up when someone said an obscene word in the classroom? Have you ever thought that the goal of life was something called *happiness*? Has your mouth ever watered at the sound of something good to eat? Have you ever bought a product because of the clever words used in a commercial? If so, you've been used by words.

All of us are used by words many times every day—used and often abused. We need to understand just *how* this happens, and just *what* we can do about it. For not until people understand how words use them can they begin to use words to communicate effectively. And not until people communicate more effectively can they solve the many problems that face the world today.

Effective communication is rarely a simple two-way process. It involves a puzzling assortment of signals both within and without the individual human mind. It demands near-total awareness of all important factors in a given situation. For these reasons, *Making Sense* tries to break out of the familiar author-to-reader textbook pattern. The book contains sixteen sections entitled "Thinking It Through." These sections offer a variety of activities to help you explore your own world of words, find your own facts, and reach your own conclusions. Some of these exercises are easy, others difficult. Some will take a few minutes, others days. But don't worry—no one is expected to do them all. Your teacher may assign certain activities or give you a choice.

This book differs from most other English texts in other ways as well. It will ask you not only to learn certain facts but also to learn just *how* you learn. It will ask you to think about *how* you think. It will stress knowing what it *means* to know. Simply "knowing" what this book says will be a waste of time. You might get 100% on all quizzes and tests, yet still be a failure.

If all this is confusing . . . it is intended to be. Wait a few chapters; the making of sense often comes slowly. For now, just remember that the real subject of the book is not *words* at all. The real subject is *you*. And tell yourself that this is not really a book "to read." Instead, it is a book "to do."

UNIT I
general semantics: mapping the territory

Up to
Trouble:
the Words Around
Us

1

Once upon a time—about 700,000 years ago, according to some scientists—the first man spoke the first word. That day was a most historic one. Perhaps it would be more accurate to say that on that day some pre-human creature used a word symbol for the first time—*and thereby became man.* For it is the use of language that defines man. He walks upright, yes, and his thumb is opposite his four fingers. More to the point, however, he is *man the word-user.*

Just what the first word was, of course, we have no idea. But one thing is certain: man has been talking himself into trouble ever since. No other animal can make that statement.

The Uses of Words

The advantages of language are well known. Man differs from other animals in his ability to use *symbols* —words or other devices that stand for something else. A verbal symbol (a word) leads us to think about something in a way that no animal is able to think. Admittedly, some animals do seem to "know" certain words. But animals react to words not as symbols but as simple *signs* that either command an action or announce the presence of a person or thing. A dog, for instance, can learn to "sit," and he will drool at the mention of "supper." Only man, however, can use *symbols* as tools of thought and communication. He can

4

think about whether or not to "sit." He can invite someone to "supper" for a week from Thursday. The words in his head enable him to remember the past and plan for the future. Spoken words allow him to communicate his ideas and feelings to others. Written words help him reach people far away in time or in space.

The grammar of our language reveals the different uses we make of words. *Nouns* name persons, places, things, and abstract ideas. *Adjectives* and *adverbs* deal with qualities and quantities. *Verbs* show actions or states of being. *Prepositions* and *conjunctions* indicate relationships between other terms. In a very real sense, all speakers of English "know" this information. Look at this sentence: *A truck big will deliver the gravels.* Does it sound wrong to your ear? If so, you "know" grammar. In this sense, *to know* means "to know how to use," not "to know the labels for." Which meaning is more important?

The Misuse of Words

The disadvantages of language are not so well known. Strangely enough, this is largely because language is so obvious. We tend to take language for granted, as a part of the world into which we were born. Like the air we breathe, our world of words, or verbal environment, is always with us. But like the air also, the verbal environment can become polluted without our noticing it.

Today this verbal pollution is approaching crises levels. It fills us with false fears; it comforts us with false hopes. It makes us forget who we really are and what it means to be a human being. It warps our ability to think straight and to see the world as it really is:

- A New York mechanic advertises himself as an "automotive internist."
- An old Chevrolet is simply a used car, but an old Cadillac is described as "pre-owned."
- The failure of two human beings to "communicate meaningfully" is blamed on something called a "generation gap."
- While a "fascist tool" from the South trades insults with "pointy-headed intellectuals" from the North, a Vice President refers to all such doubters as "nattering nabobs of negativism."
- Since World War II, over 70,000 Americans have died on foreign battlefields. Yet the country has not officially been at "war."
- A State Department spokesman believes that bombing raids (woops!—"retaliatory airstrikes") should be "mainly violins" with occasional "touches of brass."
- An Army lieutenant convicted of unnecessary slaughter in Vietnam refers to killing innocent civilians as "wasting" them. Like a bit of food or a piece of paper!
- The psychologist E. L. Thorndike wrote that a frog, placed in a pan of cold water that is heated very, very slowly, will cook to death without jumping. Slow change is sometimes not noticed. Maybe we should take heed.

The Spreading Pollution

Fortunately for our ancestors, the pollution of language was never so bad as it is today. Probably the first men to walk the globe had a pretty easy time of it. Life was simple and vocabularies were small. People were concerned with *rocks* and *rabbits,* with *roots* and *rain.* A cave was simply a place to keep dry and warm, not an "environment for living," not an "expression of personality," not a "showcase for conspicuous consumption." People were "different" from one another, not "disadvantaged" or "maladjusted" or "achievement motivated." They thought of the moon and mushrooms, not of moon landings and mushroom-shaped clouds. "Inferiority complexes" were as unknown as the planet Pluto Furthermore, people lived in small groups. If anyone did go word-mad ("All power to the Soviets"; "Down with the Fascist pigs"; etc.), the disease couldn't spread to whole political groups and nations.

The invention of writing sent human communication leaping over the natural barriers of space and time. We might suppose that writing was first used to record the useful knowledge of one generation for the benefit of the next. But this was not usually the case. Instead, writing was at an early age associated with magic and religion. The WORD itself became powerful, and those who knew its secrets were masters of this power. In ancient Egypt, for instance, the knowledge of the written word was guarded for centuries by the religious leaders. The common people apparently never considered the use of writing for practical purposes. They thought of the written word as the guardian and guarantee of religious beliefs. Its mysteries were not theirs to question. Its secrets were shared only by a select few.

Eventually, as we know, the common people won access to the benefits of writing. The invention of the printing press about 1500, and the rising demand for education that followed, resulted in a huge increase in the number of people who could read

6

and write. But the process was a slow one, as we measure change today. (Even now, a third of the world's population can neither read nor write and are called "illiterate.") Pollution levels remained low. In colonial America, for instance, ninety per cent of the population lived on the farms and in the forests. People worked with their hands, with *things,* not with pencils and pens and typewriters and paper. Few people read a daily newspaper. The Bible was the only book in many homes. Radio and television were unknown. The flood of words had not yet started.

The Dam Breaks

Consider the situation today! Words are all around us, all the time. By the billions upon billions, they tumble from the airwaves, roar off printing presses, and pop out of computers. All of them important! All fighting for our attention! They fall in saturation bombing patterns from advertisers, from politicians, from a hundred other groups with SOMETHING TO SAY. The bombarded listener rises to the booming of his clock-radio and clicks off the TV only when he goes to sleep. At his job, he is more and more likely to deal with words, not things. And young people stay in school more and more years—again, dealing almost exclusively with words.

The statistics are sobering. Many high school students have spent *one solid year* of their lives just sitting in front of a TV set. (Is this true of you? It would have taken only 2.4 hours a day for the last ten years.) The average American is exposed to some 560 advertisements a day, although he really notices less than a hundred. Americans keep about 8,000 radio and TV stations in business and buy over 60,000,000 newspapers on the average day. They send 2.5 billion Christmas cards to each other and throw away more junk mail than the rest of the world receives. (See Thinking It Through 7, page 14, for question material.)

What's Happening?

Man has always adapted to his environment. In fact, he is the most adaptable animal known to science. It should come as no surprise that recent changes in the verbal environment are now producing changes in man. Understanding the nature of these changes is difficult only because *we are the persons who are being changed*. In another few centuries, "what's happening" right now will be understood much more clearly.

One result of these changes is that man is doing what most creatures do when bombarded with anything. He is throwing up defenses. Today no one can hope to listen to *all* the words that fall on his ears. No one can possibly read *all* the print that meets his eyes. To keep some sanity while under verbal attack, people are now tending to "shut out" certain kinds of experiences. They hide themselves in invisible shells that are hard to crack. As a result, their lives are calmer. But another result is that the forces trying to break these shells have to make ever stronger attacks. TV gets more and more violent. Poli-

tics becomes the art of publicity. Advertising grows louder and louder. Movies must shock. To blast through that shell—anything goes!

A second result of the word explosion is that too many people tend to assume that the verbal environment is the only environment. Such people put their faith in words alone, ignoring the facts that lie behind them. They walk around shielded by verbal smokescreens of their own making. Mr. White, for instance, believes that all poverty is the result of "inborn laziness" on the part of the poor. Miss Black, on the other hand, tells us that poverty is the result of "unforgiveable greed" on the part of the rich. Both people have created imaginary verbal worlds to their own liking, and nothing will ever convince them they're not 100 per cent right. They do not live in the world of real people—poor, rich, lazy, greedy.

Third, there is some evidence that the verbal revolution has increased the number of "ear-minded" people. Simply stated, the theory is this: Before radio and TV, people received most of their information from the printed page—newspapers,

8

magazines, books, etc. Without realizing it, such people form mental habits appropriate to readers. That is, they are "eye-minded." They control what they read and the speed at which it is to be read. If they want to reread and study something, they do. Since reading is not a group activity, they tend to avoid getting involved with others. They remain apart and slow to react. They think of themselves as logical and thoughtful people. When they do interact with the spoken word, they like a formal lecture (the reading of written words) better than a free-flowing panel discussion. They often tend to "talk like a book." The "ear-minded" people, on the other hand, were raised on radio and TV. They like the constant babble of human voices. They are quick to react, like involvement with others, and think of themselves as "complete" only when in a group. They learn by give-and-take, not separate study. If offered three books to take to a desert island, they'd trade them all for a transistor radio.

Lastly, changes in communication have contributed to what has been called the "revolution in rising expectations." Throughout history, people have wanted better lives for themselves and their children. In this respect, of course, we modern people are no different. The difference today is that what once were idle dreams have now become real hopes. People now *expect* the "quality education" they read about in the newspapers. They *expect* the "American standard of living" mirrored on a hundred TV shows. They *expect* their "fair share" of the "prosperous Amer-

ica" promised by political leaders. When people are denied their dreams, they often just shrug and say, "Oh, well." But deny them their expectations, and they organize, they protest, they march; they demand their "rights," file lawsuits, write angry letters, go on strike, shout, and further dirty the already polluted air. Does this sound a little like a description of our country today? (Thinking It Through 8, page 14.)

If *people* are really to talk to *people,* they will first have to learn to quiet down. They must understand how words work in the middle of a verbal revolution. They need to be aware of several types of pollutants that now cloud the verbal atmosphere. Let's start with three common forms of pollution: gobbledegook, verbal barking, and meaningless mumbo jumbo.

Gobbledegook

Temperature is a most important factor in determining the ecological optimum and limits of crop growth, and therefore the agricultural exploitation of our water and soil resources.

Like precipitation measurements, temperature is probably measured within the present accuracy of our knowledge of temperature effects on resource utilization, and provides us with a standard measurement which can be linked empirically or theoretically to specific environmental applications.

Is the message clear? Read the passage again. Did you learn anything? Probably not. The writer's language confuses more than it communicates. The meaning gets lost somewhere among the weighty words and winding sentences.

Several years ago Congressman Maury Maverick of Texas grew tired of reading this kind of English in government reports. (The gobbledegook temperature passage you just read is an actual sample.) Inventing the term GOBBLEDEGOOK for such language, he launched a crusade for plain English. Unfortunately, his campaign has failed—to achieve "true operational capacity," that is.

Gobbledegook, long common in law and government, is now spreading to other fields as well. Consider these examples.

From education:

Pupil placement and articulation procedures should incorporate informal teacher observations as well as scores on standard evaluative instruments.

Translation: Teachers should use both common sense and test scores when promoting kids.

From finance:

Fundamental and technical econometric projections indicate an intermediate term reduction in P-E ratios for glamors and cyclicals alike.

Translation: The stock market's due for a fall.

In fact, the masters of modern gobbledegook can confuse almost any common thought:

The utilization of a responsive program of preventative maintenance can minimize cost projections for long-range equipment programming.

Translation: A stitch in time saves nine.

Why do people use such twisted language? One reason, certainly, is that they fail to *think* in simple, clear, logical terms. Fuzzy thought produces fuzzy sentences. Also, gobbledegook often impresses the writer with his own importance. A minor official would rather write reports on "pupil transportation vehicles" than on "school busses." Then too, the clever use of gobbledegook enables a person to sound responsible while committing himself to nothing. "My department is presently developing a number of viable policy alternatives," says a high official speaking before TV cameras. Who could disagree? What does he really mean?

Verbal Barking

Another cause of verbal pollution is the use of words as weapons. Too often people use language to impress and frighten others, not to communicate. Although this kind of language usually has some meaning, it is best translated as "Woof! Woof! Woof!"

Some kinds of VERBAL BARKING do, in fact, sound very much like the language of dogs: *The last man that messed with me woke up nine days later in an oxygen tent.* Other kinds, however, are more subtle. Salesmen sometimes use hidden insults: *Well, fella, if you're going to feel right walking around in a pair of ten-dollar shoes. . . .* Sometimes they resort to threats: *Now tell me—are you going to approve this contract, or do I have to tear it up and walk out of here?* Other people won't give us even the time of day without a growl. Still others delight in making

10

us feel uncomfortable: *What's the matter? Didn't you ever see a cat get run over before?* Long or unfamiliar words often hide aggression or contempt. Some people use terms like *precatory, prehensile,* or *avuncular* to communicate not the meaning of the words themselves but this hidden meaning: *I'm better than you are —I use bigger words.* A college girl, for instance, might turn suddenly on her brother: "Your behavior's really puerile today!" She knows very well that *puerile* is lost on him. In fact, this is exactly why she uses it. He must either ask the meaning or silently grant her verbal superiority. Either way, he loses. (Thinking It Through 1 and 2, pages 11–12.)

Meaningless Mumbo Jumbo

Remember—Whizzo tires are the only radials made in America with *interstial steel interfaces.*
Try Britesmile today. New! With *dynachlorosyll!*
Vote Row B. The building blocks of *progress!*
And I mean to restore *freedom* to the American people.

MUMBO JUMBO is the kind of verbal voodoo that pollutes advertising and politics. Often it is nearly meaningless. For instance, not one person in a hundred really knows the meaning of *interstial steel interfaces.* Words like *dynachlorosyll* communicate a sense of novelty and glamor; they do not really communicate meanings.

Words like *progress* and *freedom,* on the other hand, do convey some meaning for most people. The trouble is that the terms can mean too much. They are impressive noises to which each individual attaches the meaning he happens to find most agreeable. Whose *progress? Progress* toward what?

Or take the term *freedom.* Miss A, an English teacher, insists on her "*freedom* to teach the best of modern literature." But Mrs. B, a concerned parent who dislikes four-letter words, demands the "*freedom* to approve my daughter's reading matter." Mrs. B also upholds a new "*freedom* of choice" plan in the city's schools, while Mr. C, on the other side of town, mourns the loss of "*freedom* of local school districts." Mr. C, a service station owner, also regrets the loss of his "*freedom* to run my own business in my own way," while Mr. D, a good union mechanic, feels proud that he has won the "*freedom* to bargain collectively." With more money, Mr. D will finally be able to buy that new hunting rifle, even though a new law now restricts his "*freedom* to hunt on state lands." Meanwhile Mr. E, who detests hunters, boasts of his new "*freedom* to walk in the woods without getting my head shot off."

There is one thing, however, that Miss A, Mrs. B, Mr. C, Mr. D, and Mr. E have in common. That is the habit of voting for Congressman Politico on election day. They love it when he says that he will "restore *freedom* to the American people."

With so many of the words around us causing trouble, it is often hard to make sense of the modern world. Yet make sense we must, if the world is ever to make sense in the future. "*Freedom* is everybody's job." (Thinking It Through 3 and 4, page 12.)

Reviewing the Key Points

1. In all your communicative experiences, try to remember the four results of the "verbal revolution":
   a. People feel threatened by the flood of words. They tend to ignore certain parts of the verbal environment. Outside their areas of interest, they often seem dull and indifferent.
   b. Too many people confuse the world of words in their own heads with the world that really exists.
   c. People seem to be growing more "ear-minded." They want to become more active and involved, less separated from "what's happening."
   d. Many people now expect the kind of life that former generations were content to dream about.
2. Recognize gobbledegook as the nonsense it is. Try to understand why others use it, and avoid its use yourself.
3. Watch out for verbal barking, especially the use of difficult words to frighten people.
4. Don't be impressed by meaningless mumbo jumbo. No matter how impressive it sounds, ask yourself what it *means* (if anything).

Getting It Straight

Number your paper from one to ten and then read each sentence below. If a sentence *agrees* with what this book has said, put an A next to the number for that sentence. If it *disagrees,* write a D. And if it *neither* agrees *nor* disagrees, write an N.

1. Man is best defined by his use of symbols.
2. In an important sense, all speakers of English "know" its grammar.
3. We have less verbal pollution today than at any time in history.
4. The first writing instruments were crude pieces of hard rock.
5. All television commercials should be banned.
6. Today's youth are probably more "eye-minded" than persons over sixty-five.
7. Gobbledegook sometimes impresses the writer with his own importance.
8. Long or difficult words can be used for purposes other than the communication of "meanings."
9. Some words are virtually "meaningless" because they can mean too much.
10. Semantics will shortly replace literature in most American high schools.

THINKING IT THROUGH: VERBAL POLLUTION

1. Good English as verbal barking

Educated English is the contemptuous, audible, universal sneer of the haves for the have-nots.

—LLOYD AND WARFEL, *American English in its Cultural Setting*

12   In your experience, just how true is this statement? How often do people use "good English" to make others feel inferior? Think of a time when you were the victim of this kind of verbal barking. (Everyone has been in such a situation, at one time or another.) Explain your feelings in a short paragraph and be prepared to discuss your experiences with the class.

2. Increasing your barking abilities

One way to become a good verbal barker is to listen carefully for the latest "in" words. Here are five words currently in style, along with their "in" definitions:

counter-productive—useless or bad

The teacher's efforts to quiet the class were *counter-productive.* (In certain sophisticated circles, you can even get away with "contraproductive.")

Establishment (usually capitalized)—any organized group one doesn't like

The (business, labor, religious, education, etc.) *Establishment* is ruining the country!

feedback—results

The new dress got positive *feedback* at the dance.

resources—money or talent

The city lacked the *resources* to put its human *resources* to best use.

viable—workable

We need *viable* alternatives to war.

Start dropping these words into conversations and observe the feedback. You, too, can become a charismatic concept person.

3. Instant eloquence

Copy the following formula on paper and insert the words indicated to suit the occasion. Any word can be used in any position.

Words: peace justice freedom truth honor wisdom

What we need today is not false_____but old-fashioned_____. For surely, there is no real_____without_____. And as our forefathers knew so well, the price of _____is a little_____.

4. How well do you read?

Read the following paragraph and fill in the blanks on your paper.

Typhus fever and typhoid fever are often confused. The former is caused by *Rickettsia prowazekii* and *R. mooseri* often transmitted by *Pediculus vestimenti.* The latter, however, is associated with *Salmonella* agents and produces customary anorexia.

1. Rickettsia_____is a cause of typhus fever.
2. Typhus fever is transmitted by_____
3. _____agents are associated with typhoid fever.
4. Typhoid fever produces_____
5. Aside from words, this reading has taught me almost_____

5. How well do you speak?

Read the following paragraph aloud as though you were a TV commentator speaking right after the burial of an assassinated President of the United States.

We all know what this means. The hearts and eyes and minds of millions have been right with these events every minute of this momentous occasion. And it will take a long time to recover from what's happened here today. The future? Time runs in cycles, a wise man once said. We can only wait . . . and see. But at this moment one thing is certain, ladies and gentlemen. Look at what's on that flagpole . . . long may it wave.

Now read the same paragraph in the excited tones of a baseball announcer whose home team has just won a World Series.

Although you read the same words, you would probably not say that you read the "same thing." Think about the real meaning of the passage. Where is it to be found—in the words themselves, in the minds of the persons who speak and hear the words, or in some combination of the two? Explain your answer in a short written paragraph to discuss with the class.

6. Your likes and dislikes

Nearly everyone nowadays seems to have an intense dislike for some part of the verbal environment. In certain cases this part is found personally offensive for some reason. In other cases, however, an area of verbal experience is excluded from a person's life simply because he doesn't have time for it. To include it in his circle of awareness would upset the life style he finds comfortable.

For instance, Ms. A may dislike television because watching it regularly would not leave time for her favorite political magazines. Mr. B dislikes all political magazines because his free time is devoted to sports. Mrs. C thinks sports are "silly"; she'd rather spend her leisure hours talking to friends. Mr.

14   D, who regards all idle conversation as "gossip," enjoys driving his new car through a busy area of colorful signs near his home. Mr. E, on the other hand, dislikes the signs. He often drives three miles out of his way to avoid passing through what he calls "the eyesore of the city." Think for a moment about a few people you know well. What portion of the verbal environment do they seem to dislike? Why?

What about your own likes and dislikes? Choose one area in each category (likes and dislikes) as the subject of a short written paragraph. Try to explain the personal satisfaction found in the area you favor. What would be lost if it were removed from your life? Also explain the reasons for your "pet hate." Do you find it sickening, or do you just not have time to get involved?

7. Television and you

Some people who grew up before television became common in the late 1940's worry about the effect of TV on younger people. A few statistics on television watching are given in this chapter. Another recent study shows that by the age of fourteen, the average person has watched 18,000 killings on TV. He has also seen about 300,000 commercials.

What do these statistics really mean? Some experts argue that because TV watching is not an active pastime, it produces inactive people. Further, the bloodshed on TV is said to lessen the horror of killing and warfare. Also, the life of pleasure mirrored by commercials is said to produce people whose lives center on all the things they own or want.

This reasoning may sound logical, but in some cases it doesn't square with the facts. The present "TV generation" seems to be both more active and more opposed to war than any generation in recent American history. Also, many young people have chosen the simple life, buying less and less as the commercials grow ever more numerous.

What about your own case? Pretend that you had never even seen a TV set. Do you think your values and behavior would be any different? What about your willingness to accept the commercial paradise? Try to reach definite conclusions on these questions before discussing them with your class.

8. Your changing self

Look back at the four types of changes caused by the new verbal environment (p. 7). Considering only yourself, which kind of change do you think is most significant? Which kind is the least important? Write a paragraph explaining why you are either a good or a bad example of one type of change.

To do this exercise, you will have to get out of your "shell" and become aware of yourself as a changing person. This is a hard job for anyone. If it is too difficult, try discussing the four changes with an older person, say a teacher with thirty years of classroom experience or one of your grandparents. Explain the changes so that the individual really understands them. Write a paragraph summarizing the person's reactions.

Down
to Reality:
What is
Semantics?

The first chapter in this book attempted to look into the cloudy verbal environment of our day. Gobbledegook and misleading mumbo jumbo are on the increase. Words are used as weapons, and the new technology of communication is changing man in ways he is just beginning to understand. That chapter concluded that making sense of this new verbal environment is a *must*.

This chapter offers a method of making sense: the study of semantics.

What Is Semantics?

According to the dictionary, semantics is the study of word meanings and their changes in time. For our purposes here, however, we need a more exact definition. SEMANTICS might be defined as the study of the relationships that exist among human beings, the word symbols they use, and the world they live in. We have said *might* be defined because almost any short definition is misleading, if not wrong. In fact, a good semantic principle to start with is this: Distrust short definitions. A mouse, after all, might be defined as a small gray mammal, and an elephant as a large one. Yet an elephant is certainly not just a large mouse!

Look at the definition of semantics in the form of a diagram (p. 16).

Notice that there are at least two

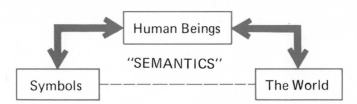

kinds of reactions possible for "human beings." First, we can react with symbols. We can add two and two, salute the flag, and read about goblins and magic castles. Secondly, we can react with the "real" things of the world. We can do dishes, shoot baskets, and take our fingers off a hot stove.

Now consider this question: With what did we react a moment ago when we defined *semantics?* With symbols, or with "reality"?

With symbols, of course. We did not touch anything or even point to any part of the "real" world. We simply defined one symbol, the word *semantics,* in terms of other symbols. If we wished to continue the process, we could define these other symbols in terms of still more symbols. The process could go on endlessly, *without once involving anything in the "real" world.* Is there no way to include "reality" in a definition?

The Operational Definition

Fortunately, there is a way to involve the "real" world in the definition of many terms. They can be defined *operationally.* An OPERATIONAL DEFINITION tells us *what to do* to experience the thing defined. We are referred to operations in the "real" world, not to still more symbols.

For example, an operational definition of *chemistry* might refer us to a certain room in a certain school building. There, most of what we saw, heard, touched, and smelled would be *chemistry.* An operational definition of *sycamore* would tell us where to find a certain kind of tree with a light, scaly bark. Looking at these trees and perhaps touching them, we would experience the "reality" that lies behind the term *sycamore.*

Look once again at the diagram, now expanded to illustrate the term *operational definition* (page 17).

When we ask for the definition of any word, what we really want is *to know* the meaning of that word. The first chapter considered two common uses of *to know:* "to know the name of" and "to know how to use." Now we have a third use: *to know* is "to have experienced."

This *experience* part of "knowing" is quite common. If a person says *I know Jane Alexander,* he means more than that he knows Jane's name, or that he knows how to "use" Jane. He means that he has had the experience of knowing Jane personally. Similarly, we say *I know New Orleans well,* or *I know Beethoven's Ninth Symphony.* Also, it should be clear that the great majority of the "definitions" we carry in our heads have been operationally acquired.

Children learn to define *shoe* by their experience with shoes. They learn to define *lie* by telling one—or perhaps by having the operational consequences performed on their backsides. A six-year-old may have learned as many as 15,000 words without having once cracked a dictionary.

The trouble is that as people grow older they tend to become more word-minded. They tend to think of definitions in terms of symbols, not in terms of experiences. This habit often leads to trouble. One young man, for instance, struggled through four years of college to get the grades needed for medical school. Finally he was admitted to the school of his choice. But he quit during the first term—working with corpses made him dizzy, nauseous, and then physically ill. He had never bothered to define *medicine* in operational terms.

An operational definition of *semantics* would refer us to the necessary experiences: Read this book and do most of the exercises. Practice the principles until they become second nature. Talk about semantics with friends who are interested. Read another good book on the subject every year for the next five years. Take college or adult-education courses offered in many cities. Only then will you really "know" the word *semantics*.

This is a tall order, of course. For true understanding we'll have to hold on, taking things one step at a time. A good place to start is with the man who made semantics such a popular study today, a man whose whole life was an operational definition of the term *semanticist*.

The Science of Sanity: Alfred Korzybski

Alfred Korzybski (1879–1950) was a Polish nobleman who spent the last half of his life in the United States. A brilliant engineer and mathematician, his interests ranged to many other fields. He was one of the best-read men of our century. Early in his productive life he turned his attention to the problems of mankind. As he put it, he turned from engineering to "human engineering." Stuart Chase offers this interesting description of the man in *Danger—Men Talking!* pages 134–135:

As a master of four or five languages —like many Poles—[Korzybski] learned to think and write in English, but he never lost his rich, rolling accent. When

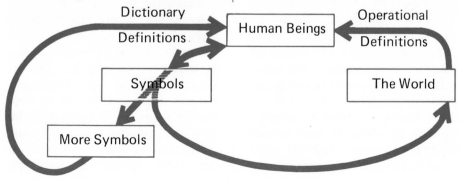

Dictionary Definitions · Human Beings · Operational Definitions · Symbols · The World · More Symbols

18

asked the difference between men and animals he would reply: "A quar-rter of an inch of cor-rtex."

When I knew him in the late 1930's, he was a heavy-set man, bald as a newel post, egotistical, opinionated, but fortunately with a sense of humor. He invariably wore a spotless khaki shirt without jacket, a costume that sometimes barred him from the tonier restaurants. When talking about abstract terms, like "liberty," he would thrust both arms into the air and wiggle the first two fingers of each hand. This was the "quote" sign, meaning "high order term, danger!"

World War I loosed its fury on the world when Korzybski was approaching the height of his powers. To him, it seemed as though civilization were going down the drain. Man's genius was being used to tear the world apart. Why was it that the same skills that had produced automobiles and bathtubs were now producing tanks and bombs? Why was it that man's great possession, his language, was being used for propaganda, not for poetry and plays? In short, why had, mankind made such a mess of things?

In the years following the war, Korzybski continued to study and think. He explained his theories in two important books, *Manhood of Humanity* (1921) and *Science and Sanity* (1933). In the first volume, he explored the idea of man as a "time-binding" creature. Plants, he reasoned, were capable of "binding" chemicals only; plants stayed in one place and maintained life by an ordered system of chemical reactions. Animals, he observed, were "space-binding" as well; animals could travel from place to place in search

of food, water, etc. Man, however, was the only "time-binding" form of life. Human beings could bind one age to another through the miracle of language. They could pass useful knowledge and customs from one generation to the next. And, unfortunately, they could also pass faulty knowledge and harmful customs. Language was both man's triumph and his tragedy. Korzybski insisted that the methods of modern science be used to re-examine man's language habits.

This huge task was attempted in *Science and Sanity,* the book in which Korzybski set forth the group of principles he termed GENERAL SEMANTICS. The word *general* was used to indicate that Korzybski's theories were not limited to language. Words are related to thought. Thought is related to behavior, and behavior is related to everything in the world around us. Korzybski wanted to stress the fact that his was a *general* system, a system that incorporated everything. Today, however, the term *semantics* is increasingly used alone to refer to the science founded by Korzybski.

Science and Sanity is a complex, far-reaching book. Portions of it still leave many readers confused. Yet Korzybski's basic ideas are not hard to understand. He noted that the "best" human beings, active and useful people who are at peace with others and with themselves, tend to be persons in close touch with "reality." Their observations of both their own inner lives and the events in the outside world tend to be accurate. Such people Korzybski termed "sane." "Insane" persons, he noted, are called that because they are out of touch with "reality"—at worst they hear "unreal" voices and see "unreal" sights. Man's basic trouble, Korzybski concluded, was that there were so few "sane" people in the world.

Did Korzybski believe that because most people were not "sane," they were "insane"? Certainly not. Obviously, most people don't hear voices or see the invisible. Yet at the same time, they are not as "sane" as they could be. Korzybski invented a new word to describe them: "un-sane."

Intensional and Extensional

Alfred Korzybski was convinced that all human beings lead a kind of double life. First, people live in an *internal* world of ideas, feelings, etc. The happenings in this world are patterns of events in the human nervous system. Secondly, people live in a world outside their skins, the external world of "reality." The happenings in this world are patterns of events best known to science.

The first world, the patterns of events inside our skins, Korzybski termed the INTENSIONAL area. The second, the patterns of events outside our skins, he called the EXTENSIONAL area (see diagram, p. 20).

Think for a moment about the two worlds in which you live. Look for instance at the outside of this book. The book *itself* is one thing; your mental image of it is quite another. The book itself exists as a pattern of events in the external world. Your mental image exists as a pattern of events inside your head. Now ask yourself this important question: Which area is more "real"? In which area is the "existence" of the book to be found? In the extensional area, of course. A book you can feel with your fingers is more "real" than the word *book* or your mental image of a *book*.

Thinking along these lines, Alfred Korzybski began to see what was wrong with the great number of "unsane" people: they confused intensional events with extensional "reality." He believed that too many people mistook the events in their own nervous systems for events in the outside world. In short, they suffered from an INTENSIONAL ORIENTATION.

In making this idea clear, Alfred Korzybski often used the terms *map* and *territory*. The words, ideas, and images in our heads, he said, are like maps of the territories that lie

INTENSIONAL PATTERNS   EXTENSIONAL PATTERNS

"cat"   An object we call "cat."

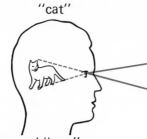

The word "cat."
The image of this cat.
Ideas about cats.
Feelings about cats.
Physical tensions aroused
by the cat: the urge to
pick it up, to kick it, etc.

A pattern of physical and
chemical events best
known to science.

outside our skins. If we were to go on a long trip with an old or incorrect map, we would become lost, frightened, angry, etc. Similarly, if the maps of words in our heads do not adequately represent the world of "reality," we become lost, frightened, angry, etc. Too many people, Korzbyski believed, live by inaccurate maps. Even worse, *they confuse their maps with the territories*. They think one *is* the other. They need to develop an EXTENSIONAL ORIENTATION. (Thinking It Through 2 and 3, pages 23–24.)

So What?

Alfred Korzybski's basic ideas are not too difficult. In fact, they are so simple that many people, on first reading them, are tempted to say:

"What's so amazing about all this? Honestly, I learned nothing new! Everyone knows that a lot of people don't know what's going on. I don't need someone named Alfred Korzybski to tell me to get in touch with reality."

Views like this tend to come from critics who have overlooked one of Korzybski's main points: There's a world of difference between "knowing" something and behaving as though we really knew it. Semantics is both a *what* to be learned and a *how* to be practiced. Look at the above quotation again. Obviously it's much easier to criticize "a lot of people" than it is to do something to help them. It's also easy to criticize the intensional orientations of others while assuming that one's own orientation is "real," "true," "scientific," etc. And such critics tend to think that what they mean by words like *reality* is exactly what Korzybski might mean. According to Korzybski, however, one reason our word maps get us in trouble is that the same word often "means" different things to different people. Consider the reactions of two people to just one common English word, *wolf*.

Mary Nettleton's "Map" for *Wolf*

1. A shaggy gray animal.
2. Mental image from old children's story, "The Three Little Pigs."
3. A "lone wolf."
4. Sly and scheming.
5. Silent and crafty.
6. About fifty pounds.
7. Kills animals for sport.
8. Lives in caves.

Hank Reed's "Map" for *Wolf*

1. A dark brown animal.
2. Mental image from movie, *Dr. Zhivago.*
3. An animal that travels in groups.
4. Crazy with hunger.
5. Howling and bold.
6. About twenty-five pounds.
7. Prefers a diet of human flesh.
8. Lives in woods.

So what?

So—Mary and Hank will always respond differently to the word *wolf.*

So—Mary and Hank will probably get nowhere in an argument about wolves.

So—Mary and Hank are both deceiving themselves about the kind of extensional wolf that exists in the real world. In truth, the wolf is a social, co-operative animal that almost never attacks man. Wolves mate for life, and the male wolves hlep bring up the playful pups. The older females are regarded as wise. Unlike humans, they do not kill for sport or use their minds to paint false pictures of other living things.

So—if Mary and Hank don't agree on a simple term like *wolf,* how can they be expected to agree on terms like *freedom, living wage, welfare state, obscene, oriental, foreigner, fair play,* etc.?

So—perhaps Mary and Hank need some semantic sanity. (Thinking It Through 1, page 23.)

What Semantics Is Not

First, semantics is not a cure-all for every one of the world's problems. The idea that man's language is the cause of *all* his problems is a foolish one.

Also, semantics is not simply a matter of agreeing on definitions. In discussions and arguments, we often hear that a certain point is "just a matter of semantics." It is important that people agree on the meanings of the terms they use. But it is equally important that these definitions square with "reality." Agreeing on falsehoods is an old human habit.

Moreover, semantics is more than a study of word meanings and how they change. Thirty years ago, the term "General Semantics" was usually used to refer to the wider study of humans, their symbols, and their world. Today the word *semantics* alone can refer to this larger area of meaning.

Finally, semantics is not constant fault-finding. Admittedly, semanticists tend to doubt the usefulness of many common words. They also distrust a number of our unconscious language habits. But it is not true that semanticists take a sneering attitude toward man's use of language. How could they? Their entire effort is based on a faith that man can understand and then master his handicaps. In fact, most semanticists have tolerant, accepting, and warm personalities.

22   Beware Beware Beware

DO NOT use terms like *intensional orientation* to criticize people you don't happen to agree with. If you're in a dispute, labeling your opponent seldom helps your cause. Labeling him with terms he doesn't understand is the kind of verbal barking that nearly always makes things worse. Even if you really think your opponent suffers from an intensional orientation, don't hurl the label in his face. Instead, ask yourself, "How can I help this person gain an extensional orientation?" This approach may not settle things right away, but it will do much more good in the long run.

DO NOT accept any theory as "true" just because it appears in this book. To do so would be to practice an intensional orientation, the very thing the book wants to avoid. Take each idea and apply it to your experience, past and present. If the idea makes sense to you, apply it to experiences in the future. If it doesn't make sense, reject it for the time being.

DO NOT assume that you're "too intelligent to bother with semantics" or that you're "not smart enough to understand all these ideas." Strangely enough, there seems to be little relationship between intelligence and semantic habits. A smart person is not necessarily extensionally orientated. Many highly intelligent people suffer from extremely intensional orientations to life. A "dull" farm worker is just as likely to be extensionally oriented as a "brilliant" college professor. Strange? Think about people you know.

DO NOT assume that everything in this book stems from Alfred Korzybski. *Making Sense* omits many of Korzybski's ideas and includes topics on which he laid little stress. Also, a few of Korzybski's views have been deliberately simplified to make them clear. (Thinking It Through 4–6, pages 24–25.)

Reviewing the Key Points

1. Remember that operational definitions are usually superior to dictionary definitions.
2. Remember the difference between an intensional orientation and an extensional orientation. The verbal maps in our heads *are not* the territories they are supposed to represent.
3. Remember that the same word often means quite different things to different people.
4. Remember that "semantic awareness" is not "intelligence."

Getting It Straight

A. On a piece of paper, match the "un-sane" items in Column A with their "sane" counterparts in Column B.

A	B
1. Totalitarian thought control	a) Operational definitions where advisable
2. Intensional orientation	
3. Complete faith in dictionaries	b) Democratic freedom of inquiry
4. Inaccurate maps	c) Accurate maps
5. "He's got to be right—look at his I.Q."	d) "As an extensionally oriented person, he's probably correct."
	e) Extensional awareness

B. 1. Be prepared to define (or identify) the following terms. If possible, do not look back at the chapter:

semantics	"un-sanity"
semanticist	intensional orientation
operational definition	extensional orientation
time-binding	Alfred Korzybski

2. For how many of the above terms would operational definitions be useful? Write operational definitions for at least two of them.

THINKING IT THROUGH: MENTAL MAPS

1. Your mental maps

It is said that no two people have mental maps that are exactly similar, even for such simple words as *book, table,* and *house.* When we use these common terms, however, our maps are usually enough alike to prevent misunderstandings. This is not the case with many other words.

Pick one of the following terms and jot down five or ten features of your mental map for that term (as was done for *wolf* on page 21). Be honest and specific.

lawyer	American Indian
college boy	President———(of the U.S.)

Through class discussion, compare your verbal map with those of other people. Where you find differences, discuss their possible causes. From what materials were the different maps constructed? Opinions of parents or friends? Ideas from the mass media? Something remembered from school or a book? Personal likes and dislikes often influence our maps, too. For instance, people who like the President will tend to judge him taller than will people who dislike him.

2. Maps around the world

You probably have a fairly complete mental map for the term *average American.* Think about this map for a moment. Now try to imagine the map

24   for *average American* in the mind of an "average" Frenchman, Mexican, Russian, or North Vietnamese. What are the differences? How do you account for them?

3. Stop! Look! and Listen!

Think of the last argument you tried to settle. Chances are you had noticed that the mental maps of one or both parties were inaccurate. (If not, the parties would have been "just fighting" to relieve their feelings about each other. You wouldn't have tried to settle things.) Describe in detail the real "territory" of the case. Also describe how the "maps" of the participants differed from the facts and from each other.

4. Sizzling maps; stark territories

The commercial production of mental maps is a billion dollar business in the United States. We call it advertising.

Advertising is an essential part of American life. Sometimes, however, the persons responsible for the ads seem to know more about slick maps than about the "product" territories the maps are supposed to represent. Sometimes too the "admen" provide glossy maps of a territory so large that the product becomes a small, vague part of some glorious Never-never Land. *They stress the map, not the product.* They want us to believe that in buying the product, we buy the map as well. Maps of fun-filled summer vacations sell automobile tires. Maps of social success sell deodorants.

Think in terms of "maps" (advertisements) and "territories" (products) as you look at the ads in a popular magazine. Try to find one ad that tells almost nothing about the territory and one ad that inaccurately describes the territory. Bring these to class.

5. The great map switch

Humor is often the result of a sudden, unexpected substitution of one map for another:

Joe: What should you say, "Five and seven *is* thirteen" or "Five and seven *are* thirteen"?

Moe: Er . . . a . . . "are"?

Joe: No, five and seven are twelve.

Obviously Moe has been tricked into using the wrong map. In response to Joe's question, Moe has pulled down a mental map called "good grammar." Joe, however, was using a map called "simple arithmetic."

Look at the two cartoons on the following page. In the first one, we see a psychiatrist listening to a wealthy patient. What makes the cartoon funny? The substitution of money for time catches us by surprise. To most people, a watch calls up a mental map labeled "elapsing time." But to the figure in the cartoon, the watch means "incoming money." Again, our maps have been switched. How are maps and territories involved in the second cartoon?

Drawing by Cobean; Copr. © 1952 The New Yorker Magazine, Inc.

Some characters in TV comedies are consistently funny because their maps are consistently wrong. From TV or magazines, collect some jokes or cartoons that depend on the map-territory relationship.

6. The maps of prejudice

Think of the most prejudiced person you know. Without naming this individual, write a paragraph describing the mental map that accompanies his or her pet hate: "Jews," "city people," "blacks," "Italians," "the rich," etc.

You should now have a rather complete "definition" of one term. Notice that the definition is in words only. In another paragraph, write an operational definition of the same term that might produce a more accurate map.

Drawing by F. B. Modell; Copr. © 1953 The New Yorker Magazine, Inc.

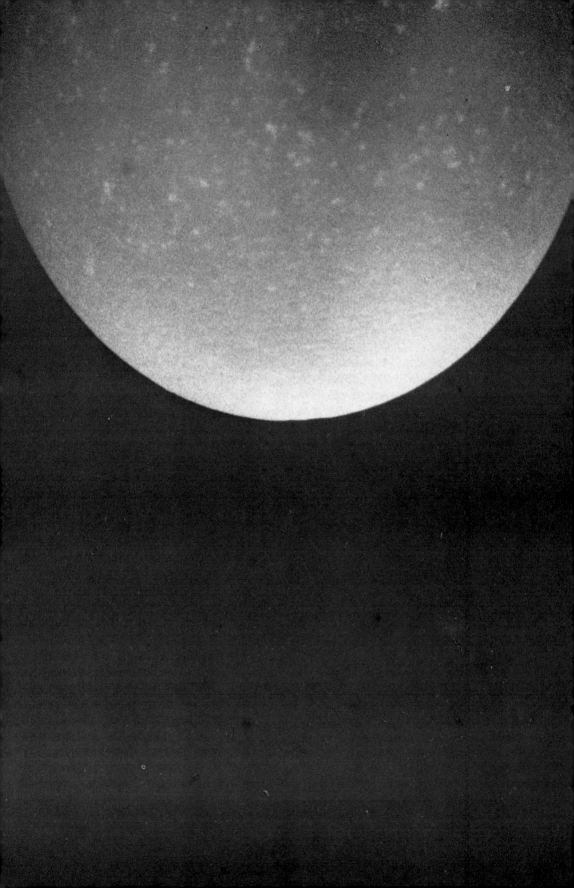

UNIT 2

looking and labeling: examining our mental maps

Perception and Projection

We have defined *semantics* as the study of the relationships that exist among human beings, the symbols they use, and the world they live in. This chapter's main focus will be on just one of these relationships, the connection between human beings and the world. It will start with PERCEPTION, the way we gain knowledge of the world through our five senses. It will answer such questions as these: "How do we know that grass is green?" "What do we mean when we say we *see* a thing?" "Just what is an *awful* smell?"

The Perils of Perception

At first thought, questions like these seem ridiculous. After all, it's obvious that "the world is full of a number of things"—candy wrappers, cabbages, bricks, doorknobs, roofing nails—more than could be named in a book of this size. We can see most of these things; some we can hear, touch, smell, or taste. Also, we can represent nearly all of them by words. We can look at the world around us and make statements like these:

"That book is blue."
"There is a chair."
"My aunt is ugly."
"The ruler is on top of the triangle."

As a matter of fact, however, not one of these four statements is nearly as "true" as it seems to be. Let's start with the first one.

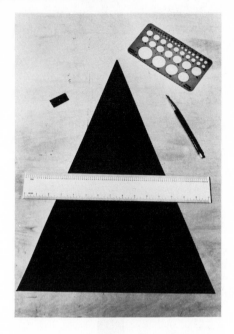

That book is blue. This sentence appears to mean that the quality we call "blue-ness" is a quality of the book. But how can we be sure of this? As the diagram makes clear, the blue color we see is not in the book itself but in the light reflected from it. We have a mental sensation of "blue-ness" because the cover of the book contains certain molecules that happen to reflect the color blue.

These molecules are not blue; they merely reflect the color blue when exposed to a source of light. In fact, *nothing* about the book *is* blue. What might happen if a lightbulb of a different color were used? Some color-blind men confuse shades of blue and green—what might happen if one of them looked at the book? The only thing that really *is* "blue" is the sensation in the mind of the person who says "blue." The slippery word *is* has tricked us into giving the quality of "blue-ness" to the book itself. In semantic terms, the sentence refers not to the book but to a pattern of events *inside* the human nervous system.

There is a chair. In a famous experiment at Princeton University, subjects were asked to look through a peephole and report what they saw. Bending forward and closing one eye, the average subject would squint through the hole and give the usual answer:

"Why, there's a chair there."

"Are you sure?"

"Of course. It's a chair."

"Take another look."

A second look, and even a third, produced the same response. Then the subject would be asked to step

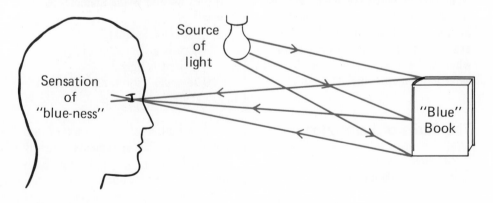

around a corner and take still another look through a peephole that gave a side view. What the subject saw was this: several pieces of wood balanced in the air with very fine wires. The object was not a chair at all; in fact, it was not even one object. Separate sticks of wood had been arranged to look like a chair from one point of view.

What was this experiment designed to prove? Simply this: that when we say "I see (something) *out there,*" what we really mean is "I see (something) *in here—in my head.*" Once again, we find that the process of seeing involves a pattern of events inside the human nervous system.

My aunt is ugly. Like the first two statements, this one includes the "little fooler," *is.* It also contains a strong "opinion-word," *ugly.* But who has ever seen "ugly" in the outside world? Words like this mirror our opinions, not the things we see. Other persons may think of the woman as *plain, firm-jawed,* or *honest-faced.* To some persons who know her well, she may even be *attractive.* And were she to live in another country or another time, she might be acclaimed *beautiful.* She *is* what she *is;* she *is not* "ugly."

The word *ugly,* like most opinion-words, tells us little about patterns of events in the outside world. When a person says "That book is good," what is he really telling us about, the book or his opinion? The book *is* what it *is;* it *is not* "good."

The ruler is on top of the triangle. Now you see it—now you don't! Look at the objects in a different arrangement (see photo at right).

What first appeared to be a large triangle with a ruler on top of it now seems to be a smaller triangle, a four-sided figure called a trapezoid, and a ruler, all lying on the same surface. In fact, the first picture (page 30) also showed a small triangle, a trapezoid, and a ruler, all on the same plane. The large triangle had no existence in the outside world. Like everything we perceive, it existed with certainty only in our heads.

These examples do not mean that we should distrust everything we see. If we want someone to hand us a blue book, we certainly don't have to say, "Please hand me that book that appears to me to reflect blue light." Neither do we have to kick every chair before we sit down in it. But we should remember that the little word *is* allows us—even forces us—to go on and on perceiving qual-

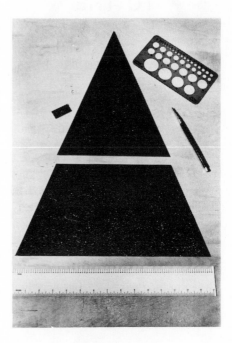

32 ities in the outside world *that simply are not there.* We should remember too that we can be fooled quite easily, and that people can perceive things differently.

The only world we know is the world in our heads. This means that each of us lives in his own world, a fact we forget only at great risk. To change an old saying, we shouldn't judge another person until we've lived for a while in the world inside his head. And this we can never do. (Thinking It Through 1 and 5, pages 38 and 40.)

Three Principles of Perception

1. We tend to see what we expect to see. In other words, when looking at new territories, we are inclined to see what the maps in our heads say will be there. For example, when you first turned the page and saw the words in the triangle, what did you see, "Keep to the right" or "Keep to the the right"? If you're like most people, you didn't notice the two *the's.*

This tendency to see with our maps, not our eyes, is a common one. All 50,000 people in the stands at a big baseball game will see the ball as a sphere, even though the human eye is not capable of such detailed depth perception at such a distance. The small white circle on the playing field appears spherical only because all the baseballs in our minds are spheres. In the same way, we see distant trees and telephone poles as round, and our mental maps add depth to a flat movie screen. If we expect to hear strange noises in the night, we will hear them. All in all, this habit of perceiving what we expect to perceive probably does more good than harm, although in rare instances it can be disastrous, as in the following case reported by Otto Klineberg:

In a series of studies Bean arrived at the conclusion that the frontal area of the brain was less well-developed in the Negro than in the White, and the posterior area better developed. He believed that this difference paralleled the "known fact" that the Negro is inferior in the higher intellectual functions and superior in those concerned with rhythm and sense perception. . . . It happened that these studies were carried out at Johns Hopkins University under the direction of Professor Mall, head of the Department of Anatomy. Mall was for some reason uncertain of Bean's results, and he repeated the whole study on the same collection of brains on which Bean had worked; he took the precaution, however, of comparing the brains without knowing in advance which were Negro and which were White. . . . Mall came to the conclusion that Bean's findings had no basis in fact. . . . There can be no doubt that Bean was sincere in his belief that he had observed these differences between the two groups of brains. It seems clear, however, that because of the expectation of finding signs of inferiority in the Negro, and because of his knowledge of the racial origin of the brains he was examining, he actually "saw" differences which did not exist.

2. We tend to see what suits our purposes at the time. For instance, suppose it's a hot July afternoon. You haven't had anything to drink since lunch. A soft drink sign on the street seems almost to leap out at you—the same sign that probably wouldn't be noticed on a cold December morning.

Also, since people have different purposes, they tend to perceive different things. Imagine yourself on the main street of a large city. It's eight o'clock on a Saturday night. Walking in front of you on the sidewalk are a policeman, a pickpocket, and a lonesome Marine. Look at the street a moment through the eyes of each of them. Is it really the same street? Hardly.

3. We tend to see what our background has prepared us to see. Suppose we could suddenly add a primitive New Guinea native to our Saturday night street scene. Chances are he'd see little except confusion —flashing lights, snarled traffic, and a bustle of people. But what would happen to us if we were suddenly put down on a wild New Guinea mountainside? We'd probably starve to death because we couldn't "see" the signs of food.

Now suppose one of the people on our city street is a very wealthy man. He has gone out to pay a charity call on a sick gardener. He walks into the gardener's house and looks around. "My goodness!" he says to himself. "All this filth! How can people live in such a pig sty?" He concludes that the gardener's wife must be one of the "lazy poor." The truth, however, could be that the wife doesn't clean up the dirt simply because *she doesn't see it*. She's always lived with a little dirt, and she won't be unhappy if she always does. But the rich man remains certain of his opinion. Like most opinionated people, he should have asked himself, "Does _____actually *see* things the way I do?"

That people see things in different ways has been proven many times by scientists. Perhaps they could have saved themselves the trouble, since people have realized this for many, many years. The poet William Blake wrote, "A fool sees not the same tree that a wise man sees." And remember the story by Hans Christian Andersen, "The Emperor's New Clothes"? It took a small child to cry out, "But look! He's not wearing any clothes at all!" (Thinking It Through 2 and 4, pages 38 and 40.)

Projection

Another children's story tells of the blind men and the elephant. Remember it? One of the blind men throws his arms around one of the elephant's massive legs. "The elephant is like a tree," he announces. Another feels the elephant's tail and says that the elephant is like a rope. "No!" cries a third, feeling the animal's trunk. "The elephant is like a

34 snake." A fourth runs his hands over the animal's side and states that the elephant is like a wall. Another grabs one of the sharp tusks and finds the elephant like a spear. Still another mistakes the elephant's ear for a large fan.

Think about this story in terms of maps and territories. The complete elephant is the territory. But the blind men, never having seen an elephant, have no "elephant maps" in their heads. Perceiving only part of the animal, they are forced to use the only maps they have: a tree, a rope, a snake, etc. Each of them, after examining only part of the territory, proclaims the whole territory to be like his particular map. In other words, he projects his map onto the territory. This process is called PROJECTION.

As the image on a movie film is projected on a screen, so our mental maps are constantly projected on the territories around us. Like the blind men studying the elephant, we can never know all the details of the world around us. Our maps are always incomplete. To complete the patterns, we project. All of us project, nearly all the time.

For instance, when we listen to the radio, we are very much like the blind men. We can't actually see the announcer or disk jockey who is the territory. But most people are unable to listen to a radio voice for very long before they begin to project a picture of what the speaker looks like. In a few weeks of steady listening, even his facial expressions become clear. And often, when we finally get to see "Woody the Wow" in person, we can't believe that the old familiar voice is coming out of such a strange face. "Why, that's just not Woody!" we exclaim.

In the same way, we project voices for people we have seen only in newspaper photographs. We look at snapshots of distant relatives and project their personalities. We look at famous works of art and project moods and meanings. Is Mona Lisa smiling or serious? The question has been argued for hundreds of years, ever since Leonardo da Vinci painted her. The answer, we now know, is that she's doing neither. The picture *is* what it *is*. One viewer projects a smile onto the canvas; another viewer does not.

Every human being projects his feelings, opinions, and shifting moods onto the territories about him. We've all had the experience of seeing a movie or TV show that left us shout-

ing for joy: "Simply great!" "Just un-believable!" "Marvelous!" As soon as possible, we see the same show again—but this time it's not nearly so good. Then we remember: the first experience happened on a day when we *felt* "simply great." Our *mood* was "just unbelievable." We had projected our "marvelous" feelings onto the show itself.

Sad feelings, too, can be projected on the territories around us. We can project our sadness so that everything is colored blue. If we're down in the dumps, no show can be "simply great." If we have a low opinion of someone, he can often do nothing right in our eyes. Most Americans, for instance, would give a good deal to have been present at Gettysburg when Abraham Lincoln delivered his famous Address. Yet here is what the newspaper *Patriot and Union* of nearby Harrisburg said about the event:

We pass over the silly remarks of the President. For the credit of the nation, we are willing that the veil of oblivion shall be dropped over them and that they shall no more be repeated or thought of.

Lincoln's "silly remarks," as we know, have by now been thoughtfully repeated millions of times. The Harrisburg newsman had done his readers a disservice. He had projected his opinion of Lincoln into the speech itself. (Thinking It Through 6–7, page 40, and 9, page 41.)

When Projections Go Astray

In what other ways can our tendency to project lead us astray?

First, we are often tempted to supply our own meanings for vague or confusing terms. Our language, good as it is, does not always make extensional meanings clear. For this reason, we are constantly forced to project our own meanings. What Mrs. A means by *freedom* is not what Mr. B means by *freedom,* and Miss C projects still a third meaning into the word. "Tomorrow I want *all* the homework passed in," Mr. D tells his class. The next day he is surprised when three students hand him all their old homework papers for the term. What he meant, he now explains, was that *all* the students should do their homework for tomorrow. A few minutes later he says he wants "the large dictionary kept on top of the bookcase." One student rises to bring him the dictionary. "No!" he protests. "I mean I want it kept on the bookcase at all times, not passed around the room!" "What *do* you mean?" the pupils ask —and they are right. *Habitual use of these four words (What do you mean?) is a key to clear understanding.*

Other projections that often cause trouble are those arising from our fears, suspicions, and worries. It seems to be human nature to project too many hostile meanings into the words and actions of others. To get back to our classroom, let's suppose that Mr. D has decided to use the period to discuss and return some original poems passed in a week earlier. He singles out Cathy for special praise. A sensitive girl, Cathy looks uncomfortable as her work is read aloud. When the bell rings, Mr. D returns the papers and the students

RUN

leave the room. Going through the door, Jill says to Cathy, "You're a real poet, yahnowet." Jill means the words as a sincere compliment; but Cathy, fearful of being thought too tender or "poetic," projects her own meaning into Jill's remark. To Cathy, Jill is being critical. Cathy is so upset that she accidentally lets her poem slide off a pile of books she's carrying. Mr. D, on hall duty, finds it a minute later. Projecting his worry that he has seriously offended Cathy by reading her poem aloud, he decides that she dropped the paper as a deliberate insult. Now he is upset —so upset that he decides to start his next class with a spot test on the homework reading. The class groans. The students can't understand the reason for the test; they have been doing the homework regularly. They know, and the whole school knows, that theirs is Mr. D's favorite class.

Deciding that the groaning is a bit too loud, he says, "Now don't take advantage of your special position." As he says this, however, he happens to be looking at Melodie, one of the five black members of the class. Always suspicious of prejudice in others, Melodie projects her private meaning into "your special position." To her, the words mean "your racial difference." Mr. D cannot understand it when she writes BLACK IS BEAUTIFUL in big letters across the top of her quiz paper.

Still another danger involving projection arises from our tendency to project our own mental maps into the heads of other people. This happens when we assume that others have maps like ours; that they perceive, think, and feel as we do. "Oh, Dionne won't mind lending me fifty cents," we say, assuming that Dionne feels as we do about lending money.

"Uncle Tony's going to love this jackknife for Christmas," we think, little troubling ourselves with Uncle Tony's mental map for the object "jackknife."

Uncle Tony's mental maps are not ours; but like ours, they are the result of the perceptions and projections of one individual. Each and every human being lives in an intensional world of his own, a private universe created out of his own experience in agreement with his own needs. This means that every person is a unique person. *No one who ever lived, in whatever country or in whatever age, lived in a world exactly like yours.* Without you, your world would not exist. And since it's your world, others should, to a certain extent, respect your rights of ownership—as you, hopefully, respect theirs (Thinking It Through 8 and 10, page 41.)

Reviewing the Key Points

1. Remember that our perceptions are affected by our expectations, our backgrounds, and our immediate purposes. The more these differ among people, the more their mental maps can be expected to differ.
2. Distrust the word *is*. No book *is* blue.
3. Don't project your own meanings into the words of others. Instead, ask "What do you mean?"
4. Remember that our feelings and emotions color the world we see. Don't be so suspicious that you project hostility everywhere.
5. Don't project your private mental maps into the minds of others.

Getting It Straight

A. Read the sentences below. If a sentence *agrees* with what the book has said, put an A next to the number of the sentence on your paper. If a sentence *disagrees,* write a D. If a sentence *neither* agrees *nor* disagrees, mark it with an N.

1. The word *is* can trick us into seeing qualities in the real world that actually exist only in our heads.
2. We should disbelieve everything we see.
3. We tend to see what we expect to see.
4. Our immediate purposes influence our perception.
5. Our backgrounds have little to do with perception.
6. Americans tend to project more than Europeans.
7. Both good and bad feelings can be projected into territories.
8. *What do you mean?* should be used more often.
9. People seldom go wrong in projecting hostile meanings into the words of others.
10. We should guard against projecting our own mental maps into the minds of others.

B. Write down the three principles of perception listed in the chapter. Give a good example of each. Then write down three types of projection and give an example of each.

THINKING IT THROUGH: THE EYES OF THE MIND

1. What do you see?

Look at the picture on page 39. Do you see a stylish young woman or an old hag? Look again till you see both figures. The young woman's chin is the old woman's nose.

2. Testing your perception

We know that a person's purposes affect his perception. If you have no purpose in perceiving something, you may not perceive it—*even though you have "seen" it thousands and thousands of times.* Test yourself on these questions:

1. Is a red stoplight above or below the green light?
2. President Franklin D. Roosevelt's likeness is one side of some dimes. What is on the other side?
3. If you were outside in the sun at 2:00 p.m. today, how long would your shadow be?
4. Put both hands down by your sides where you can't see them. Can you describe how the thumb differs in construction from the fingers? Now lift your left hand and examine the lines in the palm. Can you tell how these lines differ from those on the right palm? Look.
5. What color is the top bar on the American flag? Which has more stars, the top row or the second?

3. Outlawing "is"

Alfred Korzybski considered the little word *is* the most troublesome in the English language. He often used sentences with *is* to illustrate his point that the patterns of language (and thought) do not correspond to patterns of events in the outside world. He thought that constant attention to the danger of *is* could greatly improve our extensional orientation.

As we have learned, the word *is* often forces us to project upon the outside world qualities found only in our heads. No book *is* blue. Also, although we know that "the word is not the thing," the term *is* often makes it seem as though the word were the thing. "This," we say, "*is* a door." But the real thing —the door that we can see and touch—obviously *is not* the word *door*. We should be careful not to mentally substitute the equal sign (=) for the word *is*.

Examine each of the following sentences. First try to think "beyond language" to what the sentence really "means." Then try substituting the equal sign for *is*. Think about how the terms on one side of the sign differ from the terms on the other. Finally, substituting other words for *is*, take a piece of paper and rewrite the sentences to make them better copies of the outside world. You may need to use two or more sentences to explain some of the meanings adequately.

Sample: In the moonlight, the valley is black and white.

Rewritten: In the moonlight, the valley looks black and white.

1. Fluorine is a chemical element.
2. The third math problem is the hardest.
3. Seeing is believing.
4. Believing is seeing.
5. War is war.

Do you agree with Korzybski on the danger of *is?* Explain why or why not in a short paragraph.

4. Your mental vision

In the section on perception we read that we "see" with our minds as well as our eyes. Alfred Korzybski recommended that students of semantics prove this by a simple experiment. Have someone cut out several newspaper headlines of letters of equal size. Then tell this person to hold up one of these headlines and walk away from you. When you can no longer read it, tell your friend to stop. Experiment with different headlines until you find the point just beyond the distance at which you can make out the words. Then have your helper hold up a new headline. You will, of course, be unable to read it. But if the person tells you what the headline says, the letters will suddenly become clear. Your mind will have helped your eyes to see!

5. Yes or no?

Imagine an absolutely dark closet and a red apple. You put the apple in the closet and close the door tightly. Now answer this question:

Is the apple red?

Either *yes* or *no* is a satisfactory answer, depending on what we think the question really means. Write a short paragraph giving both your answer and your interpretation of the question.

6. Test your projections

Ink blots are often used to discover the ways different people are inclined to project. The blots themselves are pictures of nothing (except, we might say, of ink blots). But different people can often "see" different things in them. Nature lovers will see butterflies and birds. Fearful people will see goblins and monsters. Imaginative people will see the faces of clowns, etc.

Someone in the class may be asked to make some ink blots for this purpose. (India ink on hard-surfaced paper works best.) Then, your teacher might hang about ten of the best ones in the front of the room for a week or so. Look at them often to "see" what you "see." Finally, discuss your projections with other members of the class. What can you say about the person who insists he sees nothing but ink blots?

7. Of what is your dream?

People who project to an abnormal degree are called insane. Such persons are able to project people and things into their environments, then to believe that these people and things really exist. They can project the sound of the human voice so that it really seems to be coming from the outside world.

Actually, all of us have abilities that are strangely similar. We dream part of every night—that is, we witness happenings which are nothing but our projections. Since these nightly projections are so much a part of our lives, it is odd that we know so little about them. For instance, do you dream in color? Do you really "hear voices" in dreams, or do you somehow know what other people are saying without actually "hearing" them? Do the events in dreams happen faster or slower than those in real life? Do you ever "see" yourself in a dream? Do you ever have a dream in which you are not involved?

Make a note now to do some research on these questions. Remember them the next time you find yourself drifting into and out of a light dreamy sleep. Then discuss your findings with other members of the class. You will probably be surprised at how much people's dreams (and projections!) differ.

8. Hostility everywhere!

We all know people who are too quick to take offense. These suspicious persons see hostility in the most innocent remark and in the slightest action. As a learning game, pretend you are one of these people for half a day. The one rule of the game is this: try to interpret *every* remark and *every* action as a threat. For instance, if someone says, "Nice day, isn't it?" tell yourself, "She thinks I'm too stupid to discuss anything but the weather," or "Her being so nice means she wants something from me." Don't say these things aloud; continue to "act yourself." At the end of the time you'll be exhausted, but you will have learned what makes some people tick!

When the experiment is over, discuss your experiences with the class. Some persons will have had a much easier time of it than others. Did anyone in the class have trouble finding remarks to misinterpret? Was anyone successful in misinterpreting everything that was said?

9. Swinger for a day

Try to spend a day living by the mental maps of someone else. The person should be someone whom you know quite well but who is different from you. It can be anyone—a teacher, a clergyman, a parent, another student, etc. Don't just pretend to be the person or act the part, but really try to *be* the person inside. This is impossible, of course, since our intensional worlds are essentially private. You can go a long way, however. Start by preparing quietly for at least an hour. Fill in the details on at least ten maps you think the person lives by. Then *be* a swinger! *Be* a rabbi! *Be* a scholar! *Be* a bum! See everything through the other person's eyes, and try to react with his reactions. Write a short report of your experiences to share with the class.

10. Polishing the Golden Rule

The semanticist tries to show how faulty language habits result in misunderstandings, hurt feelings, and confusions of all sorts. A rather common language habit is repetition of the Golden Rule—and not even this escapes the semanticist's inquiry. Explain what a semanticist might find wrong with the Golden Rule: "Do unto others as you would have others do unto you." Try to rewrite it in the light of modern semantic knowledge. You may need to look back at the last two paragraphs of this chapter.

Words, Words, Words: How Many of What?

Words are rascals. This is the rule of semantics. And here are some of the reasons:

- We don't know exactly what words are.
- We have only a rough idea of how many there are.
- Most of the time, we're unaware of how they affect our lives.
- Words seem to have "meanings," and in a sense they do. But in another sense, only people have "meanings," which they express by words.
- The "meaning" of a word is not entirely contained in the word itself. Meaning depends on context, on when and where is the word used.
- Even to talk about words—takes words. But let's go on trying.

The Number of Words

According to one method of counting words, there are about 600,000 of them in the English language. They range in length from *a* to *pneumonoultramicroscopicsilicovolcanokoniosis,** and the list is added to at the rate of almost one a day. No one person knows all the words in the language. The first grader may know 5,000; the good high school student, 50,000. And no matter how many words a person knows, he uses most of them only rarely. In everyday life, the most common 2,000 words account for ninety per cent of the total number of words used.

* A disease of the lung caused by a kind of rock dust.

Figures like these are meaningless, however, unless we first agree on just what a "word" is. Just what makes one word "different" from another? If we add the common suffixes (*s, ed, ing,* etc.) to the list of English words, it grows to well over a million. Is *eats* a "different word" from *eat?* It simply depends on how we define *word.* And if we consider that many common words have several different meanings, the list grows even longer. After all, cattle that are raised on a *range* in New Mexico are cooked on a *range* in a Kansas City apartment. *The American College Dictionary* lists 104 meanings for the little word *run.* Does this mean that *run* should be counted as one word or as 104 words? (See diagram, page 44.)

Furthermore, even if questions like these could be settled, more questions would remain. For instance, there is the question of the many two-word combinations in English (*turn on, tear down,* etc.). Since these combinations are often thought of as single words, shouldn't they be counted as words? Look at what can be done with the little word *put:*

1. The teacher finally *put across* the hard idea.
2. Mr. Ives *put away* some money for a rainy day.
3. The British *put down* the rebellion.
4. The Prime Minister *put down* his thoughts on paper.
5. The ship *put in* to harbor for the night.
6. She *put off* her trip to the dentist.
7. Clara didn't mean to *put off* George.
8. Don't *put on* such a sad face!
9. Dolly *put out* the fire.
10. Why are you so *put out* about it?
11. The pup was *put out* of the house for chewing a shoe.
12. The insurance salesman *put over* the whole plan.
13. The President *put through* his whole program in the first session of Congress.
14. *Put up* or shut up!
15. They should *put up* a monument to your ignorance!
16. Mrs. Farmer *put up* some beans last summer.
17. If Mr. Piker would only *put up* some money!
18. Then Mrs. Piker wouldn't have to *put up* her own hair.
19. They *put up* at a motel just out of town.
20. I won't *put up* with this any longer!

Now, *put to* yourself this question: if *extinguish* is a word which means *put out,* why isn't *put out* a word? We think of *put out* as a single word, and we pronounce it as a word. We only write it as two words.

Now we've arrived at the really hard problem. Actually, the way we think of words, as well as the way we pronounce them, often differs greatly from the way we write them. Most people think of both *bedroom* and *living room* as single words, yet the first term is written as one word, the second as two. Most Americans pronounce, think of, and even write *alot* and *boyfriend* as single words, yet dictionaries prefer *a lot* and *boy friend.* If we forget about writing and listen to the way people speak English in their various styles, the question of what a word is becomes very complicated! Read the following sample of "English as she is spoke":

rum·bly (rŭm′blĭ), *adj.* **1.** rumbling. **2.** attended with, making, or causing a rumbling sound.

Ru·me·li·a (rōō mē′lĭ ə), *n.* **1.** a division of the former Turkish Empire, in the Balkan Peninsula: it included Albania, Macedonia, and Thrace. **2. Eastern,** a former autonomous province within this division, which later became S Bulgaria. Also, **Roumelia.**

ru·men (rōō′mĕn), *n.*, *pl.* **-mina** (-mə nə). **1.** the first stomach of ruminating animals, lying next to the reticulum. See diag. under **ruminant. 2.** the cud of a ruminant. [t. L: throat, gullet]

Rum·ford (rŭm′fərd), *n.* **Count.** See **Thompson, Benjamin.**

ru·mi·nant (rōō′mə nənt), *n.* **1.** any animal of the artiodactyl suborder or division, *Ruminantia,* which comprises the various "cloven-hoofed" and cud-chewing quadrupeds: cattle, bison, buffalo, sheep, goats, chamois, deer, antelopes, giraffes, camels, chevrotains, etc. —*adj.* **2.** ruminating; chewing the cud. **3.** given to or characterized by meditation; meditative. [t. L: s. *rūmin-ans,* ppr., ruminating]

Ruminant stomach
A. Duodenum; B. Abomasum; C. Omasum; D. Esophagus; E. Reticulum; F. Rumen

ru·mi·nate (rōō′mə nāt′), *v.,* **-nated, -nating.** —*v.i.* **1.** to chew the cud, as a ruminant. **2.** to meditate or muse; ponder. —*v.t.* **3.** to chew again. **4.** to meditate on; ponder. [t. L: m.s. *rūminātus,* pp.] —**ru′mi·nat′ing·ly,** *adv.* —**ru′mi·na′tion,** *n.* —**ru′mi·na′tive,** *adj.* —**ru′mi·na′tor,** *n.*

rum·mage (rŭm′ĭj), *v.,* **-maged, -maging,** *n.* —*v.t.* **1.** to search thoroughly or actively through (a place, receptacle, etc.), esp. by moving about, turning over, or looking through contents. **2.** to bring or fetch (*out* or *up*) by searching. —*v.i.* **3.** to search actively, as in a place or receptacle, or among contents, etc. —*n.* **4.** miscellaneous articles; odds and ends. **5.** a rummaging search. [ult. f. (older) F: m. *arrumage,* n., der. *arrumer* stow goods in hold of ship; orig. uncert.] —**rum′-mag·er,** *n.*

rummage sale, a sale of unclaimed goods at a wharf or warehouse, or of odds and ends of merchandise at a shop, of miscellaneous articles (old or new) contributed to raise money for charity, etc.

rum·mer (rŭm′ər), *n.* a large drinking glass or cup. [cf. Flem. *rummer,* G *romer;* orig. uncert.]

rum·my[1] (rŭm′ĭ), *n.* a card game in which the object is to match cards into sets and sequences. [orig. uncert.]

rum·my[2] (rŭm′ĭ), *n., pl.* **-mies. 1.** *Slang.* a drunkard. —*adj.* **2.** of or like rum. [f. RUM[1] + -Y[1]]

rum·my[3] (rŭm′ĭ), *adj.,* **-mier, -miest.** *Chiefly Brit. Slang.* odd; queer. [f. RUM[2] + -Y[1]]

ru·mor (rōō′mər), *n.* **1.** a story or statement in general circulation without confirmation or certainty as to facts. **2.** unconfirmed gossip. —*v.t.* **3.** to circulate, report, or assert by a rumor. [ME *rumour,* t. OF, t. L: m. *rūmor*] —**Syn. 1.** talk, gossip, hearsay.

rump (rŭmp), *n.* **1.** the hinder part of the body of an animal. **2.** *Chiefly Brit.* a cut of beef from this part of the animal, behind the loin and above the round. **3.** the buttocks. **4.** the last and unimportant or inferior part; fag end. **5. the Rump,** *Eng. Hist.* the remnant of the Long Parliament established by the expulsion of the Presbyterian members in 1648, dismissed by force in 1653, and restored briefly in 1659–60. [ME *rumpe,* t. Scand.; cf. Dan. *rumpe* rump, G *rumpf* trunk]

Rum·pel·stilts·kin (rŭm′pəl stĭlt′skĭn), *n.* the dwarf in German legend who agreed to spin great quantities of flax required by the king of his new bride. The girl-bride in return agreed to go off with the dwarf if she should not guess his name within a month. At the last moment she succeeded and he vanished.

rum·ple (rŭm′pəl), *v.,* **-pled, -pling,** *n.* —*v.t.* **1.** to draw or crush into wrinkles; crumple: *a rumpled sheet of paper.* **2.** to ruffle; tousle (often fol. by *up*). —*v.i.* **3.** to become wrinkled or crumpled. —*n.* **4.** a wrinkle or irregular fold; crease. [t. MD: m. *rompel* n., or t. MLG: m. *rumpel*]

rum·pus (rŭm′pəs), *n.* *Colloq.* **1.** disturbing noise; uproar. **2.** a noisy or violent disturbance or commotion.

rum·run·ner (rŭm′rŭn′ər), *n.* *U.S. Colloq.* a person or a ship engaged in smuggling liquor.

Rum·sey (rŭm′zĭ), *n.* **James,** 1743–92, U.S. inventor (of steam-driven boat).

run (rŭn), *v.,* **ran, run, running,** *n., adj.* —*v.i.* **1.** to move the legs quickly, so as to go more rapidly than in walking (in bipedal locomotion, so that for an instant in each step neither foot is on the ground). **2.** to move swiftly by other means of locomotion than legs. **3.** to move swiftly, as a vessel, vehicle, etc. **4.** to make off quickly; take to flight. **5.** to make a rapid journey for a short stay at a place: *to run up to New York.* **6.** *Racing.* **a.** to take part in a race. **b.** to finish a race in a certain (numerical) position: *he ran second.* **7.** to stand as a candidate for election. **8.** to migrate, as fish: *to run huge shoals.* **9.** to migrate upstream or inshore from deep water to spawn. **10.** to sail or be driven (ashore, aground, etc.), as a vessel or those on board. **11.** to ply between places, as a vessel or conveyance. **12.** to go about without restraint (often fol. by *about*): *to run about at will.* **13.** to move easily, freely, or smoothly: *a rope runs in a pulley.* **14.** to flow, as a liquid. **15.** to flow along, esp. strongly, as a stream, the sea, etc.: *with a strong tide running.* **16.** to melt and flow, as varnish, etc. **17.** to spread on being applied to a surface, as a liquid. **18.** to spread over a material when exposed to moisture: *the colors in a fabric run.* **19.** to flow, stream, or be wet with a liquid. **20.** to discharge, or give passage to, a liquid or fluid. **21.** to overflow or leak, as a vessel. **22.** to creep, trail, or climb, as vines, etc. **23.** to pass quickly: *a thought ran through his mind.* **24.** to continue in or return to the mind persistently: *a tune running through one's head.* **25.** to come undone or unravel, as stitches or a fabric. **26.** to be in operation, or continue operating, as machinery. **27.** *Com.* **a.** to accumulate, follow, or become payable in due course, as interest on a debt. **b.** to make many withdrawals in rapid succession. **28.** *Law.* **a.** to have legal force or effect, as a writ. **b.** to continue to operate. **c.** to go along with: *the easement runs with the land.* **29.** to pass or go by, as time. **30.** to keep the stage or be played continuously, as a play. **31.** to go or proceed: *so the story runs.* **32.** to extend or stretch: *shelves ran round the walls.* **33.** to have a specified character, quality, form, etc. **34.** to be of a certain average size, number, etc.: *potatoes running large.* **35.** to pass into a certain state or condition; get; become: *to run into debt.* —*v.t.* **36.** to run along (a way, path, etc.). **37.** to traverse in running: *to run the streets.* **38.** to perform by or as by running: *to run a race.* **39.** to contend with in a race. **40.** to enter (a horse, etc.) in a race. **41.** to run or get past or through: *to run a blockade.* **42.** to bring into a certain state by running: *to run oneself out of breath.* **43.** to pursue, or hunt (game, etc.). **44.** to cause to ply between places, as a vessel or conveyance. **45.** to convey or transport, as in a vessel or vehicle. **46.** to cause to pass quickly: *to run one's eyes over a letter.* **47.** to keep operating or going, as a machine. **48.** to expose oneself to, or be exposed to (a chance, risk, etc.). **49.** to put up (a person) as a candidate for election. **50.** to sew (fabric) by passing the needle in and out repeatedly with even stitches in a line. **51.** (in some games, as billiards) to complete a series of successful strokes, shots, etc. **52.** to bring, lead, or force into some state, action, etc.: *to run oneself into debt.* **53.** to cause (a liquid) to flow. **54.** to give forth or flow with (a liquid). **55.** to pour forth or discharge. **56.** to cause to move easily, freely, or smoothly: *to run up a sail.* **57.** to pierce or stab (fol. by *through*). **58.** to drive, force, or thrust. **59.** to conduct, as a business, an establishment, etc. **60.** to extend (a thing), as in a particular direction: *to run a partition across a room.* **61.** to draw or trace, as a line. **62.** to melt, fuse, or smelt, as ore. **63.** to smuggle (contraband goods). —*n.* **64.** act or spell of running, as in hastening to some point or in rapid flight: *to be on the run.* **65.** a running pace. **66.** act or spell of moving rapidly, as in sailing, moving on wheels, etc. **67.** the distance covered. **68.** a rapid journey for a short stay at a place: *to take a run up to New York.* **69.** a spell or period of causing something, as a machine, to run or continue operating. **70.** the amount of anything produced in such a period. **71.** a line or place in knitted work where a series of stitches have slipped out or come undone. **72.** a continuous course of performances, as of a play. **73.** onward movement, progress, course, etc. **74.** the direction of something: *the run of the grain of wood.* **75.** the particular course or tendency of something: *the run of events.* **76.** freedom to range over, go through, or use: *to have the run of the house.* **77.** any rapid or easy course or progress. **78.** a continuous course of some condition of affairs, etc.: *a run of bad luck.* **79.** a continuous extent of something, as a vein of ore. **80.** a continuous series of something. **81.** a set of things in regular order, as a sequence at cards. **82.** any continued or extensive demand, call, or the like. **83.** a spell of being in demand or favor with the public. **84.** a spell of causing something liquid to run or flow. **85.** the amount which runs. **86.** a flow or rush of water, etc. **87.** a small stream; brook; rivulet. **88.** a kind or class, as of goods. **89.** the ordinary or average kind. **90.** that in or on which something runs or may run. **91.** *Chiefly Brit.* an enclosure within which domestic animals may range about: *a chicken run.* **92.** a way, track, or the like, along which something runs or moves. **93.** a trough or pipe through which water, etc., runs. **94.** the movement of a number of fish upstream or inshore from deep water. **95.** large numbers of fish in motion, esp. inshore from deep water or up a river for spawning. **96.** a number of animals moving together. **97.** *Music.* a rapid succession of tones; a roulade. **98.** a series of sudden and urgent demands, as on a bank, for payment. **99.** a series of successful shots, strokes, or the like, in a game. **100.** *Baseball.* the score unit, made by successfully running around all the bases and reaching the home plate. **101.** *Cricket.* the score unit, made by the successful running of both batsmen from one wicket to the other. **102.** *Naut.* the extreme after part of a ship's bottom. —*adj.* **103.** melted or liquefied. **104.** poured in a melted state; run into and cast in a mold. [ME *rinne(n),* OE *rinnan,* c. G *rinnen,* Icel. *rinna.* form *run* orig. pp., later extended to present tense]

In recent years linguistic scientists have tried hard to get all the world's languages down on paper. Many of these languages belong to small primitives tribes and exist only in spoken form. The linguist's task is not an easy one. He must first listen carefully to the sounds of the strange language, recording them in a kind of professional shorthand. Then he has to listen for sound combinations, or words, and at the same time try to observe what the speakers are doing or thinking. Slowly he begins to assemble a glossary of the new language, a listing of the sound combinations, or words, and their meanings.

Imagine you are such a linguist working on the language of Americans. Suppose that you had absolutely no knowledge of written English. One of your stops is a corridor right outside a school lunchroom. Two natives approach each other. Both appear to be adolescent males. What would you make of this odd language?

Native 1: Hwarya, Sam. Di-jeet yet?
Native 2: Naw. Ain't gonna.
    1: Wassa matta? Sicker sumpin?
    2: Jeez! Gimmea break.
    1: Doncha wanna eacher lunch?
    2: I shoulda stoodin bed.
    1: Jeet breakfast?
    2: Baco neggs.
    1: Yin trouble?
    2: Gwon! You're worsn molady.
    1: Hwatcher nex class?
    2: Mercanlit. Lassa Mohicans.
    1: Jeez. Gonna gwin?
    2: Gotta. Gotcher watch?
    1: Ten twon.
    2: Seeya.
    1: Ya.

Language and Thought

How many words are in the English language? The answer to this question depends on how we define *word*. This fact, rather than the actual number of words that might be counted, is of interest to the semanticist. He does not really care to make long lists of words and definitions. This is the task of the LEXICOGRAPHER (leks-uh-KOG-ruh-fur).

Neither does the semanticist care particularly about the fine points of grammar. *That book is blue,* after all, would strike a GRAMMARIAN (gruh-MARE-ee-un) as a perfectly acceptable sentence. Instead, the semanticist is interested in how people use words, and how words use people. He's interested in discovering how language habits affect our thought and action. He's interested in the way words get confused with the things they are supposed to stand for.

The *name* of a thing is not really a "part" of that thing. A name is simply a label that speakers of one language apply to a certain portion of their extensional world. Speakers of another language probably have a different name for the same "thing." Speakers of still other languages may have no single name for it, or they may have several names for different types of the "thing." There is no necessary relationship between the "things" of the world and the words we use to name them. Names are not things. Maps are not territories. Intensional patterns are not extensional patterns.

Today the idea that *words* are not *things* seems obvious. We laugh at the story of the little girl who said, "Pigs are called *pigs* because they are so dirty." The sentence amuses us because we know in our own minds that there is no logical connection between the word p-i-g and dirt. But the idea was not always

THE ANIMALS

They do not live in the world,
Are not in time and space.
From birth to death hurled
No word do they have, not one
To plant a foot upon,
Were never in any place.

For with names the world was called
Out of the empty air,
With names was built and walled,
Line and circle and square,
Dust and emerald;
Snatched from deceiving death
By the articulate breath.

But these have never trod
Twice the familiar track,
Never never turned back
Into the memoried day.
All is new and near
In the unchanging Here
Of the fifth great day of God,
That shall remain the same,
Never shall pass away.

On the sixth day we came.

—EDWIN MUIR

so clear. The wise men of ancient Greece used to argue whether or not the name of a thing were one with its "essence"—that is, a part of the thing. The ancient Hebrews considered God's name so much a part of Him that it was not supposed to be spoken here on earth. In medieval Europe the *name* of God was used as proof of the *existence* of God (if the name and idea existed, therefore the "thing" existed). And even nowadays, the individual who buys a Plymouth *Road Runner* or a Ford *Mustang* feels that the name is somehow an essential part of the new car. Although the car would remain the same "thing," the person would probably not buy it if it were named the Plymouth *Turtle* or the Ford *Flounder*.

Our tendency to confuse words with things is the result of our having grown up confusing the intensional and extensional worlds. As we learned about one, we learned about the other. At birth all was confusion. Our unfocused eyes saw only a meaningless blur. Then, slowly, we began to organize the world around us, to distinguish particular objects. First, probably, came the pattern of features on our mother's face. At four months we were fascinated with our hands. Then we discovered our feet, a rattle, the red spots on a blanket, etc. Before our first birthday we became vaguely aware that all these things had names.

This was the breakthrough! Those small pudgy objects we could wave in the air were no longer just two of the many unnamed things that often appeared before our eyes. Instead, they were *hands*—like Mommy's, like Daddy's, like Auntie Peg's. Why, everyone in the house had hands! (Everyone except Fido, that is. His were called *paws,* even though they were as small and as clumsy as ours. That meant they were different kinds of things; they were called by different words.)

In this way, the word *hand* helped us learn about the thing we came to call a "hand." The same was true of the words *feet, rattle,* and *spot.* The world of words helped us organize the world of things. For in the intensional world, most things were organized for us. The confusion of people around us became simpler when we learned the labels *man, woman, boy, girl,* and *baby.* We organized our room in terms of four *walls,* a *floor,* and a *ceiling.*

As we grew up, thousands of other words—from *store* to *soldier* to *ocean* to *God*—helped us organize our neighborhood, our world, and our universe. We learned about the extensional world as we learned about the intensional world.

Often we learned to distinguish particular objects only *because* they had names. If you grew up in the country, for instance, you might have learned to distinguish a *harrow* as a separate kind of thing because you were taught its name early in life. A city child, however, to whom harrows and hayrakes were interchangeable things, might have beat you in distinguishing a *taxi* as a separate kind of thing.

Young children are not able to think in terms of forms, patterns, or general ideas. They would find the material being presented in this book almost meaningless. They tend to think in terms of real things or people they can see or remember. They believe that it is the extensional world that they organize and learn to understand. The truth, of course, is that to a great extent the world is organized by our language for us. When we think, we have to think with the words that have been given us. These words fit together in only certain kinds of patterns. And these patterns may be quite different from the extensional patterns they are supposed to resemble.

A few examples will make this idea clear. Several centuries ago, the human body was thought to contain four principal liquids, or *humors.* In a healthy body, these humors— blood, phlegm (FLEM), black bile, and yellow bile—were in balance. Too much or too little of one of them, however, brought on disease. The doctor's job was to control the humors with practices such as bloodletting. For years, medical science made little progress because the words with which physicians had been taught to think were poorly related to "reality." Not until doctors stopped organizing the human body in terms of "humors" could the age of modern medicine begin.

Word problems of this sort continue to bother us today. One school principal, for instance, struggled unsuccessfully for several years to raise the quality of education in his building. Then he discovered his mistake. He had been thinking in terms of *teaching,* not *learning.* After all, he realized, schools are built and staffed not so that teachers can teach but so that students can learn. The substitution of one word for another re-

48 organized his thinking and led to a rapid improvement in the school. Similarly, there is much talk today about the "Negro problem." *What "Negro problem"?* As many blacks have pointed out, "white problem" is probably more accurate. People who have been trained to think in terms like "Negro problem" are, semantically speaking, very much like the ancient doctors thinking about their "yellow bile." *Names are not things. Maps are not territories. The intensional is not the extensional.*

Meanings and Contexts

Another basic danger involving words is the tendency to assume that their meanings are independent of the persons who use them. True, we do have dictionaries, the purpose of which is to list the "meanings" of the words in the language. But a dictionary definition is only a notation of the meaning *usually* given a word at the time the dictionary was put together. It does not tell us what any one person means when using the word in a certain situation. When we ask the question *What do you mean?* we are seldom asking for a dictionary definition of a word. Instead, we want to know what idea is in the mind of the person who uses the word. If we insist on thinking of "word meanings" only, forgetting about "people meanings," communication can break down completely. In an important sense, "meanings" are not found in words. Meanings are found in people's heads, as might be seen in the following experiment conducted by a professor:

This was one of the favorite demonstrations of Dr. Irving J. Lee of Northwestern University. A facetious student once referred to him as "the only man on the faculty who can't draw a triangle." He had devised a way of misinterpreting every kind of instruction that was ever given.

Here are some of the instructions most frequently given by any group:

Draw three straight lines connected: he drew them as three sides of a box, or as continuing parts of a single line.

Draw three straight lines touching at their tips: he drew an arrow.

Draw three straight lines connecting them so that they make three angles: He drew them in the form of an X with a line connecting the two lower points. This, of course, made a triangle but with an extra V on top. If they protested that he had now drawn a triangle, he would then ask, "Is this really what you had in mind by a triangle? Have I done exactly what you wanted? Would you be satisfied with an employee who came this close to the assignment? I think not. Try again."

Draw three straight lines connecting them so that they make three and only three angles: he drew a K.

Make three straight lines enclose an area: he drew an A.

Draw three dots: He would put two dots on the blackboard and one on the floor.

Put three dots on the blackboard: he made three dots all on top of each other.

Put three dots on the blackboard not on top of each other: he put one dot on the back of a reversible blackboard, or on the frame of a stationary one.

Put three dots all on the black part of the blackboard: he did as expected.

Now connect the dots: he drew a circle connecting them.

Connect the dots with straight lines: he connected the three dots with only two straight lines, making a V shape.

Connect all three dots with three straight lines: he would take a pencil and draw the third line on the blackboard so that the class couldn't see it.

Now go over the third line with chalk: he used the side of the chalk and smeared it all up.

Put the dots back the way you had them: he did as expected.

Now connect all three dots with three straight chalk lines: he drew dotted lines, or slightly wavy lines, then stood at the side of the blackboard, where he was looking along its surface, and said, "They look straight from here."

It has been said that no word ever "means" exactly the same thing twice. This is so because nearly every time a word is used, it is used by a specific person in a specific context—and no two people or situations are exactly the same. Pronounced in a certain way, *sure* can mean "no," and *no* can mean "yes." A rich man's *good restaurant* is not a poor man's *good restaurant*. A *quiet crowd* in a ballpark makes much more noise than a *quiet crowd* in a library. And reaching the *end* of a chapter is not reaching the *end* of a book. (Thinking It Through 1–2, page 50.)

Reviewing the Key Points

1. Be alert to the fact that to a great degree, the world is organized for us by our language. This organization may or may not be that of the extensional world.
2. Remember to search for word meanings in people's heads, as well as in dictionaries.
3. Remember the importance of contexts in determining meanings.

Getting It Straight

On paper, write sentences or short paragraphs answering as many of the following questions as your teacher directs. You may need to look back at the chapter.

1. What are four difficulties encountered in trying to find the total number of English words?
2. What different aspects of language are of interest to the lexicographer, the grammarian, and the semanticist?
3. What is one reason why people often forget that the name of a thing is not part of the thing itself?
4. What do we mean when we say that our language helps organize the extensional world for us?
5. What is wrong with the statement that the meanings of words are to be found in the dictionary?
6. How does context help determine meaning?

50 THINKING IT THROUGH: A LOOK AROUND

1. Bits and pieces

Back in Chapter 2, we read that semantics was a *general* subject. This means that we should be able to relate semantics to much of what we see and hear in the world around us.

On the following pages are some small bits and pieces of that world. Try to relate each of them to your semantic knowledge. Be prepared to discuss your feelings. If you have trouble, think about maps and territories, intensional and extensional orientations, the way words contain "meaning," and the importance of contexts.

LOVE

There's the wonderful love of a beautiful maid,
And the love of a staunch true man,
And the love of a baby that's unafraid—
All have existed since time began.
But the most wonderful love, the Love of all loves,
Even greater than the love for Mother,
Is the infinite, tenderest, passionate love
Of one dead drunk for another.

—ANONYMOUS

2. Examining your own world

Now it's time to take a look around yourself. Perhaps you have already noticed several items or events in your environment that brought something in this book to mind. If not, look for them. They can be reports of things you saw or heard, photographs, cartoons, poems, advertisements—*anything*. Find at least two bits and pieces of your own world. Bring them to class.

Words
at Work:
Labeling
Our Mental Maps

Man has been looking out at the world for a long, long time. He's been looking out, perceiving things, and naming them. In the Old Testament, we read that although it is God who creates, it is man who names *(Genesis* 2:19–20). There is a great truth here, for *naming* is definitely a human activity.

Classifying the Confusion

When we name, we do several things. First of all, we classify. When we call a certain object a *book,* for instance, we are stating that it is like other objects of a similar kind. We are placing it in a class of similar objects, a mental pigeonhole we have labeled *book*. And so our minds contain thousands of classifications, each one naming a certain portion of our environment. We have divided the extensional world up into thousands of little boxes labeled with the words in our language. Sometimes these intensional classifications correspond to "reality"; sometimes they do not.

Frequently, in fact, the words we use make us see clear-cut classifications that do not exist in nature. Actually, our environment is more changeable and overlapping than commonly believed. This confusion allows speakers of different languages to classify experience in different ways. Color is a good example. To speakers of English, it seems "obvious" that blue and green are two different colors. To speakers

54

of Navajo, however, it seems just as "obvious" that our blue and green are merely different shades of a color they have learned to call by a single name. Moreover, some Indians appear to classify color not as a quality but as a kind of action. For instance, instead of *The barn is red,* they would say *The barn reds.* To us, sentences like this sound "illogical" —but where is our "logic" to be found? In this case, our only "logic" is the "logic of language." It is no more illogical to say *The barn reds* than it is to say *The cheese smells.* Both sentences make a verb out of what we usually think of as a quality. Similarly, a Navajo might argue that it is "illogical" for English speakers to refer both to black *things* and to the black "no-thing-ness" of night by the same term. He uses two different words for what he classifies as two different ideas.

Is "hunger" a thing, a quality, or an action? Speakers of different languages say *I have hunger, I am hungry,* and *I hung*er. The Danes have separate words for "boy cousin" and "girl cousin," and the Germans have one word, *Geschwister,* for "brothers and sisters." The Chinese baby becomes "one" year old at birth, while the American baby does not become "one" until he begins his *second* year. The Eskimos have some twenty words for our *snow,* and the French have no term for our *vacant lot.* Differences like these lead the world's peoples to view the world in slightly different ways. And when the interests of many nations are involved, agreement on a name does not always mean agreement on the classification that goes with it. (Think-

ing It Through 3, page 60.) The International Olympic Committee experiences this difficulty in attempting to define what is an "amateur":

By international agreement, participation in the Olympic Games is restricted to "amateur" athletes. But no agreement has ever been reached on exactly what the term *amateur* means. Every four years, the battle over the word *amateur* threatens to overshadow the battles among the athletes themselves.

According to the International Olympic Committee, an amateur athlete is one who engages in a sport for enjoyment, not for money. An amateur cannot be paid, "directly or indirectly," for his skills. Under this definition, a wealthy American whose inherited fortune enables him to spend most of the year skiing can compete as an amateur —as long as he's never accepted money for his skiing.

"But is this fair?" ask the Russians. They point out that in the Soviet Union, young men cannot inherit large fortunes; all property belongs to the state. "If it is fair for private property to pay for the training of a skier," the Russians maintain, "it is fair for government property to do so." So the Soviets openly put their skiers on the state payroll.

"Foul!" cry the Austrians. "Look at what the Russians are doing—paying their skiers! If it is fair for the Russians to pay their ski team, it's fair to let Austrian skiers accept money from the manufacturers of ski equipment. After all, this isn't really paying the skiers for skiing!"

Is this money a "payment" or not? Are college athletic scholarships "payments"? Should payments for one sport prohibit an athlete from competing in another sport in the Olympics? Are payments for teaching a sport the same as payments for playing the sport? And what about payments from related fields? For instance, can a swimmer accept payments for working as a lifeguard?

As the Olympic rule book grows thicker and thicker, the rules themselves grow fuzzier and fuzzier. At present, to take one example, a swimmer can work as a lifeguard—but not within three months of an Olympic meet! What is an *amateur*? The world waits.

The Consequences of Naming

Names are the building blocks of language. If we are to communicate at all, we must have names for the many things we want to talk about. Yet names can become the stumbling blocks of language as well. We already know that we tend to think with the names that our language has given us. If these names don't fit the facts ("Negro problem," etc.), our thinking doesn't fit the facts either. What other dangers are involved in the process of naming?

First, it seems to be human nature to assume that the act of naming results in power over, or understanding of, the thing named. To know a name is to have control. This tendency was true of the earliest humans, and it is true of us today. In primitive religions, to know the names of the gods and goddesses was to have some control over the forces of the universe. Among modern children, to know the names of Santa's reindeer is somehow to understand them better. All of us ask for the name of a piece of music when we hear it for the first time, although no one can explain exactly how the name increases musical understanding. In the same way, we don't feel comfortable until we know the name of a painting or piece of sculpture. We demand names for our clothing styles and names for our diseases. In school we learn the names of a few state capitals and assume that we understand our country better. Some adults learn the names of the President's cabinet members, thereby becoming experts on the inner workings of government. Actually, of course, knowing a name is simply knowing a name. What's in a name? Usually nothing—unless we learn to look behind the label.

A second danger of naming is that all peoples of the world tend to assume that the labels of their own language are "logical." This tendency sometimes makes international communication difficult, if not impossible. We like to believe that our names are "natural," that they describe our environment as it "really is." As we've seen, however, this one-to-one correspondence between names and things is false. To some degree, the shape of a man's language is the shape of his world. To achieve the best possible communication with a foreigner, a person must learn the foreigner's language so well that he knows the foreigner's world. Among closely related languages, this is not too difficult. English, for instance, translates fairly accurately into German, French, and most other European languages. Between English and Russian, however, the differences are greater, and between English and Chinese, greater still. Unfortunately for history, the differences between English and many

American Indian languages are very great. This fact, in part, accounts for the sorry record of our Indian relations. Neither the white man nor the Indian understood that although their words could be translated, their worlds remained minds apart.

Finally, since to name is to classify, to name is to put different things under a single label. The convenience of this single label often hinders us from seeing important differences. For instance, once a child has classified two or three items he doesn't like as "vegetables," he will probably reject any "vegetable" on the basis of the name alone. If it's a "vegetable," he doesn't like it—and that's all! The label hides the differences, and the child doesn't see that many other labels for vegetables are possible: classifications based on color, consistency, taste, cooking procedures, etc.

A small child, certainly, can be forgiven for letting a word stop his observation and inquiry. But what about the adult who doesn't like "teenagers"? Isn't he doing exactly the same thing? "I don't like vegetables!" "I don't like teenagers." "I don't like intellectuals!" "I don't like American cars!" The world is a simple place for those who slap easy labels on everything in sight. It's an intensional world of the worst order! (Thinking It Through 2, 4, and 8, pages 60, 61, and 63.)

Denotation and Connotation

Look carefully at the following statements. Do the two sentences in each pair mean the same thing?

1. a. The money was donated by affluent people.
   b. The money was donated by rich people.

2. a. The aged man walked with a cane.
   b. The old man walked with a cane.

3. a. Miss Bruce is the slender type.
   b. Miss Bruce is the skinny type.

4. a. Mr. Yen, the typing teacher, is a Chinese.
   b. Mr. Yen, the typing teacher, is a Chinaman.

5. a. The poet writes of his life as a vagabond.
   b. The poet writes of his life as a tramp.

It's hard to say whether the two sentences in each pair mean the "same" thing. On one hand, a dictionary would tell us that *affluent* means the "same" as *rich,* that *aged* means the "same" as *old,* etc. On the other hand, we feel that the different words suggest slightly different meanings. "Slender" suggests the graceful and easy motions of being thin; "skinny" suggests hollow cheeks and sharp elbows.

The difference between a word's dictionary meaning and the other meanings it somehow suggests is the difference between denotation and connotation. A word's DENOTATION (dee-no-TAY-shun) is its dictionary meaning. A word denotes what it points to in the extensional world. As they exist in "reality," there is no difference between a *Chinese* and a *Chinaman.* As they exist in our intensional worlds, however, there is a difference. To most people, the word *Chinaman* CONNOTES coolies pulling rickshaws, small cellar laundries, odd music, and perhaps even cruelty. This is the reason, of course, that persons of Chinese ancestry rightly wish to be called *Chinese*. The word carries a more favorable connotation than the unfortunate term *Chinaman*.

CONNOTATIONS (kon - uh - TAY - shuns) are all important in language, much too important for us to forget. We all know people who use words as though their dictionary definitions were all that mattered, forgetting that connotations are part of "meaning" too. When troubles arise, such persons defend themselves by protesting, "But all I said was. . . ."—ignoring the fact that denotations are seldom "all" that one says. Admittedly, there are many "neutral" words, but even these can be given connotations by context or tone of voice. Compare these two statements:

The moon on the breast of the new fallen *snow*
gave the luster of midday to objects below.
Snow is frozen water vapor in crystalline form.

In the first example, *snow* connotes the beauty of a moon-flooded winter night. In the second, however, the romantic connotations give way to scientific ones. Compare these two sentences:

If I could lose twenty more pounds, I'd call myself *thin*.
You're so *thin*, if you turned sideways you wouldn't cast a shadow.

The connotations of *thin* are surely more pleasant in the first example than in the second. (Thinking It Through 1, 5 and 7, pages 59, 62 and 63.)

Magic Words 57

Today we are bombarded with words used mainly for their connotations. These terms often lack really meaningful denotations. They are used to get us to behave in certain ways. Because they are so marvelously effective, they can be called MAGIC WORDS.

Magic words come from all sources, but the master magician is the businessman. For instance, many real estate agents sell only *homes,* never *houses*. The word *home* connotes family life, happiness, and security, while a buyer is apt to think of a *house* in terms of concrete, lumber, and next year's taxes. These homes have rooms that are either *spacious* (too big) or *cozy* (too small). Their bathrooms are called *conveniences*. If a home is too dilapidated to be rebuilt by word magic, it becomes a bargain as a *handyman's special*. And the buyer will never be asked to *sign the contract* of sale; instead, he will *approve the agreement*. "The right words in your mouth," says one expert, "can mean money in your pocket."

The art of advertising is largely the art of using magic words. Terms like *Pentachlorodyne* and *Zymex-D* denote absolutely nothing to the consumer. Instead, they connote all the mysteries of modern science. In the intensional world of the advertiser, "light brown" becomes *desert sand,* and "prunes" become *black diamonds*. Smiles come from pills and all money seems to come from your friendly bank. Sex sells everything, from arch supports to automobile tires to the most prudish of schoolroom classics. (See illustration, page 58.)

58 Cars take on life as Mavericks, Hornets, Gremlins, Barracudas, Dolphins, Impalas, Beetles, and even Ambassadors. Hitch your Pinto to a Texaco Star! Transportation without connotation? What fun is that? (Thinking It Through 9–10, page 64.)

There's an old saying that horses *sweat,* men *perspire,* and women *glow.* In the denotational sense all three terms, as used here, refer to the same process. Once again, it's word magic that makes the difference. The connotations of *sweat* ill become Miss, Mrs., or Ms. America. Whatever their differences, they all *euphemize.*

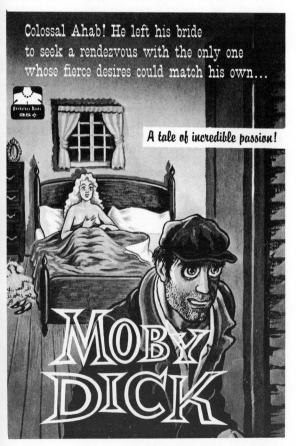

Colossal Ahab! He left his bride to seek a rendezvous with the only one whose fierce desires could match his own...

A tale of incredible passion!

MOBY DICK

EUPHEMISM (YOO-fuh-miz-um) is the substitution of an inoffensive term for one whose connotations might offend. The word can also refer to the inoffensive terms themselves. For example, *disadvantaged* is a euphemism for *poor,* as *comfortable* is a euphemism for *rich.* Euphemisms are commonly used in discussing very personal subjects, such as the human body, its functions and diseases, and death.

Because they depend on connotations, euphemisms often seem to have no "reason" or "logic" behind them. The euphemisms of one generation often strike the next generation as silly. Today, for instance, supermarkets print the word *thigh* on packages containing a certain cut of chicken. Not so a generation ago! The word would have offended many people, who then used the euphemism *second joint.* If this seems absurd, remember that a hundred years ago the word *leg* was not spoken in polite company. In some groups one even referred to the *limbs* of a chair!

An interesting group of euphemisms surrounds the very emotional subject of death. About 1920 *undertakers* became *morticians* (mor-TISH-uns). Now they are *funeral directors.* They take over when a *terminal illness* has caused someone to *pass away.* The *remains* are placed in a *casket* and prepared for *interment* in a *memorial park.* What good English words are being concealed by these euphemisms? Are the hidden terms really shocking? If not, why are they sometimes not used? (Thinking It Through 11–12, page 65.)

Reviewing the Key Points

1. Remember that your verbal classifications may not exist in the world outside your head.
2. Distrust feelings of understanding and control that come from simply learning the name of something. Ask yourself, "What have I actually learned *about* it?"
3. Remember that really learning a foreign language involves more than translating words on a one-to-one basis.
4. Don't let labels conceal important differences. All "vegetables" are not alike.
5. Remember that the "meaning" of a word includes both its denotation and its connotation.
6. Don't let magic words lead you into false beliefs or ideas.
7. Remember that euphemism is a matter of politeness or etiquette, not reason or logic.

Getting It Straight

Write sentences or short paragraphs answering as many of the following questions as your teacher directs. You will probably need to look back at the chapter.

1. What are four results of the process of naming?
2. What is the difference between denotation and connotation?
3. Why is connotation an important factor in language?
4. What are magic words, and where are they often used?
5. Why are euphemisms not found in all fields of human interest?

THINKING IT THROUGH: WORDS AND THOUGHT

1. What's in your name?

Write your full name neatly on paper. Pronounce it slowly, enjoying each syllable. Now print it in clear block letters. Try to see it in the following contexts:

THE MEMOIRS OF_____: Volume I

WANTED BY THE FBI:_____

_____REFUSES NOBEL PRIZE

THE_____SHOW: Channel 4 at 8:00 p.m.

How well does your name fit in these blanks? How well do *you* fit? Are these two questions the same? How well does your name fit you?

60   The name is not the thing. A person's name is not the person—a fact most of us have trouble remembering. If we know someone named *Cheryl,* it's hard to imagine her with any other name. Her name seems almost a part of her. And equally important, it's hard to think of the word *Cheryl* as simply a denotative label. The name *Cheryl* seems to connote a certain type of person. Similarly, our mental maps probably tell us something about a *Maxine* or a *Patrick,* even though we may never have met the territories (people) involved.

Connotations cling to names as names cling to people. We often react to names as if they were people. In a sense, to have a name is to be that name. Long ago, girls were often given the names of qualities their parents thought desirable, such as *Charity, Patience, Submit.* (Today we have names such as *Grace, Faith, Hope, Joy.*) Also, slaves were commonly given only one name, for to deny someone a complete name was to deny him his rights as a complete person. In contrast, dignified persons have often borne the weight of three names: *Henry Wadsworth Longfellow; Franklin Delano Roosevelt; Norman Vincent Peale.*

What about your name? Are you a *Hugo* trying to be a *Hal?* A *Lena* trying to be a *Joy?* Describe in detail what you feel to be the connotations of your first and middle names. In what ways do these connotations fit you? In what ways do they not fit? If given the choice, would you choose another name? If so, what? In the back of a good dictionary you may find a special section on common names.

2. Names as tools of thought

In a way, thinking is a circular process. We have to think with the words we know—and these very words frequently influence what we think. In some schools, for instance, *graduation* is called *commencement* in the hope that it will be seen not as an "end" but as a "beginning." Persons who favor changes in the tax laws commonly speak of tax *reform.* In the last fifty years, *colored person, Negro, Afro-American,* and *black* have all been socially favored at different times. Persons who once detested *socialized medicine* now willingly accept the benefits of *Medicare.* Other persons tell us that their *worries* vanished when they learned to label them *concerns.* Words *do* make a difference!

Examine some of the labels in your own mind. Try to find one term that has influenced your thinking in ways you hadn't realized. Look particularly at terms that carry powerful conotations or do not adequately describe the territory. Then explain in detail how the term tends to affect your mental map. If you have trouble, consider your use of the following: *drop-out, honor student, Department of Defense, drug problem, good English, tax loopholes, welfare state,* and *higher education.*

3. The world in pieces

We have learned that every language splits up human experience in its own "logical" way. Speakers of one language often need two or three words to say

Drawing by Kovarsky; Copr. © 1955 The New Yorker Magazine, Inc.

what speakers of another tongue can say in one. And even when word-for-word translation is possible, the two terms often have slightly different meanings. A tragic example of this is the Japanese reply to a surrender ultimatum delivered not long before the first atom bomb was dropped on Hiroshima. The key word in the Japanese reply was *mokusatsu,* which was translated *ignore.* The Japanese warlords had met, and they had chosen to *ignore* the American demands! On with the war! Unfortunately for history, the American translator was working on a word-for-word basis. The Japanese word *mokusatsu* does not have the rude connotations of the English *ignore.* Moreover, its denotations cover a much wider area, ranging from our *ignore* to "consider thoughtfully but not comment on at this time." This last meaning was probably what the Japanese had intended. If *mokusatsu* had been translated differently, World War II might have come to a much quieter close.

If you are learning a foreign language, you have probably noticed several of these differences. Get out your language texts and see whether you can list on paper five examples of how another language views the world differently. If your own experience is limited, try to find someone who speaks a foreign language well. Ask him for five examples that have come to his attention. And if you're totally locked in the world of the English language, just try to remember that yours is not the only possible world.

4. Comfort me with names

Recently a man entered a doctor's office with an itchy splotch on his right leg. The doctor examined the area, nodded professionally, and wrote out a prescription.

"But this red place—what *is* it?" asked the man.

"I'm sorry," said the physician. "We doctors know what this is, but we don't have a name for it."

The man looked sad.

"Would a name make you feel better about it?" the doctor asked.

The man's eyes gleamed.

"Then we'll call it a high-class form of athlete's foot," the doctor continued. "There's a name. Are you satisfied?"

Smiling broadly, the man took the prescription and left.

Have you had a similar experience recently? Has a *name alone* given you understanding or made you feel more in control? Think of the names of pieces and types of music, diseases, games, living things, products, and various human activities. The important thing here is that the *name alone* must have made you feel better, not any true understanding or knowledge of the extensional area involved. Make a note of your experience to share with the class.

5. The conjugation of adjectives

In the past, students of English were taught to conjugate verbs, listing in order the various forms of a verb: I *am;* you *are;* he or she *is.* British philosopher Bertrand Russell once joked that we conjugate adjectives too: I am *slender;* you are *thin;* he or she is *skinny.*

There is truth in this observation. To refer to similar extensional facts, we often use terms with pleasant connotations when speaking about ourselves; neutral terms when speaking about the person we're talking to; and negative terms when speaking of others. Sometimes nouns are substituted for adjectives:

I am *thrifty.*   You are *economical.*   He is *cheap.*

I am *modest.*   You are *humble.*   She's a *mouse.*

I am *humorous.*   You are *funny.*   He's a *cornball.*

Write on a piece of paper ten adjectives you might honestly use to refer to yourself. How many of these can be "conjugated"? Try to do at least five.

6. A NOW language

Speakers of any language are forced to use the words they've inherited from past generations. Unfortunately, however, the needs of the present often differ from the needs of the past. English is full of words that most people know, but for which they have little use. Since most of our distant ancestors lived on farms, our agricultural vocabulary is especially rich. How often do you use *stallion, mare,* or *foal?* Is the distinction between *hay, straw,* and *fodder* important in your life? What about *legume, mulch,* and *heifer?*

On the other hand, we often lack convenient words for the newer objects in our environment. We are forced to say long terms like *audio-visual equipment room, modular scheduling, off-track betting office, data processing machine,* and *central air-conditioning unit.*

On paper, draw up a list of five words you could easily live without. List another five terms that might well be replaced by shorter words of your own choosing. If you have trouble finding these jawbreakers, remember to concentrate on the new. Look around and start naming.

7. Your pet labels

We have learned that changing a label often results in changing behavior. The principal in Chapter 4, for instance, changed the goal of his school from *teaching* to *learning* and standards went up. An *insomniac* (in-SOM-nee-ak) learned to fall asleep by substituting *relaxing* for *sleeping* as his goal. Another man couldn't change his smoking habits until he analyzed his problem semantically. He decided that thousands of advertisements had given the word *cigarette* connotations too glorious to resist. After substituting *cancer stick,* he found that he really didn't have to smoke a pack a day, after all.

How about the labels in your life? This question is not an easy one. For most of us, labels are so much a part of life that it's hard to see how they influence us. Most dictionaries give *pupil* and *student* a slight difference in meaning. Look the words up. Would a change from one to the other help you? And think about the words *learning* and *understanding*. Which is your aim in school? Some students have been helped by a shift to the second term.

Try to find one or two labels you could change to your advantage. Explain how one label affects your thinking and how another label might bring improvements. If you have trouble, write five short sentences starting with *I am.* Then look at your "self" words from Exercise 5, page 62. Are they the terms that will do you the most good? As a last resort, you might consider your reaction to the following words: *happiness, work, anger, popularity, leisure time,* and *sin.*

8. You, the classifier

When we name, we classify. And not all people classify in the same way. Have you ever observed a small child playing with plastic blocks of different colors, shapes, and sizes? He will put them in piles, first according to one classification, then according to another. In the same way, he learns to classify with words. He learns that the term *chair* includes not only the hard wooden object in the kitchen, but also the bulging soft object in the living room. A week later he learns that the term *bench* includes the long hard object on the porch, but not the long soft object in the living room. This is a *sofa.* Classification, he learns, is a matter of habit as much as of logic.

Look around carefully the next time you enter the home of a family that owns a lot of books. How are the volumes classified on the shelves? By subject matter? By size? By their owners? By colors? Different families agree among themselves to classify in different ways.

Consider the classification "my English class." Obviously, several sub-classifications are possible. Which come to your mind first? Boys and girls? Good,

64

average, and poor students? Classifications based on race or family background? Popularity groupings? Interest groupings? Think of some more methods of classification. Which of these do you think is most important? Be honest. Do you think all members of the class would agree with your choice? Would all members of all English classes in the United States agree? What factors in your background and present situation accounted for your choice? What influences might account for other choices?

Try this experiment in classification. Think of an odd system of classifying your fellow students into three groups. For instance, you might use birds: each person must be a *mud hen,* a *robin,* or a *sea gull.* (Cars, foods, occupations, historical figures, and TV personalities also offer interesting possibilities.) At home, write your classifications on large cards, and in your notebook list each class member under one of the three headings. On the day assigned by your teacher, post your cards on three sides of the classroom, if possible. Allow a minute or two for people to make their choices in silence. Then have each person get up and stand under his label. Look at your notebook listings. How right were you? Where differences occur, discuss them with the person involved, and with the class. Don't simply argue; discuss your classifications thoughtfully. The purpose of the discussion should be for you to learn something about the reasons you classify certain people in certain ways.

9. Discovering word magic

Stroll through a variety store collecting examples of word magic. (If this is not possible, open any general magazine.) Look particularly at the names of products (*Cover Girl*), colors (*sunset glow*), ingredients (*lanolex plus*), and features (*quality kissability*). Find five examples you think unusually effective. List them on a piece of paper. Also note down their denotations (if any) and their connotations (go into detail on all they suggest).

Discuss these lists with your classmates to determine:

1. magic sounds or letter combinations,
2. words (or word parts) commonly used, and
3. the underlying human emotions and ideas that give magic words their effect (fear, greed, envy, love of power, faith in science, and others).

10. You write the law

Is advertising honest? Many people would answer this question with a loud *no!* These persons are so disturbed by advertising that they continually call for new regulation by the government. Other persons, however, think that while advertising is not exactly "honest," no one "really believes it," and therefore it does little harm. What is your opinion?

The Federal Trade Commission tries to keep advertisers honest by making them prove all claims. This law sometimes takes years to enforce, but enforcement is at least possible. A certain brand of beer, for instance, either does or does not produce a "longer-lasting head" than most other brands. A certain kind of bread either does or does not contain "three times the vitamins and minerals" of the average loaf. These facts can be determined in scientific laboratories.

The trouble with present laws is that they deal mainly with *denotations,* whereas advertising deals mainly with *connotations.* And connotations are so unfactual and vague that they're hard to pin down in legal language. Try to define a "misleading connotation" in an advertisement. Try to write an "honesty-in-connotations" law that you think would help you as a consumer and could be easily interpreted by judge or jury. Give it a try. If you can do it, bring it to class. Your teacher might send a copy to your Congressman without delay!

11. The hidden shockers

An old language habit is to try not to take the name of the Lord in vain. Because this kind of language shocks many people, euphemisms have come into use. Today most of these euphemisms are so common that we no longer think of them as substitutions for terms that might offend. Still, they start with the sound of either a hard *g* (*gosh!*) or a soft *g* (*jeepers!*). How many others can you name? Does it surprise you to learn that they were once recognized as substitutions and frowned on by many people? Do you think of any of them as euphemisms now?

12. Euphemism in the modern age

Many people believe that euphemism is becoming a thing of the past. This is true—with respect to the euphemisms of the past. In your own lifetime, many of the old "shockers" have come out of hiding, into the sight and hearing of the average person. Every year words are used on TV, or in the movies, for the first time. The older euphemisms are "passing away."

At the same time, however, whole new groups of euphemisms have sprung into being. Most of them concern the "sensitive" subjects of our time, such as race, intelligence, social and economic standing. Others concern governmental policies we don't like to think about in true extensional terms. See if you can find out what your grandparents would have said in place of the following euphemisms:

1. A mother: "My daughter qualifies as an *exceptional child,* but my son is in a *special education* class."
2. A mayor: "We still have the problem of *substandard housing* in this city."
3. A businessman: "My ads should appeal to the *beautiful people.*"
4. A Congressman: "My main purpose will be to give the *disadvantaged* a better break."
5. A Senator: "Let's face the fact that the country needs an increase in *internal revenue.*"
6. A general: "With more *preventative airstrikes,* we would have won the war."
7. A teacher: "Last year Bernard was a *disciplinary problem.*"

UNIT 3

a mental trap:
the allness attitude

Allness
and Indexing: etc.,
etc., etc....

Since the time of Alfred Korzybski, teachers of semantics have taught one lesson that no one ever forgets. It's a lesson that interests most students and pleases most teachers. A miracle lesson? Hardly—it has one flaw. It takes days, even weeks, to present. To save your time, we'll go through a brief summary here.

Allness and Apples

Tomorrow your teacher starts the class by standing in front of the room holding an apple. The instructions are simple: "I want you to tell me all about this apple."

The students nod happily. Their only worry is that the teacher's off-beat beginning will slide into a boring ending. They can certainly tell all about the apple in a short time. Then what will happen?

"It's red," begins one student.

"It weighs about a third of a pound," says another.

"It has a stem," chimes in another. "The stem is about one-eighth by three-quarters of an inch."

The teacher writes these observations on the board, and continues writing as the class tells more about the apple. The teacher lists items relating to color, size, shape, taste, smell, and touch. Before long the front board is covered, and the

teacher goes to a small board at the back of the room. The students still have something to say:

"It's white on the inside."

"White and moist—apples are mostly water."

"There are little white spots on the outside, too."

"And there are seeds inside."

"How many?" asks the teacher.

No one knows.

The teacher hands the apple to a girl in the back row. "Tell me about these little rust spots—how many, what size, and where are they?"

The girl examines the brown spots and gives her observations. The teacher continues writing. Other students handle the apple. The teacher writes data about the size of the depressions at the two ends, the shape of the black "navel" at the bottom, the shiny quality of the skin after so much handling, etc.

The bell rings. There is no homework.

The next day, the students enter the room to find that the boards have been washed clean. They breathe a sigh of relief—but the teacher still wants to know "all" about the apple. Again the apple is passed around the room, and again the teacher starts writing. This time, however, the teacher seems to want more than surface observations. The teacher really wants to know *all* about the apple:

"Exactly how thick is the skin?"

"What is the 'core,' really? How does it differ from the rest of the apple?"

"What do the seeds look like on the inside?"

"Is the apple's moisture in the *cells* of the apple, or is it just oozing around between them?"

"How many cells are there in this apple, anyway?"

"And how are the cells organized inside?"

"A month ago this apple was probably green. What substance in its skin has changed so that it now looks red?"

The students can answer none of these questions. The teacher admits to not knowing the answers either. But arrangements have been made for a biology teacher to visit the class the next day. The rest of the period is spent writing a list of questions for the biologist to answer.

But the following day, the biologist can answer only about half the questions. He draws a diagram of the inner structure of an apple seed.

He explains the make-up of a typical *rosaceous* (ro-ZAY-shus) cell. He goes into detail on the apple's relatives and in-laws. The rest of the questions, he says, are matters of physics or chemistry.

When the biologist leaves, the teacher again challenges the class to tell *all* about the apple. By this time the students have gone through interest, amusement, confusion, boredom—and a strange return of interest. "Why *isn't* it possible to find out *all* about the apple?" they ask themselves. They listen to the teacher's proposal:

The following day, the class will not meet. Instead, the teacher will make arrangements around the school for the students to do research on apples. Some pupils will go to the library. Others will go to the physics room. Still others will go to the chemistry lab, and a few will revisit the biologist. The remaining questions are given to individual students for short reports. If all the answers can be found, the class will know all about the apple.

With absences and delays, about ten days go by before all the reports are turned in. Finally the last student is finished. All questions about the apple can now be answered with facts. One by one, the students read their reports. Nobody can think of a question about the apple that has not been answered.

"Marvelous!" exclaims the teacher when the last report is read. The teacher beams at the students a moment, and then walks over and unlocks a small closet on the right side of the room. The teacher pauses and says to the class:

"Just one more thing. Like anything else, an apple is made of atoms. Did anyone find out what an atom is?"

"Electrons, protons, and neutrons," says a boy.

"Perhaps positrons," adds a girl.

"Those are only *words*," says the semantics teacher. "Tell me all about the *things*."

"I can't," says the boy. "No one has ever seen whatever it is the words stand for. Scientists don't know if electrons are matter, energy, or a combination of both."

The teacher nods. From a shelf in the closet, the teacher takes a plate, and on the plate is the same old apple. Now, however, the apple has spent too many days in an overheated schoolroom. The students can smell it right away. Its skin is dull, dry, and wrinkled. It leans toward a side that is turning soft and brown. The teacher takes hold of the stem and lifts it a few inches. Plop. The stem breaks and the apple falls.

"Now I'll tell you the real trouble with your reports," says the teacher. "They explain the apple as I first showed it to you. They don't tell me all about *this* apple."

"But it's not the same apple!" a student protests.

The teacher smiles and says, "A week ago Tuesday, I put this apple on the closet shelf and locked the door. I'm the only person with a key. A minute ago, I reached up and took the apple down again. *Of course* it's the same apple!"

The class groans.

"Don't you think we should start again?" asks the teacher. "We certainly don't know all about this de-

caying apple I have here on the plate."

The class groans again.

"Do you think you could *ever* tell me *all* about this apple?"

The class answers together: "No!"

The teacher holds up an eraser. "Or this?"

"No!"

"Or this?" Now it's a piece of chalk.

"No! No! No!"

Allness Attitudes

The lesson has taken two weeks—and the class has learned a lot about apples! But the students now know that the apple itself is not really the point of the lesson. Much more important is the semantic principle in-volved, one few of the students will ever forget:

NO ONE CAN KNOW ALL ABOUT ANYTHING.

Think about this statement. At first it might seem too simple to consider for more than a minute. It's rather obvious, after all, that man's knowledge is never *complete*. But think a little further. If we can't know all about a little thing like an apple, how can we possibly know all about such a puzzle as another human being? And how can we possibly know all about groups of human beings, or about any part of their complicated existence? Yet every day we hear people stating or implying that they do know all:

"With five years on the job, I guess I should know how to do things around here."

"Oh, I know all about that."

"You're telling *me* about the cost of living?"

"I know Brooklyn like the palm of my hand."

"If you've known one Puerto Rican, you've known them all."

"Let me explain to you about the Republican Party."

People who talk like this suffer from ALLNESS ATTITUDES. They assume that they know what no one can know—*all* about a certain subject. They assume that their mental maps tell them all about the territories. They are not really living in the real world. They are like sleepwalkers in a land of intensional dreams.

Allness attitudes are harmful for several reasons. Almost always, they tend to block communication. Who wants to discuss a subject with someone who seems to know all about it? Since you can't change his mind or teach him one new fact, you feel you're wasting your time. The person with an allness attitude is unable to learn and unable to change. His mental maps are locked in the vault of his mind, and he's thrown away the key. (Thinking It Through 1–2, pages 78–79.)

Overcoming Allness Attitudes

Since allness attitudes are so common, they are easy to observe in other people. But discovering them in ourselves is a harder matter. And harder still is to direct our lives so that they lead toward a future of flexibility, not the ambush of allness. Fortunately, Alfred Korzybski suggested some semantic skills that can make our task easier.

"The map does not represent all the territory," wrote Korzybski. Look at that quotation again. It is an easy sentence to understand, but a hard one to live by. This is so because *allness attitudes often make life more comfortable.* The person who "knows it all" has nothing new to worry about, nothing to disturb his misleading dreams. It's easy and pleasant to live in a world one knows all about—easy and pleasant and *dangerous.* Modern science tells us that we can't know all about the world or anything in it. Our mental maps are always incomplete, whether we like it or not. To live with these incomplete maps takes courage. The semantically sane person has this courage. He knows that un-sane and anxious persons have to fill in every detail of their intensional maps. He knows too that the comforts of such people are false comforts.

Another method of overcoming allness is to practice using terms like *to me* and *I think.* These expressions make it clear that our observations and opinions have definite limits. The person who forms the habit of using them in his speech, writing, and thought will also form the habit of "non-allness":

> "*To me,* Southern California is the only place to live."
> "*I think* Lincoln was a finer man than Washington."
> "*In my experience,* German shepherds are vicious dogs."
> "*Probably* the Mets are a better team than the Tigers."
> "*From my point of view,* modern art stinks."
> "*It seems* it's going to rain this afternoon."

We should remember, then, that allness is sometimes a pleasant trap to fall into and that the habitual use of phrases like *to me* can help. (Thinking It Through 3–9, pages 79–82.)

Extensional Devices

What else can we do to avoid allness attitudes?

Alfred Korzybski recommended the use of what he termed EXTENSIONAL DEVICES. These are small additions to writing, speaking, and thought that tend to move us more into the realm of "reality." Here are four of them:

74

1. ETC. This little symbol can pack a big meaning. We usually translate the Latin *et cetera* as "and so forth" or "and so on." But to Korzybski the term meant "all we don't—and can't—know about something," "all that words cannot contain," or "all that language and thought leave out." He suggested using it often to remind others—and ourselves—that no matter what we say, we can never say all.

For example, think about the sentence *In college Jack studied business.* Didn't Jack study anything else in college? And didn't his "business" courses include a lot of math, psychology, history, etc.? To say simply that *Jack studied business* is to simplify the facts. The addition of *etc.* to the sentence would make us think of all the possibilities that the sentence leaves out. The *etc.* would imply that we can't know all about Jack's college experience. Or consider this sentence: *The people of the world are weighing communism and democracy.* How is the sentence improved by changing it to read *The people of the world are weighing communism, democracy, etc.*?

Without a doubt, the use of *etc.* is a good habit. The only question is how much to use it. Since words, etc., can never say all, does this mean we have to use *etc.* after every sentence, etc.? Of course not. Korzybski himself used it only occasionally in his writing, just enough to keep the principle in the reader's mind. As a tool of thought, on the other hand, it probably cannot be overused.

2. QUOTES. A few semanticists have suggested that we try to avoid the use of words whose meanings are not clear to everybody. These semanticists consider terms like *freedom* and *soul* to be "meaningless noises." Alfred Korzybski, however, had another idea. He would have us continue using words like this as long as we put *quotations marks* around them. The quotes indicate that we can't know *all* about vague words that often mean different things to different people. In this book, for instance, words like *reality* usually appear in quotes to show that we can't know *all* about them. Other words appear in quotes when their meanings differ slightly from the

usual ones. As we've seen (page 18), Korzybski often used his fingers to insert "quotation marks" into his speech. An odd habit, perhaps, but a useful one.

3. DATES. "But it's not the same apple!" a student cried out at the end of the long lesson. *"Of course it's the same apple,"* the teacher argued. What do you think? Could the passage of ten days' time change the original apple into a "different" one? If it had been another object—an eraser, for instance—would there have been any argument? What did the student mean by the word *same?* What did the teacher mean?

The truth is that the apple was the "same" in some respects and "different" in others. The teacher might have improved communication by holding up the "finger quotes" when saying the word *same.* Or the teacher might have stepped to the blackboard and written the following:

apple (October 12) is not apple (October 26)

And the teacher might have added:

eraser (October 12) is not eraser (October 26)

you (October 12) are not you (October 26)

war (1865) is not war (today)

United States (1789) is not United States (today)

Obviously, the apple had changed. What had not changed was the student's mental map of the apple. When he said it was not the "same" apple, he really meant that the extensional apple (the one that existed in the real world) and the intensional apple (the one that existed in his mind)

were dissimilar. He had forgotten to update his mental map.

Since the time of the ancient Greeks, man has known that "all things change, all the time." There is, however, one important exception to this rule: our mental maps. The extensional world changes constantly; the intensional world does not change without our help. When we forget that each of our mental maps should have a date on it, we risk allness attitudes.

Most people have proven this fact to themselves several times. For instance, have you ever suddenly met someone you hadn't seen since the second grade? Or have you ever returned to the scene of your earliest years? If so, the changes probably came as a shock to you. Most of us think of people and places as we last saw them—no matter how long ago this may have been. Older people tend to suffer more from this form of allness simply because they have lived longer. For example, one man will tell us "all about the French," even though he hasn't been to France since World War II. Another knows all about farming because he grew up on a small dairy farm during the depression of the 1930's. Now *the French (1940's)* are certainly not *the French (today).* Neither is *farming (1930's)* like *farming (today).* As a person's mental maps get older, they represent less and less of the changing territories.

So, to avoid allness we should date not only our own mental maps, but also the maps that other people give us. This is especially important when reading books written long ago. Mark

76 Twain's *Tom Sawyer,* for instance, was published in 1876. Today we can't really understand it unless we remember that Twain's mental maps were those of the 1870's. To make sense of the book we have to see his *street* as *street (1870's),* his *church* as *church (1870's),* and his *teacher* as *teacher (1870's). Teacher (1870's)* is certainly not *teacher (today),* as you can see from The State of New York Regulations for Teachers, 1872:

1. Teachers each day will fill lamps, clean chimneys and clean wicks.
2. Each teacher will bring a bucket of water and a scuttle of coal for the day's session.
3. Make your pens carefully. You may whittle nubs for the individual tastes of the pupils.
4. Men teachers may take one evening a week for courting purposes, or two evenings a week if they attend church regularly.
5. After ten hours in school, teachers should spend the remaining time reading the Bible or other good books.
6. Women teachers who marry or engage in unseemly conduct will be dismissed.
7. Each teacher who smokes, uses liquor in any form, frequents pool or public halls, or gets shaved in a barber shop, will give good reason to suspect his worth, intensions, integrity, and honesty.
8. Each teacher should lay aside from each pay a goodly sum of his earnings for his benefit during his declining years so he will not become a burden on society.
9. The teacher who performs his labors faithfully and without fail for five years will be given an increase of twenty-five cents per week in his pay providing the Board of Education approves.

4. INDEX NUMBERS. In Chapter 5 we learned that when we give something a name, we put it in a category. We classify it with a number of "similar" things. Thus when we label the object you are looking at now a *book,* we are classifying it with the Gutenberg Bible, the latest hit novel, and the collected writings of Chairman Mao. It's clear that the differences among these three are much more important than their similarities—yet they all come under the label *book.* A name calls attention to the ways things are alike.

Names tend to stress similarities and hide differences. Since names are a vital part of language, we can correctly say that language tends to hide differences. Persons ignorant of this fact easily fall into allness attitudes:

a. "Mommy, I hate *vegetables!"* (All vegetables?)
b. *"Holidays* are a big bore!" (Even Christmas morning?)
c. *"Germans* are serious, sensible, and stable." (Adolf Hitler?)
d. *"Blacks* are lazy and rude." (Dr. Martin Luther King?)
e. *"Teenagers* are lazy and rude." (You?)

Statements like these betray STEREOTYPED THINKING. The persons who make them have lazy minds that deal only in similarities, not differences. They are hurting themselves, for their thought patterns are false to facts. More important, perhaps, they are hurting others.

We find stereotyped thinking in all walks of life, at all levels. Avoiding the practice is difficult, for STEREO-TYPES develop wherever words are found. Alfred Korzybski noted that the basic problem was to get people to remember differences when using words based on similarities. What device would do this? Being a mathematician, Korzybski used a kind of shorthand, index numbers:

"vegetable" = $vegetable_1 + vegetable_2 + vegetable_3 \ldots vegetable_n$

"holiday" = $holiday_1 + holiday_2 + holiday_3 \ldots holiday_n$

"German" = $German_1 + German_2 + German_3 \ldots German_n$

In other words, there is no such thing as a typical or representative "vegetable" in the outside world. *Vegetable* is simply a word we use to stand for a class that includes *this* head of cabbage ($vegetable_1$), *that* bunch of lettuce ($vegetable_2$), *this* rather limp green bean ($vegetable_3$), etc. The small n represents the last possible vegetable we might imagine. We can translate it *each and every.* Try inserting *each and every* after the italicized words in sentences (a.) through (e.) above.

Does it make a difference? Now try seeing a small n after each of the words. Can you imagine it? Good. The person who can see that tiny n probably wouldn't be foolish enough to say one of the sentences.

If any part of semantics has spilled over to the general public, it is this matter of index numbers. Critics of Korzybski sometimes laugh at their use. They think of semanticists as people who walk around muttering to themselves, "Cow_1 is not cow_2 is not cow_3." On the other hand, many people have found that index num-

DON'T BE MISLED BY WORDS— DOG_1 IS NOT DOG_2

"I love dogs. Man's best friend, you know."

"We'd better read that chapter on index numbers tonight."

bers and the small n have helped them avoid stereotyped thinking. What is your opinion? Should index numbers be used in writing and speaking, or should their use be confined to the area of thought? History will decide the question, and as for now, $semanticist_1$ is not $semanticist_2$ is not $semanticist_3$.

1. Remember that we can't know all about anything.
2. Don't let the false comforts of allness attitudes affect your thinking. The semantically sane person has learned to live with uncertainty.
3. Learn to use qualifying terms, such as *to me, it seems, I think.*
4. Use Korzybski's extensional devices frequently in thinking and occasionally in speech and writing:
   a. *Etc.* Words always leave something out.
   b. Quotes. Words often have slippery meanings.
   c. Dates. Mental maps do not change without our help.
   d. Index numbers. War_1 is not war_2 is not war_3.

Getting It Straight

Read the following sentences. Then, copy them on paper, adding semantic truth to each sentence by adding an extensional device where needed. Use *etc.,* quotes, dates, and index numbers. Pretend you are the speaker of sentences 1, 5, and 10.

1. After her trip, my second grade teacher showed us slides of Alaska.
2. Mr. Shlan committed suicide because he got fired.
3. Crime is caused by poverty.
4. The dancer leaped over the dancer and landed in the arm's of the dancer.
5. I know Dayton well, for I lived there till I was six.
6. Many communist countries call themselves democratic.
7. The president shook hands with the president before they went in to see the President.
8. Allness attitudes can be lessened by index numbers.
9. To have an extensional orientation is to be in touch with reality.
10. I can't understand this toothache—the dentist said my teeth were perfect.

THINKING IT THROUGH: ESCAPING ALLNESS

1. You, the stereotype

You have certainly had the experience of being treated as a stereotype. Everyone has, and it's not pleasant. After learning one little fact about you, someone with an allness attitude assumes he knows you better than you know yourself. No matter how much you want to be treated as an individual, you are treated as a type. You feel rather like a butterfly the person has caught, killed, labeled, and collected in a book of specimens. There is no escape.

Choose one such experience as the topic of a short paper. (It may be necessary to change the name of the person who stereotyped you.) What was the basis of this stereotype? Did it spring from your race? Your name? Your background? Did it have to do with your size, your looks, or one example of behavior? Explain the person's stereotype in as much detail as you can. Explain how you differed from the stereotype. Explain what you did, if anything, to try to make the person see you as an individual.

Read your paper to your classmates and discuss possible ways of breaking out of the stereotypes of others. It is not an easy question.

2. Examining your own stereotypes

Not long ago a student of general semantics sat reading in the living room of his home. His father strolled in and asked, "What are you reading now, Paul?"

"Korzybski," Paul replied, without looking up.

"Korzybski?" his father grunted. "Who does he play for?"

"All of us," Paul said to himself. Then he got to wondering. Why did his father always come out with that old joke whenever he heard a Polish name? Certainly two stereotypes were involved. One was the stereotype of the Pole as big and dumb. The other was the image of the football player as big and dumb. Since two things equal to a third thing are equal to each other, it was "only logical" that *Poles* equalled *football players!*

Paul decided to do some research on these stereotypes. He looked at rosters in a pro football handbook and found Polish names a small minority. He looked up "Poland" in an encyclopedia and found the names of geniuses in many fields—Paderewski, Chopin, Korzybski, Korzeniowski ("Joseph Conrad"), etc. He discovered too that the Poles were one of the last groups to come to America in large numbers. Right up through the 1920's, they found job opportunities in a booming American economy. If they were "dumb," then, it was because they were among the last to learn the English language. If they were big and strong, Paul reasoned, it only made sense. Who would one expect to immigrate to America, a frail little man or a worker with a strong back?

What stereotypes are you most familiar with? Do some research into their origins. Consult books and ask people who might know. The following are especially interesting: the black as shiftless, lazy, and stupid; the Jew as a smart city businessman; and the Chinese as a ruthless craftsman of evil. These stereotypes are false. The interesting thing is that there are factual reasons for their development. Find them.

3. Indexing your prejudices

To be prejudiced means to *pre*judge, to judge on the basis of labels, not the facts behind them. All of us have some prejudices, even the person who says, "My only prejudice is against prejudiced people." If you believe you have none, read through this list: *poetry, labor leader, capitalist, atomic power, black* *power, teacher, fish, WASP, made in Japan, foreigner, Kelly, Cohen, hippie, ex-convict, politician, snake.* Can you honestly say that not one of these labels brought a trace of judgment to your mind?

It's not easy to conquer our prejudices, even though we may "think" we ought to. The study of semantics has helped many people in this struggle. Here are four things you can do:

1. Realize that to the degree you are prejudiced, you are unscientific and semantically retarded. Be ashamed of yourself.

2. Try to find the origin of your prejudice. Does the word *poetry* start your suspicions sizzling? Why? Too much memorizing in the eighth grade?

3. Try not to use the labels that trigger your allness attitudes. Instead, use terms that get behind these labels. "Poetry" can mean sonnets, light verse, limericks, haiku, lyrics, Longfellow and Frost. "Fish" can mean flounder, halibut, swordfish, tuna, shad and cod. Say "I've tried mackerel three times, and I don't like mackerel," not "I've tried mackerel three times and I hate fish."

4. Use index numbers in your thinking. New Yorker$_1$ is not New Yorker$_2$ is not New Yorker$_3$. New Yorker$_n$ *cannot* be rude, dishonest, or immoral, even though these qualities may now be features of your stereotyped "New Yorker."

Start with a few of your smaller prejudices first, and record your progress for a possible future report. Don't be surprised if your more serious prejudices take months or years to overcome. Prejudice$_1$ is not prejudice$_2$ is not prejudice$_3$.

4. Your "love" index

Index numbers are usually applied to nouns. It is also useful to apply them to verbs that can mean many things. For instance, take the verb *to mean* itself.

This means$_1$ trouble! (will result in)

Mr. Smith means$_2$ business today. (is intent upon)

I don't know what he means$_3$. (wants to communicate)

The prefix *un-* means$_4$ *not.* (is verbally equal to)

Marcia means$_5$ to do very little. (intends)

The verb *to love* can also confuse us if we fail to index. Its major meanings, in fact, are denoted by different words in some languages. See how many shades of meaning you can find for your "loves." Show that these meanings really are different by writing a separate sentence for each. Put a new index number next to *love* each time you use it with a new meaning. Also, try to write a short definition for each meaning (as with *to mean,* above). How many meanings can you find? Do you think it's "logical" to use the word *love* for all of them?

5. . . . and "dating" habits

Forgetting that our mental maps have dates often causes trouble. Sometimes the results are tragic. In 1972, for instance, a thin, ragged Japanese man was found hiding in the woods in the Pacific island of Guam. He'd been there over twenty-five years, ever since American soldiers had captured Guam during World War II. Why hadn't he come out of hiding? His mental maps told him that Americans were vicious enemies who would shoot him on sight. He knew the war had ended, but he'd forgotten that Americans (1944) were not Americans (today).

Has failure to date ever led you into surprise or trouble? Do you always take unobserved change into account? Think of one bad experience you've had because your mental maps were not up to date. The change may have occurred in yourself, in another person, or in a place. Could attention to dates have helped you? If so, how? Describe in detail.

6. You be the judge

The nine Justices of the Supreme Court struggle constantly with the problem of dating. Their map is the Constitution of the United States. Their never-ending task is to update the meaning of the words in the Constitution. For instance, Article VIII of the Bill of Rights states that the courts shall not impose punishments that are "cruel and unusual." Does this mean "cruel and unusual" (1790's) or "cruel and unusual" (today)? The latter, of course. In the 1790's, when the Amendment was added to the Constitution, the death penalty—often public hanging—was considered a fair and usual punishment for several types of crime. Today, however, many people consider the death penalty a "cruel and unusual" punishment for any crime, including murder. In a legal sense, what does "cruel and unusual" mean? It means what the Supreme Court said it meant the last time they updated the map.

On May 16, 1954, segregation by race in public schools was legal. On May 17, 1954, the practice was illegal. This famous change came about without amending the Constitution and without the passage of a single law. The Supreme Court simply updated the Fourteenth Amendment, which declares that no State shall deny any person "the equal protection of the laws." The Justices declared that segregated schools could no longer be considered "equal." "Equal" (1868) was not "equal" (1954).

Article II of the Bill of Rights was added to the Constitution in 1791:

A well regulated Militia, being necessary to the security of a free State, the right of the people to keep and bear Arms, shall not be infringed.

Pretend you are an Associate Justice of the Supreme Court. Write an opinion updating what you think this Amendment should mean in modern practice. In forming your "judicial opinion," you should consider these questions:

1. What was evidently the purpose of the 1791 promise that the people could "keep and bear Arms"?

2. Is this purpose still a necessary purpose today? If not, do the people still have the right to "keep and bear Arms"?

3. What did the term "Arms" mean in 1791? Did it include cheap handguns that could be advertised in comic books and sold in corner stores?

4. Did the Founding Fathers intend the right to "keep and bear Arms" to apply to *anyone, anywhere,* at *any time?* Should we consider any restrictions today? If so, what restrictions? And would they violate the Constitution? Why or why not?

Remember, a good justice is supposed to *interpret* the Constitution (the map) to suit the needs of a changing society (the territory). He cannot, with a stroke of his pen, change the Constitution itself. In your written opinion, you cannot make judgments that are in clear violation of the words of the Constitution. Your job is to explain how Article II should be interpreted today, and to give the reasons for your thinking.

7. All₁ is not all₂

Students of semantics sometimes confuse the meaning of the term *allness attitudes.* It refers to attitudes that imply a person knows what it is impossible to know—*all* about a certain territory. It does not mean that the word *all* should never be used. Which of the following statements show allness attitudes? Which do not?

1. All human beings have been born.
2. All human beings love to learn new things.
3. Americans hate war.
4. Stones have weight.
5. Girls are better English students than boys.

8. A day without allness

Ridding ourselves of allness attitudes is a hard job. Try it for one day. Have the courage not to judge or jump to conclusions before you know all that can be known. In your speech, writing, and thinking, indicate you don't know all by using terms like *to me, personally, from where I stand, in my experience,* and *I think.* Remember the use of *etc.,* index numbers, and dates. In your writing, put quotation marks around vague, fuzzy terms, and use "finger quotes" when speaking. (If other people think you're crazy, you may have to assure them that you're trying to be semantically sane.)

After this experiment, discuss your experiences with the class. Did you find it hard to think about the way we think for a whole day? Did you find it impossible at times to "think before thought"? What did you learn about your usual behavior? How long do you think it would take before habits of non-allness became automatic? During this class discussion, *no one is to say anything that betrays an allness attitude.* Penalties, however, should not be cruel or unusual.

9. Allness in literature

Years ago, a writer of fiction usually pretended that he knew—or could know—all about his subject. He told readers everything they needed to know, leaving little to the imagination. Like a verbal magician, he skipped around in time and space. He even skipped around in his characters' minds, telling first the thoughts of one person, then the thoughts of another. In literary terms, he was an *omniscient* (om-NISH-unt) author: he knew everything.

Today the omniscient author is disappearing. The modern writer often tells his story from the point of view of one character, telling nothing that this character does not know. The reader is never told *all*. Sometimes, in fact, the reader is told so little that the result is confusion. This tendency is especially true in modern poetry. Here is a modern poet's interesting approach to the subject of allness. What do you make of the poem?

                    Re
(here) (   ) (   )
(   ) (there) (   )
(   ) (   ) (here and there—I say here)
(   ) (I do not say now) (   )
(I do not say it now) (   ) (   )
(   ) (then and there—I say there) (   )
(   ) (   ) (say there)
(   ) (I do not say then) (   )
(I do not say, then, this) (   ) (   )
(   ) (then I say) (   )
(   ) (   ) (here and there)
(   ) (first here) (   )
(I said here second) (   ) (   )
(   ) (I do not talk first) (   )
(   ) (   ) (there then)
(   ) (here goes) (   )
(I do not say what goes) (   ) (   )
(   ) (I do not go on saying) (   )
(   ) (   ) (there is)
(   ) (That is not to say) (   )
(I do not say that) (   ) (   )
(   ) (here below) (   )
(   ) (   ) (I do not talk down)
(   ) (under my words) (   )
(under discussion) (   ) (   )
(   ) (all there) (   )
(   ) (   ) (I do not say all)
(   ) (all I say) (   )

            —VITO HANNIBAL ACCONCI

Case Study: "Jane the Brain"

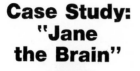

Name	Jane M.		Age 16	Height 5'5½"

Name *Jane M.*   Age *16* Height *5'5½"*

Weight *112* Hair *Black*   Eyes *Brown*

Health *Good – history of anemia*

I.Q. *119* Average: frosh *94* soph *92* jr   sr

Activities *Newspaper; Honor Society; Class Secretary*

Sports *none*

In the spring of her junior year in W_____ High School, Jane M seemed to change overnight. Once agreeable and serious, she grew moody and bitter. Her marks went way down. Several of her teachers tried talking to her. When they met with no success, they sent notes to the guidance counselor, Mr. F. Soon Jane received a slip ordering her to report to the guidance office during a free period. She entered to find Mr. F shuffling through some cards and papers on his desk.

Mr. F: Oh, hello, Jane. Sit down. . . . I've got your records here. You can't blame me for wondering what's happened this spring.

Jane (quickly): I didn't fail anything.

Mr. F: I know, but . . . .

Jane: Then why am I here?

Mr. F (smiling): Well, it's just that . . . Jane, we've never seen much of you in the guidance office. We all figured you for a pretty smart girl.

Jane (sarcastically): Thanks.

Mr. F: Well—?

Jane: Do you think the smart girls get the highest marks?

Mr. F: *Smart*—you know what I mean.

Jane (Nodding): Maybe I'm smarter now.

The rest of the interview went no better. "A disaster," Mr. F said to himself as Jane left the room. He resolved to dig out the facts and get to the root of Jane's problem. In the days that followed, he interviewed her teachers. He talked to some of her classmates on an informal basis. Every so often he called Jane in to check his findings with her. As she became more cooperative, he began to reconstruct her case.

The trouble had apparently started one day in English class. Mrs. A, the teacher, had got nowhere with a discussion of Thomas Hardy's *Return of the Native*. As the period dragged on, she had called on Jane more and more. Jane hadn't known many of the details, even though she'd "read" the assigned chapters the night before. At the bell, Mrs. A had called Jane to the desk.

Mrs. A: You're not letting this spring weather make you lazy, are you, Jane?

Jane (with an embarrassed smile): Lazy? No.

Allness. Mrs. A has stereotyped Jane as "best student in class."

Mrs. A: You've been doing so well—all year—and now, what's happened to my best student? I really do hate to see you fall off so.

Jane: Fall off? (disturbed) I really did try to read that book. I was up till almost midnight. I read every word. But that's all they were: words!

Mrs. A: Come now, Jane.

Jane: Honest!

Allness. Jane (September) or Jane (May)?

Mrs. A: I know you, Jane. I know you can do it if you try. Some people have an excuse for not performing, but you—?

Is Jane's thinking
justified?

Jane (trying to nod politely): I'll try. (Thinking as she leaves: *The nerve of that woman! Here I've been supporting her all year long—giving her the big fat answers she couldn't get from anyone else. And now, when one of her books finally bores me too, what does she do? Turns on me like a cat! That's gratitude for you!*)

Jane fumed through her next class, World Civilization. She felt little better the following period in chemistry. The teacher, Mr. W, began the class by handing back a test.

Mr. W: Larry, here. Armand, good paper. Lisa, nice job. Peter. Mindy. Candy, keep it up. Jane. Ken, you surprise me. . . .

Projection. Later it
was determined
that Mr. W omitted
praise for Jane because he thought
mentioning her
name after every
test would prove
embarrassing.

Jane (Thinking: *He's congratulating everyone with a good paper—everyone except me. Now why? I got a ninety-six. But Jane is supposed to get high marks, he thinks! Jane's like a computer—she doesn't have to be rewarded! Jane, Jane, the mechanical brain!*)

Mr. W: Now, first let's go over a few questions most people missed on the test. Number five, for instance. Who got that right? . . . Jane, didn't you?

Does Jane herself
believe the "smartest-in-class"
stereotype?

Jane (reading in a flat voice): A metal is an element whose oxide is the anhydride of a base. (Thinking: *Why am I so angry? Is it a sin to be the smartest one in this class?*)

Mr. W: Good. (Smiling) Wrong side of the bed this morning, Jane? (Thinking: *I shouldn't have called on her. She's embarrassed.*)

Jane: No, I'm sorry. (Thinking: *It's this school that's wrong, not me. A bunch of lazy kids, and teachers that should give me half their paychecks. These teachers are all alike.*)

Teacher$_1$ is not
teacher$_2$

Later, on her way to French, Jane found herself walking beside Armand P, who was in most of her classes. At the time, Armand considered himself Jane's friend.

Armand: How did you do on the chem test?

Jane (sharply): Ninety-six. Why?

Armand (surprised): What ails you, Jane the Brain?

Jane: Don't call me that!

Armand: So what's the matter? I've been calling you that for three years!

Aggressive use of
language.

Jane: Get lost, Armie, will you please? Go catch up with your sybaritic friends.

Armand: Huh?

What connotation is involved in *normal*?

Jane: Do I call you "Armie the Normal"? That's what you are, do you know that, Armie? Normal!

Armand: So, what's wrong with that? If we were all geniuses, where would you be?

Jane: Okay! Okay!

The French class started with the usual daily quiz on the homework. Jane found herself doing a strange thing—writing down wrong answers on purpose. Why? She didn't quite know. She was tired of being labeled "Jane the Brain." And why was it smart for her to stand for it any longer? After all, she thought, the school wouldn't collapse if "Jane the Brain" didn't play her part for a while. In the days that followed, she deliberately got C's and D's on tests. She did just enough homework to get by. In a month she found herself talking to Mr. F in the guidance office. Not until the fourth interview did Mr. F get to Jane's real problem.

Mr. F: Jane, you know the old children's saying, "Sticks and stones will break my bones, but—"

Jane: "—names will never harm me."

Mr. F: Right! There's probably no more untrue saying in the world. Names *can* do a lot of harm, Jane, and I think that's what we should do some talking about.

Jane: You mean "Jane the Brain"?

Mr. F: Of course. Now, listen to these facts and tell me if I'm right. You came in as a freshman from S_____ Elementary, out in the east end. You were worried about competing with kids who came from the bigger schools. So you worked like a demon for that first report card. You surprised even yourself by getting a ninety-five average. Right so far?

Jane: I guess so.

Mr. F: And it was about that time this "Jane-the-Brain" business started. That's just a label, Jane, It's not *you*.

Jane: I know, but . . . The kids weren't mean. They used it in fun.

Mr. F: All the worse. In a way, they believed the label. So did most of your teachers. And so did you.

Jane: What do you mean?

Mr. F: I mean you seem to have taken the label seriously.

Jane (trying to laugh): How do *you* know what I take seriously?

Mr. F: Your marks, Jane. (Tapping her guidance folder.) We've got a lot of information here on your scholastic ability, going all the way back to first grade. It's my opinion that your class marks are too high for you. They're out of line with your true abilities.

Jane: You mean I'm stupid?

Mr. F: Of course not! You're an intelligent girl, a good bit above average. But you're not a genius. . . . (smiling) Does that hurt?

Jane: No. . . . It's nice to know.

Slowly, Mr. F enabled Jane to see herself more clearly. In semantic terms, her basic trouble was that her mental map of herself didn't correspond to the territory, the real Jane. She had half believed the "Jane the Brain" stereotype. Didn't her high marks prove it? Thinking herself highly intelligent, she had worked very hard for the marks she thought a highly intelligent person ought to receive. This had meant staying up late nearly every night doing homework and reports. And after nearly three years, it had meant breaking under the strain. Jane's job now was to find a mental map of herself that she could live with comfortably. This time she based her map on facts. By the end of the year she was a relaxed "B" student.

THINKING IT THROUGH: CONSIDERING THE CASE

1. A friend in need

This case study does not tell us if Jane had any really close friends in school. A good friend who was with her on her troublesome day might have been able to help. Suppose yourself to be this friend. You're shocked to see a pleasant, sincere person turn suddenly bitter and suspicious. But you know Jane well enough to understand her problem accurately. How might you help her? What would you say?

Remember, you cannot simply tell Jane the truth. Although she has given up trying to get high marks, she still believes herself to be extremely intelligent. This belief is wrong, but it is the source of what pride she has left. You cannot suddenly take it away from her. It took Mr. F four interviews to get to Jane's problem, and it might take you this long. Write down some of the things you might say during your talks with Jane. Make notes too on how you think Jane would react.

2. Role playing

Test your ideas for helping Jane by role playing in class. One of you may be selected to play Jane (or perhaps "Jack"). This person should re-read the case study several times so that she (he) can really "become" Jane (Jack) in a role-playing situation. Use no notes and let the conversation be spontaneous. Remember, the role playing will probably be only as successful as your preparation for it. Also, the role playing will go better if you create a realistic setting.

For instance, have Jane seated alone in the cafeteria. Her angry silence is broken by an old friend who wants to make a try at restoring their former relationship. . . .

Continue the role playing with other "Janes" and other "friends." Of course, not all "Janes" will react in quite the same way. Nor should they. The "friends" will have to remain flexible.

After each sequence, discuss the following questions:

1. Were Jane's reactions in keeping with her character? Did she make it too easy or too hard for her friend?

2. What was the friend's basic plan of approach? Did this plan have any unforeseen flaws?

3. Was Jane offended by allness attitudes on the part of the friend? How much talking was Jane encouraged to do?

4. What principles of semantics did the friend manage to suggest? Did he get across the idea that Jane suffered from being stereotyped? (Semantic terms should probably not be used if Jane is unfamiliar with them.) That some of her teachers had allness attitudes? That she did a good deal of projecting? That Jane (freshman) was not Jane (junior)? That teacher$_1$ was not teacher$_2$?

5. No matter how unsuccessful the interview may have been, did the friend try to leave future opportunities open? Did he approach the interview with a "make or break" attitude that might have ended the friendship forever?

3. Real playing

Chances are that within the last few months you've tried to help someone with a "real problem." Think back over your efforts. How successful were you? What mistakes did you make? What semantic principles were involved in your thinking, and in the thinking of the person you tried to help? If the situation arose tomorrow, how would your involvement be different? Write a report, using the form shown for Jane's meetings with Mr. F (pages 85–88). Add to the left hand column comments indicating your mistakes, if any. You may change names, dates, locations, and situations (slightly) to protect the feelings of others.

UNIT 4

time out for silence:
body english, etc.

Ideas Without Words: Non-Verbal Communication

The vocabulary of communication takes some odd turns. We commonly say that we "see" (understand) what someone means. We also say that silence "speaks," sometimes "louder than words." In the last chapter, for instance, one of the things that disturbed Jane was her chemistry teacher's failure to say a kind word when he returned her paper. To both Jane and the teacher, although for different reasons, his silence was meaningful. Both understood that he had used silence to communicate. That is, he had used a form of NON-VERBAL COMMUNICATION, communicating without words.

All of us use non-verbal communication. In fact, whether we realize it or not, we practice it most of the time. Even in the absence of words, we can't help communicating. Think of the last time you had to stand before the class to give a speech or report. You probably thought of yourself as the communicator in the situation—but wasn't your audience communicating too? Your fellow students either sat erect and alert or slouched in their seats. Their faces showed amusement, interest, or boredom. They looked at you or they stared out the window and stole glances at the clock. At the time, you were quite aware of this communication, even though it was unconscious on their part. (Thinking It Through 1, page 100.)

Does the way a person walks tell you anything about the person? Does it *communicate*? Of course it does. Some people lope along with a springy, athletic step. Others walk their straight paths with a firm, determined stride. Still others move with a hip-swaying roll. Yet how many of us think very often about how we walk? And even if we do, who really knows what he looks like? Who has ever seen himself from twenty feet to the rear? And how many of us are aware of how we perform the thousands of other actions that communicate—sitting down and standing up, getting off a bus, drinking a glass of water? Yet these routine acts betray a great deal. Even the shyest people cannot hide their true natures, for their actions reveal their shyness.

The line between conscious and unconscious communication is not always clear. Think about the seat you occupy in English class. Unless the teacher assigned seats, you probably had something of a choice. What does your selection communicate to the teacher? Did you think about this communication on the first day of class? For instance, did you choose a seat in the front row because of poor eyesight, or because you wanted to let the new teacher know you were eager and interested? Did you choose a rear seat to show that you didn't care, or simply to have the security of seeing the whole class in front of you? Chances are that different members of the class would answer these questions in different ways. People vary greatly in their awareness of different ways they communicate to others. This is why a girl can consciously spend a long time every morning on her face and hair, then unconsciously ruin the whole effect by chewing gum with her mouth open.

A good time to observe truly unconscious behavior is when a person is thrown off guard for a moment. What do you do when you feel threatened or embarrassed? Most people revert to some "infantile" form of behavior. This is easily observed in small children: the thumb goes into the mouth. Adolescents and adults tend to release their tensions in personal grooming. Girls and women reach up and fiddle with their hair. Boys and men examine their fingernails or brush imaginary crumbs off their chests.

From a semantic point of view, a crucial question about unconscious behavior is what other people project into our actions. If we want someone to think we're lazy, that's one thing; but if someone projects laziness into our every act, that's another. "Whatever makes him think I'm lazy?" we wonder. Unfortunately, such questions are hard for the individual to answer. We can't see ourselves from the outside, and our friends often remain friends because they overlook our failings or refuse to tell us. The truth often hurts: "Stop biting your nails." "Stand up straight." "Don't slurp your soup." "Don't fidget so much!"

Yes, most of us want to know how to fidget less and enjoy it more. We want to know—but we don't want to be told! (Thinking It Through 7–8, page 104.)

The Shape of Ideas

The tools of communication are many. Usually we use words. But sometimes we use non-verbal tools. Our wordless ideas take on form and color. Our thoughts become the shapes and signals that other people recognize as having meaning.

Here are five shapes commonly used to communicate. What do they mean to you?

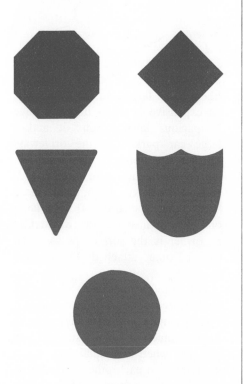

If you're used to road signs, the meanings should be "loud and clear." The first shape, the octagon, is that of a stop sign. The diagonal square carries a warning—a curve, perhaps, or an intersection. The triangle means "YIELD," and the shield marks a national highway.

The last shape, the circle, usually warns of a railroad crossing. An experienced driver reacts as much to the shapes of these signs as he does to the words or symbols they carry. He also reacts to their colors. What color is each in your state?

Shape and color communicate in more ways than we usually realize. Think for a moment of the business district where you shop. Think of the people on the street. Hasn't their clothing been chosen largely for the messages carried by shape and color? Other messages seem to be transmitted by the women's hair styles, from the sculptured, traditional look to the carefree short cut, to the Afro. The long hair of some boys and men was originally a symbol of the free man, as opposed to the short hair required of the slave. Still more messages come from the symbols that identify certain businesses, as well as from the buildings these businesses occupy. A supermarket is likely to have a glass front, but a bowling alley of the same size and construction will have a solid front. Brands of gasoline are signaled by the shapes and colors of both the signs that bear their names and the service stations that sell them. Old movie houses are marked by their marquees, overhanging roofs originally used to protect patrons in bad weather. The wooden Indian is gone from in front of the cigar store, but the red and white barber pole turns on and on. Originally, this device symbolized the barber's second role as a surgeon. How many people today look at a barber pole and think of bandages and blood? (Thinking It Through 5, page 102.)

Space, Time, and Meaning

TEXACO. SHELL. GULF. SUN-
OCO. Shapes and colors often
scream their meanings in ways we
know well. Space, however, is a
more subtle tool of communication.
Yet people have been claiming and
defending land and property for hundreds of thousands of years. The
"space age" started with the first
man.

Observe your "space habits"
closely to understand them. For
instance, if called into one of their
offices, would you sit closer to the
principal or to a guidance counselor?
Probably to the guidance counselor.
The "formal" distance of six to eight
feet between you and the principal
would communicate your respect for
his position. The "informal" two to
four feet between you and the guidance counselor would communicate
your willingness to let him help you
on a personal basis.

There would be other spatial differences as well. The principal's office would probably be much bigger,

since in most things, size signals importance. The principal's desk is
likely to be larger. In the same way,
an expensive house is likely to have
a spacious lawn around it and a
large car parked in the driveway.
Smaller sizes, on the other hand, often show attachment or close friendship. A small car is somehow more
"cozy" and "personal" than a large
one. It can also tell the world that
its owner is the sort of person who
can become attached to a good
machine.

All Americans know a rather
complicated code of "space signals,"
even though they may never have
thought much about the subject. For
instance, when two equals are standing talking to each other, their heads
are likely to be from eighteen inches
to four feet apart. A smaller distance,
especially less than a foot, makes
us feel uncomfortable, while a wider
space makes the conversation seem
formal and strained. Quickly imagine this picture: a fifth-grade teacher
is scolding a boy who has been kept
after school. How far apart do you

see the two people? Chances are that the teacher would either try to get right on top of the boy, within the eighteen-inch "zone of discomfort," or stand back at the "formal" distance to communicate importance.

Like space, time can be used to communicate. The semantic importance of time is indicated by the odd fact that we often speak of it in the language of money. We *spend* our minutes as we *spend* our pennies. We *save* time, and occasionally we *waste* it. We envy people who seem to *have* more of it than we do. We *use* it to impress others, and we *give* it freely to people we like. Suppose, for instance, that a friend calls you up after supper tonight to ask for an assignment he or she missed. You could probably give the information in a very short time and then end the phone call. But would you really hang up right away? No—and neither would the caller. Instead, you and your friend would spend several more minutes talking about almost any subject that came to mind. The important thing would not be what was said; it would be that each of you reaffirmed your friendship by giving some time to the other.

The "time code" Americans live by is at least as complicated as their "space code." A minute late to class is somehow recognized as being "longer" than the ten minutes you may be late to a party. A businessman will try to be right on time for an appointment he has requested. Yet when he returns to his own office, his time sense changes. He may not hesitate to keep others waiting many minutes in his outer office for appointments they have requested.

And if he and his wife are invited out for dinner that night, they will try to arrive at their hostess' home a "proper" five to ten minutes late. If they accidentally get there "on time," they may even drive around the block a while to avoid breaking the unwritten rules of time. (Thinking It Through 2–3, pages 101–102.)

The Barriers of Customs

Travelers to foreign countries often think they can have no communications problems if they have first learned the language. As many tourists have discovered, however, this belief is not true. Travelers have to know both the verbal and the non-verbal language of the countries they visit. They need to know how the natives treat space, color, time, etc. If they do not learn these non-verbal codes, they are in danger of projecting meanings that have no basis in fact.

For United States citizens these dangers arise even with our close neighbors, the South Americans. In our country, as we have noted, lawns are important. But most South Americans prefer the courtyard to the lawn. The South American wants a wall around his property, a wall that clearly separates his space from that of others. He also likes to stand quite close to a person he's talking to, inside the North American's "zone of discomfort." Moreover, he thinks little of being half an hour late for almost any appointment. For these reasons, the North American who doesn't know the Latin's non-verbal system is likely to project

98

some very inaccurate ideas. He sees the walls as symbols of suspicion and distrust. As he slowly backs across the room from a "pushy" Latin, he wonders why all South Americans assume such "close friendship" on first meeting. When the Latin doesn't arrive on time for a meeting, he feels insulted. And later, when the South American doesn't even bother to apologize, he feels that insult is being piled on insult!

The farther we go from home, the farther we find ourselves from our own system of non-verbal communication. For instance, the Japanese smile has caused trouble for many Americans. What a Japanese regards as an automatic sign of friendliness makes us uncomfortable. When a Japanese flashes his wide smile of approval, we tend to see it as a definite sneer. Neither do we understand that the laughter of a Japanese is likely to communicate embarrassment. The Japanese laugh does not have to be *at* something. The Japanese hiss can be a sign of praise.

Until recent years, the Japanese considered kissing in public wildly indecent. When the sculptor Rodin's famous statue, "The Kiss," was exhibited in Tokyo, it had to be placed behind a special screen. It was too immoral for public display.

Literature without Words

Non-verbal literature? This sounds like an impossibility, since literature, we think, *is* words. In recent years, however, non-verbal poetry has become something of an international fad. Sometimes called *concrete* poetry, it depends on the shape of a poem to carry most of the meaning. A few words can be used, but design and arrangement must come first. The non-verbal must count for more than the verbal. In the following "poem," for instance, the German *Apfel* translates easily into the English *apple*. Can you find the other word?

How does shape reveal sense in the following two "poems"? (Thinking It Through 6, page 103.) 99

silencio silencio silencio
silencio silencio silencio
silencio   silencio
silencio silencio silencio
silencio silencio silencio

rendering the legible illegible
rendering the il**legible**
rend**erlegible**
rendegible

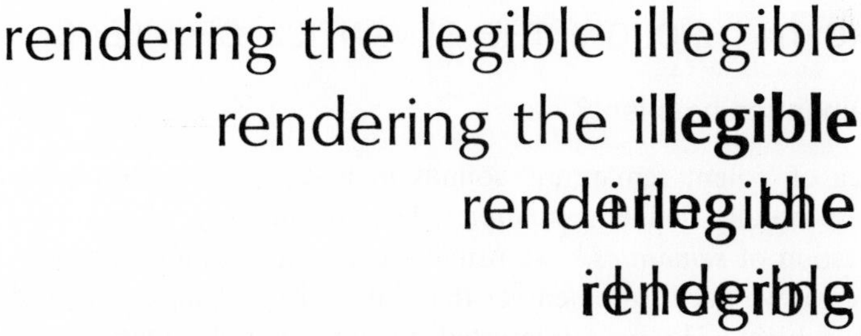

Reviewing the Key Points

1. Remember that you project "meanings" into the "meaningless" actions of others. They also regard your unconscious behavior as a form of communication.
2. Become more aware of the importance of non-verbal communication. Observe the messages carried by shape and color. Think about the codes of space and time.
3. Remember that an understanding of "non-verbal language" is essential to international communication.

Getting It Straight

Read the sentences below. If a sentence *agrees* with what the book has said, put an A next to the number of the sentence on your paper. If a sentence *disagrees,* write a D. If a sentence *neither* agrees *nor* disagrees, mark it with an N.

1. We always know when we are communicating non-verbally.
2. The line between conscious and unconscious communication is sometimes unclear.
3. Thumb-sucking is more common in boys than in girls.
4. It is often difficult to discover what we communicate non-verbally.
5. The barber pole originally symbolized the candy canes distributed with haircuts.
6. Latins differ from North Americans in their treatment of space and time.
7. Latins prefer walled-in courtyards to lawns because of the frequent revolutions in their countries.
8. All Japanese customs are easily understood by Americans.
9. Interest in concrete poetry has grown in recent years.
10. Mathematics should be classified as a non-verbal communications system.

THINKING IT THROUGH: THE SEMANTICS OF SILENCE

1. Can semantics be silent?

The idea of "silent semantics" sounds at first like a contradiction in terms. After all, as usually defined, *semantics* deals exclusively with words. When we say "a question of *semantics*," we usually mean "a question of *words*."

Once again, we need to remember that Alfred Korzybski considered semantics a *general* subject. He was interested in how people react to *everything*—everything in their environments, and everything inside their skins. He noted too that people can react in several ways. They can react *verbally*, with spoken or unspoken words. They can react *emotionally*, with feelings like fear, love, and anger. They can react *physically*, with actions or bodily tensions. They can also react in other complicated ways we do not yet fully understand.

Korzybski believed that these types of reactions could not really be separated from one another. That is, we never react *only* verbally, *only* emotionally, *only* physically, etc. A verbal reaction is always, to some extent, emotional and physical as well. Thus part of a so-called verbal reaction is always silent.

To get across the idea of the sum total of our reactions, Korzybski invented the term *semantic reaction*. A person's SEMANTIC REACTION is his complete reaction as a complicated human being. It may or may not include words. Part of it is always silent.

Test the idea of a semantic reaction by looking at the picture on page 101. Of course, every viewer of the photo will have his own complex reaction. Just concentrate on yours. What emotion did you first feel? What was your verbal reaction (what did you "tell yourself")? Can you really separate the

emotional from the verbal? Did your reactions change in any way as you continued to think and react emotionally? Did any two reactions conflict with one another? What were your physical reactions? Did you feel physically repelled or attracted by anything in the photograph?

Try to explain your semantic reaction to the picture in a few well-written paragraphs. The questions above are just starters, for your reactions are your own. Be honest.

2. A study in space

How do you treat the space in a typical classroom? Where do you like to sit? Why? Do you choose this location with any conscious intent to communicate? When seated, do you rest your feet on the chair ahead? Do you drape your arms over the chairs next to yours? Or do you regard these spaces as "belonging" to other students?

Make a short study of your attitude toward space in a classroom. If you can, contrast your habits with those of two or three other students. You might include the attitudes of some typical teachers as well. How much space does a teacher seem to claim? The area around the desk? The front of the room? The whole

102   room? How does a teacher communicate these attitudes? What does the practice of assigning seats indicate about a teacher's attitude toward classroom space?

3. Your "time table"

Use this short exercise to discover part of your personal time code. Tell how late you would have to be in the five situations below for each of the following to be appropriate: (A) no apology necessary; (B) a word or two of apology; (C) a short explanation or excuse; (D) a long and detailed excuse; (E) better not to show up at all.

1. Late to your present English class.
2. Late meeting your best friend on a sunny streetcorner to go to a movie.
3. Late to an interview for a summer job.
4. Late calling a friend you said you'd phone "about eight."
5. (Boys) Late arriving at the home of your date for the biggest dance of the school year.

   (Girls) Late appearing in the living room after your date has arrived on time to pick you up.

Discuss your answers with those of classmates. How do they compare? See if you can discover the maximum and minimum limits of the time codes in your community. Disregard the few "way out" answers.

4. What's your problem?

Think of a personal situation you could act out non-verbally before the class. For instance, you might be caught wearing your best party dress in a sooty rain. You might be thrown over Niagara Falls in a barrel. Or you might simply be sitting at home working on an assignment for school. How might you indicate these activities?

Think of an interesting situation you believe you could act out successfully within a few minutes. Practice it, using only imaginary props. Finally, offer your non-verbal presentation to the class. Discussion should concern the originality and difficulty of the idea, as well as the variety of non-verbal clues you used to get your message across.

5. More shapes and colors

This chapter mentioned a few distinctive shapes and colors you might see on a busy street. The next time you are in a business area, make a list of at least five more. A good way to do this is to pretend you can't read. Could you recognize a bank as a bank? Could you tell a Ford from a Chevrolet? If so, how? Try not to use objects themselves as clues to their own identity. For instance, do not say you recognized a vegetable stand because of the vegetables on it. Instead, try to find man-made examples of "non-verbal language."

6. Getting your thoughts in shape

a. Try your hand at composing a "concrete" poem. Start on a simple level by making the shapes of a few words suggest something about their meanings:

Copyright 1960 by Saul Steinberg

b. Now it's time to put a more complicated thought into shape. Try to use as few words as possible and to give these words the shapes and colors that reinforce their meanings. You may want to cut letters out of newspaper headlines. What pictures or symbols will convey your meaning? What sort of artistic whole can you construct out of your materials? On the opposite page is an example of non-verbal poetry by an American poet, Kenneth Patchen. Can you do as well? Bring your efforts to class.

7. The signals you send

As the chapter stated, it's often hard to find what other people project into our unconscious non-verbal behavior. Discover something about your own habits by working with a close friend. Don't simply ask him about yourself; you'll probably get nowhere. Instead, you should first write down three of your own "bad habits." These should be mannerisms into which you believe other people project ideas about your character. Then exchange papers and discuss whether you were right or wrong. You will probably discover that most people worry constantly about the wrong things.

Choose one of your unfortunate habits and see whether you can correct it by conscious attention. Don't begin with serious problems like nail-biting or a duck-walk. Select a simple habit that will yield to your will. Check your progress frequently with your friend.

8. A touchy subject

Peoples of different countries have different space and time codes. In much the same way, they also have rather formal but unwritten codes of who may touch whom, and when. For example, Russian men often embrace when they meet, while American men usually do not. These "touching codes" vary widely from one nation to another, and even within the boundaries of a single country. "Shockingly indecent" dancing in one place may be "just friendly" a hundred miles away. The codes also vary with circumstances. Bodily contact in a crowded hallway does not have the same meaning it would have in an uncrowded one.

Through classroom discussion, try to construct a code for the formal touching system in your community. How old does a child have to be before it's considered bad for him to hug his mommy's knee for protection? How old are children when they stop touching each other casually at play? At what age does the pat on the head stop? And what is the touching code among adolescents? Would you put your hand on the shoulder of anyone you are walking with? If so, how many people? Under what circumstances could the teacher touch you without offense? Remember to restrict your inquiry to the formal code that is used for communication. Remember too that the touch itself is not as important as what it's supposed to mean.

Some experts who have studied this subject have concluded that the American adolescent is about the most "untouched" human being on earth. Do you agree? Why?

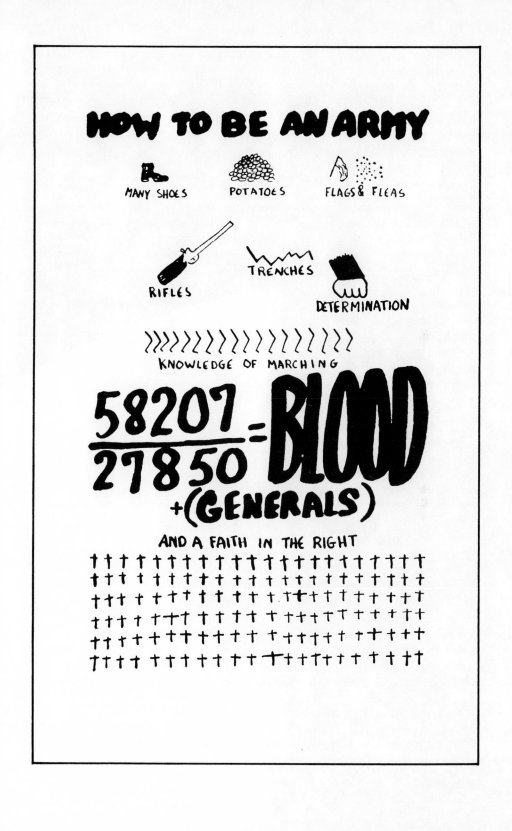

UNIT 5

another mental trap: the two-valued orientation

Back to Words: Our Two-Valued Maps

After a short "time out" for silence, now it's time to get back to words. Again we take up the semanticist's important task of discovering how language affects thought and behavior. So far, our survey of semantics has mapped a good deal of territory. We've investigated our perception and classification of the world around us. We've learned to beware of projection and allness attitudes. With this chapter we'll move a step beyond allness. What other verbal habits can lead us astray?

From One to Infinity

As we've learned, a person with an allness attitude on a certain subject thinks he knows everything about it.

He sees the situation only one way —his way. "My mind is made up;" he seems to say, "don't confuse me with the facts." His cast-iron opinions make the rest of us suffer. Usually we suffer in silence, although we often find ourselves wanting to stand up and protest:

> "Now look at this from my point of view."
> "Wake up and find out what's going on!"
> "But there are two sides to every question."
> "Look, there are two kinds of people in this world."

From a semantic point of view, it's just as well that we usually keep such protests to ourselves. Look at the statements again. Unlike allness attitudes, they seem to indicate that

110   a situation can be seen in two ways. But notice that they also imply that a situation can be viewed in *only* two ways. The words *either* and *or* can be seen lurking between the lines:

> EITHER my point of view OR your point of view.
>
> EITHER asleep and ignorant OR awake and knowing.
>
> EITHER my side OR your side.
>
> EITHER my kind OR your kind.

Now we can begin to understand why we don't often say such statements aloud. We know from experience that they don't do much good. This is so because they offer our listener only two alternatives—his or ours. Statements like these are likely to keep arguments going, not to settle them. Agreements are seldom reached when people think in *either-or* terms.

Unfortunately, thinking in *either-or* terms is an old human habit. Consider the mythical "average man." He looks out at the world and sees either "communist" countries or nations of the "free world." He looks at his countrymen and sees either "whites" or "blacks." At any given moment, he expects to be either "happy" or "sad." His life is either a "success" or a "failure." His children are either "dumbbells" or "smart kids." In short, he suffers from a TWO-VALUED ORIENTATION.

A two-valued orientation is a serious kind of mental disability. Although our territories are usually multi-valued, our maps often remain two-valued. Thus our maps do not adequately represent the territories. For instance, the "either-communist-or-free" orientation leads us to ignore the dictators that rule some "free" countries and the socialist economies of others. We know too that communism (Russia) is not communism (China) is not communism (Yugoslavia), etc. The "either-white-or-black" orientation blurs the fact that about 60,000,000 Americans have mixed blood. Countries like South Africa, that insist on drawing official racial lines on an either-or basis, find the task nearly impossible, as in the following case reported by James A. Michener:

The saddest case I heard about during my South African visit concerned a white mother who took her daughter to beginners' school. While there, she spotted another little girl who looked suspiciously dark. Alerting the police, she had the child and her parents taken before the Race Classification Board. This group of pseudo-scientists inspected the family, paying great attention to the texture of hair, thickness of lips and especially the presence or absence of freckles. "Freckles are a good thing to have in South Africa," my informant told me. "You'd get by. You have freckles."

This family had none and the Board decreed that all three members had been illegally passing themselves off as white. They were reclassified as Coloured. This meant that the child had to be dismissed from school; since the term had started, she could enter no other. The father had to quit his job, for it was reserved for whites. The family had to evacuate their home, selling it in a forced sale at a loss, and move to a ghetto.

Said the mother who had prompted the investigation, "They got what they deserved. After all, they were posing as something they weren't."

As for the "either-happy-or-sad" orientation, haven't you ever been both happy and sad at the same time? And how often is a man *really* a "success" or a "failure"? The majority of men occupy the large middle ground in between. In the same way, the great majority of children are of average intelligence. Study the diagram below.

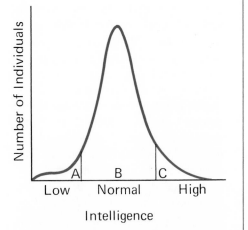

Low   Normal   High

Intelligence

This diagram is an accurate map of a clearly defined territory—the tested intelligence of American children. It shows us that the percentage of children having either very high or very low intelligence is quite small. Notice that the line resembles a "bell-shaped curve." It starts up at a very slight angle, rises rapidly as it approaches "middle ground," declines sharply on the right side of the "normal" group, and then tapers off to nothing. This is the shape of most human territories. It is how they should be mapped. We would get a bell-shaped curve if we graphed such things as heights, weights, incomes and years in school. In most respects,

a two-valued orientation is false to facts.

We might now discover an important cause of *either-or* thinking. Look at the diagram again. How many words can you think of to describe the individuals represented in area A? (*Unintelligent, stupid, slow,* etc.) How many for area C? (*Bright, smart, intelligent,* etc.) How many for area B—*where most of the individuals are found?* Probably none at all. (Words like *average* and *normal* do not refer specifically to intelligence.) Now suppose the diagram represented heights. We have the word *short* for one end of the scale and the word *tall* for the other, but what word do we have for the center? What single word comes between *thin* and *fat*? Between *poor* and *rich*? Between *uneducated* and *educated*?

Our language often gives us convenient single words for the extremes, but no word(s) for "the great in-between." Since we tend to classify and think with the words we know, our mental maps commonly focus on the extremes and obscure the middle. *To a large extent, two-valued orientations are the result of a two-valued language.*

Because our language has this built-in bias, two-valued orientations are difficult to change. Yet change them we must. Semantic sanity depends on MULTI-VALUED ORIENTATIONS. (Korzybski preferred the term INFINITE-VALUED because it reminds us that we cannot know *all* the possibilities in any situation.) The first step in ridding ourselves of two-valued orientations is to realize the harm they can do. (Thinking It Through 4, page 118.)

As indicated above, two-valued orientations give rise to endless arguments. A situation exists, and two people propose two different solutions. They explain, they defend, and they argue. At worst, they come to blows. They agree on little except that the problem has only two possible solutions. Either one side or the other must "win." Obviously, the problem cannot be solved without humiliation of one of the parties.

In many cases, however, a multi-valued approach can be made to work. Instead of arguing, the two parties tell each other, clearly and simply, *why* they feel as they do. Each tries to understand the real interests of the other. Finally, the two cooperate in trying to find the solution that will go farthest in meeting the real need of each. Sometimes the result is simply a compromise. At other times the solution is completely new. It is an answer that would never have been found had the parties engaged in two-valued argument.

Not only does two-valued thinking cause friction between people, it also can lead to trouble for the individual person. Suppose, for instance, that a man wants to quit smoking. He is a "smoker" (a carton a week) who wants to become a "non-smoker." In his mind, he must be *either* one *or* the other. He quits for three days and thinks of himself as a "non-smoker." Then one morning he breaks down and accepts a cigarette from a fellow worker. Woops! He's a "smoker" again. He buys a pack on his coffee break and a carton on his way home from work.

Next week, he tells himself, he'll make another try at becoming a "non-smoker." He does not realize that his heavy smoking will probably last as long as he holds a two-valued orientation to his problem. A multi-valued orientation would suggest a pipe or occasional cigar. It would remind him that there are as many kinds of cigarette smokers as there are people who smoke cigarettes. Some inhale deeply; others hardly at all. Some smoke only half of each cigarette; others burn their fingers for the last hot "drag." Some smoke three cigarettes a day; others smoke three packs.

Young people can do themselves serious harm by taking a two-valued approach to the future. "I'm going to be an engineer," one boy tells himself throughout high school. The alternatives? He has none—except a label spelled f-a-i-l-u-r-e. In his mind, he's going to be *either* an engineer *or* a failure. In his sophomore year of college, unfortunately, he gets low marks in two math courses. He is forced out of the engineering program. Now, of course, he's a "failure." He drops out of college and finds a dropout's job, still not realizing that the future is almost always multi-valued.

A two-valued orientation often invites disaster. Think about some people you know. Actual cases are not hard to find. A high school girl, for instance, prides herself on being "honest." She believes that everyone is essentially "honest" or "dishonest." This orientation serves her well until her senior year. In the spring, she gets so involved in the senior play that she has to copy part of a history paper to get it in on time. Her mistake is discovered, and soon all her teachers know that she's "dishonest." Some people, in this situation, would shrug their shoulders and live up to the label. This girl, however, struggles with the label until the strain forces her to drop out of the senior play. She still fails to see that there are many degrees between "honesty" and "dishonesty." There is no bell-shaped curve in her mind. Instead, her mental map looks something like this:

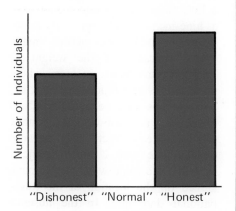

Throughout history, two-valued thinking has been a threat to human progress. Today, for instance, the surgeon's skill is ranked among the highest of medical specialties. Not so a few hundred years ago! In that era, people took a two-valued approach to the subject of occupations. (The habit lingers with us today.) A person worked *either* with his hands *or* with his head. He was either a "menial" or a "professional." Since surgery was done with the hands, it was not considered a proper job for a gentleman. The doctor had to employ a "menial" (usually a barber) to do the actual cutting, while he stood by and directed. For many years, the art of surgery progressed hardly at all. Physicians themselves had the "either-or disease." (Thinking It Through 1–3, pages 116–117, and 5–6, pages 118–119.)

The Facts about "Facts"

Two-valued orientations are sometimes signaled by the presence of certain words. We already know about *either* and *or*. We should also be suspicious of pairs of words like *fact* and *fiction, true* and *false,* and *real* and *unreal*. These slippery words can lead us to think in either-or terms. They can make us see two where there may be many.

Here is a list of ten statements. Give each of them some thought. How many would you accept as "facts." Which would you classify as "non-facts"? Why?

1. You have both a first and a last name.
2. All Americans have both first and last names.
3. President Lincoln's first name was Abraham.
4. Some farmers in Iowa will raise corn next summer.
5. At this moment you are reading a book.
6. Santa Claus has eight reindeer.
7. Sirloin steak is better than hamburger.
8. Christ was born on December 25.
9. George Washington crossed the Delaware in a small boat.
10. There are too many commercials on TV.

114   All these statements would probably be accepted as "facts" in the everyday thinking of most people. Did you accept them all? If you did, think about the list again. For instance, if Santa Claus does not exist, how can it be a "fact" that he has any number of reindeer at all? And how do you really know that Washington crossed the Delaware in a small boat, or even that he crossed it at all? Can a famous painting be enough to establish a "fact"?

If you didn't label all ten statements as "facts," you probably have objections to the exercise itself. It's not fair, you think, to be asked to put all ten statements into only two baskets, "facts" and "non-facts." Some of the statements seem "truer" than others. Some are "true" for different reasons. Some may be "true" for you, but not for everybody.

These objections are sensible. They reveal a multi-valued orientation. If we think about it, we will see that we commonly label several different kinds of statements with the single term *fact:*

1. OBSERVATIONS. These are the "facts" we know from personal experience. If Mr. A testifies in court that he saw Mr. X running out of a bank right after a robbery, he is giving an observation. (He may be mistaken, of course; human perception is not foolproof.) Statements 1 and 5 above are probably best termed *observations,* since you know them from your own experience.

2. REPORTS. Because our own experience is limited, we often have to depend on reports of the observations of other people. If Miss A testifies that Mr. B told her he saw Mr. X running out of the bank, she is giving a report. (And the court would probably rule it out as "hearsay" evidence.) Most historical "facts," like 3 and 9 in our ten statements, are best called *reports,* since they are far removed from our own experience. Historians usually consider the evidence of two unbiased persons sufficient to establish a historical "fact."

3. AGREEMENTS. Why is it a "fact" that there are three feet in a yard? Only because people have agreed on these standards of measurement. If British history had been a little different, we might now have a nine-inch "foot" and a four-foot "yard." Today we accept many "facts" because of the weight of tradition, particularly in areas where observations and reports are lacking. No one has ever seen Santa Claus or talked to a person who has. Santa's reindeer are a "fact" only because people have agreed on the subject. In much the same way, people have agreed on the location of the international date line. In the absence of observations and reports, people have agreed that Christ's birthday shall be celebrated on December 25.

4. INFERENCES. An inference is an extension of what is known. It goes beyond observations and reports. If all the Americans in our experience have had both first and last names, we might make the inference that "all Americans have both first and last names." In this case the inference is not a "fact," since many birth certificates bear only last names and initials (such as "J.D." or "K.C."). Other inferences, however, like statement 4, are more reliable.

5. VALUE JUDGMENTS. It is a fact that people have opinions, but these opinions themselves are seldom "facts." *"Most people think* sirloin steak is better than hamburger" is the kind of "fact" that could be established by observations and reports (a public opinion poll, for instance). But considered by itself, "Sirloin steak is better than hamburger" is best termed a *value judgment.* Would all TV executives agree that there are too many commercials? If not, statements about "too many commercials" should be recognized as value judgments, not facts. Of course, there are some value judgments on which nearly all Americans seem to agree: "It is wrong for people in China to eat dogs." Even here, however, it is better to separate the report (Chinese eat dogs) from the value judgment (It is wrong). Don't many persons in India think it is "wrong" for us to eat cattle? Are they entitled to their opinion? Or are they entitled to their "facts"?

In recent years words like *fact, truth,* and *real* have come to have the ring of authority. They are spoken continually by persons who urge us to abandon our "time-worn traditions," our "false mythologies," our "outmoded stereotypes." To be modern, it seems, is to be in touch with the "facts." To semanticists, all this is very fine—up to a point. Semanticists know only too well that the world is crying for change. They would agree that we should argue only *with* the facts, and that stubborn facts are the first cousins of stubborn people. But they would also maintain that today's fact-worshipper often suffers from a two-valued

orientation: *either* modern and factual *or* old and untrue. Semanticists would ask what *kinds* of "facts" are being shouted from every rooftop—prejudiced observations? biased reports? inferences and value judgments dressed up as facts? (Thinking It Through 7–10, pages 120–123).

As the American writer Stephen Crane knew, the truth is seldom so simple as some would have us believe:

"Truth," said a traveller,
"Is a rock, a mighty fortress;
Often I have been to it,
Even to its highest tower,
From whence the world looks black."

"Truth," said a traveller,
"Is a breath, a wind,
A shadow, a phantom;
Long have I pursued it,
But never have I touched
The hem of its garment."

And I believed the second traveller;
For truth was to me
A breath, a wind,
A shadow, a phantom,
And never had I touched
The hem of its garment.

Reviewing the Key Points

1. Remember that two-valued orientations often result in trouble. Remain flexible and multi-valued. Ask yourself frequently, "Is this really an 'either-or' question?"
2. Distrust words like *fact, true,* and *real.* Remember that the label *fact* commonly covers observations, reports, agreements, inferences, and value judgments. Thinking in these terms will make you more multi-valued.

Getting It Straight

A. Be prepared to explain how each of the following terms is used in semantic analysis:

two-valued orientation	observation	inference
multi-valued orientation	report	value judgment
infinite-valued orientation	agreement	

B. On a sheet of paper, try to classify each of the following "facts" as an observation, report, agreement, inference, or value judgment. Suppose yourself to be the speaker of statements 1, 2, and 3. If you want to classify a statement in two or more ways, do so and explain why.

1. I got caught in the rain yesterday.
2. Today I feel a cold coming on.
3. The rain caused me to catch cold.
4. There are 360 degrees of arc in a full circle.
5. Pitcher Steve Blass won two games for Pittsburgh during the 1971 World Series.
6. The rigorous New England climate is more healthful than that of the South.
7. Santa Claus lives at the North Pole.
8. New York is bigger than Chicago.
9. New York is better than Chicago.
10. The sun will rise tomorrow.

THINKING IT THROUGH: THE "EITHER-OR DISEASE"

1. The power of Janus

In ancient Rome, Janus was the god of beginnings and endings. He had two faces that looked in opposite directions. From him we get the name of the "middle" month, January. We also get the expression *Janus-faced,* or "deceitful." People have always felt disturbed by the presence of two opposite qualities at the same time. Our two-valued orientations lead us to expect *either* one *or* the other.

Strange as it may seem at times, having two "opposite" emotions or ideas simultaneously is not uncommon. For instance, nearly everyone has had the sudden impulse to steal something in a store. The urge is overcome (hopefully!), leaving us with mixed feelings. We feel honest because we didn't carry out the theft, yet we feel dishonest because we came very close. Although we feel virtuous, our thoughts of the minute before put us to shame.

Think of an experience that left you confused by conflicting emotions. Perhaps you decided to return a stolen gift to the store where it had been shoplifted. Perhaps you told an "honest lie." Perhaps you broke down after winning some intense competition, happy with your prize but sad that all your friends couldn't have won too. Describe your experience in a report of about 150 words. How would an awareness of the *either-or* fallacy have enabled you to understand yourself better?

2. It's always here and now

A multi-valued orientation toward the future is essential in all areas of life. We must remain flexible. This doesn't always mean we have to give up our goals. It does mean, however, that we must be willing to change our goals as life changes our opportunities.

How two-valued is your approach to the future? Will you be like the dying man who thought his life a failure because he was still a few dollars short of his cherished million? Write one of your serious goals at the top of a piece of paper. Under it put down three specific circumstances that might make this goal impossible. Now explain fully what you think you would do in each of the three situations. If you have trouble, all the more reason to grit your teeth and go on writing. This is a necessary exercise, not a pleasant one.

3. Either sheep or goats

Have you ever been the victim of another person's two-valued orientation? Such a person insists on classifying others as either sheep or goats—while you think of yourself, perhaps, as a rare sort of woodland deer. As a result, you feel the most important thing about you is going unnoticed: your individuality.

This kind of either-or thinking is often practiced by persons who are themselves members of the "superior" group. In some schools, for example, one finds a clique of students who have been together since the earliest grades. "You're either one of us," their attitude seems to say, "or you're not *and never can be.*" In the business world, men with college degrees sometimes form the Snob party, all others being the Slobs. Among occupational groups, too, the two-valued orientation is sometimes used to establish a "superior" position. Recently the Police Commissioner of New York City defended his force by saying, "The policeman is not just another city employe. He is not a sanitation worker.

118   He is not a fireman." In other words, a municipal worker was *either* a "policeman" *or* "just another city employe." This made the firemen angry. "The Police Commissioner would do well to just shut up!" a prominent Fire Officer snapped.

Try to recall a case in which you were the victim of an unfair two-valued orientation. If you have trouble thinking of one, recall your frustrations as a girl, as a boy, as a teenager, and as a member of a racial, religious, or ethnic group. Choose one unhappy experience that resulted from another person's either-or thinking. Explain the details fully in a few paragraphs. For extra credit, add an example of an unreasonable two-valued orientation of your own. This will probably be more difficult, since we're often unaware that our either-or classifications do harm to others.

4. Improving the English language

The Chinese language differs from English in many ways. Each has its advantages and disadvantages. One strong point of Chinese is that it allows for more "middle ground." People who know both languages say that Chinese is not as likely to lead to two-valued orientations.

Look at the ancient Chinese symbol, "yin and yang," below. Notice that although the two sides are "opposites," they seem to blend together, to penetrate one another, and to be parts of a larger whole. Speakers of English would do well to make this symbol a part of their mental maps.

Along these lines, can you think of any way the English language might be made less two-valued? For instance, you might invent some new words for the many "in-between's" that now go unnamed. Or you might choose to handle the extremes with prefixes and suffixes. There are many possible systems. Think of one and give a few examples of your own.

5. Our multi-valued world

How two-valued is your approach to international affairs? Does your mind treat the nations of the world like characters in an old western movie, either "good guys" or "bad guys"? Do you really believe there is a "Third World?" If you do, are there only three? Do you believe that each nation should be allowed to develop independently in its own way?

Try to find a social studies teacher who will come to your class to discuss these important questions. First make sure that your guest fully understands the difference between a two-valued orientation and a multi-valued orientation. Then ask how two-valued thinking affects world affairs. What results from this attitude: "If Nation X is not our friend, it must be our enemy"? How should the United States react to similar attitudes on the part of other powers?

If you cannot talk with a social studies teacher, simply discuss these statements in class:

All-out war is almost always two-valued.
True peace is almost always multi-valued.

6. Get set to "double think"

Since we can think about thinking, we can apply two-valued thinking to the subject of two-valued thinking itself. In other words, we can assume that our thinking is *either* two-valued and bad *or* multi-valued and good. This assumption is not always true. Two-valued orientations are occasionally useful.

In the first place, we often face situations that offer only two courses of action. Suppose you wake up on a weekday morning with a sore throat and a headache. You can *either* stay at home *or* go to school. There may be many reasons for your final decision, but basically there are only two choices. (Once the decision has been made, however, the person with a multi-valued orientation again has the advantage. He might miss school but try not to miss all that went on in school. He might call up a friend for the day's gossip and homework. He might re-read the assignments that his classes were to discuss that day. For him the day would not be completely "school" or completely "non-school." He would remain flexible.)

In the second place, even where three or more choices are possible, it is sometimes best to limit ourselves to two. For example, most Americans believe in the two-party system. They base their belief on the history of our nation and the experience of other countries. They know, of course, that our two large parties completely please almost no one. But they also know that our two-party system seems to function better than a multi-party system that offers everyone his exact choice. (Here again, however, the two-valued approach can be carried too far. Try to explain why.)

Think of a two-valued orientation you would defend as a useful one. If you have trouble, think about concerns that really bother you—the use of drugs, for instance. A two-valued approach would place you squarely on either the *yes* or the *no* side of the drug question. A multi-valued orientation would lead you to evaluate each drug on its individual properties. Which orientation would be better for you? Why? (Remember that Alcoholics Anonymous insists on an intense two-valued orientation.)

Write a short statement defending your two-valued approach to a complicated question. Read it to the class. Does everyone agree?

Choose an area you think you know something about. It can be a school subject or a field of general interest like politics or music. Examine some of the "facts" in this area. See if you can discover examples of observations, reports, agreements, inferences, and value judgments.

As an example, suppose you choose physics. Any of the "facts" you prove experimentally in the physics lab are *observations*. Most of the "facts" in your textbook, however, are *reports;* you have not observed them yourself. An *agreement* is an understanding among physicists that has no basis in nature: that 100°C shall be equal to 212°F, for example. An *inference* is an extension of the known into the unknown, such as the statement that the invisible atom is like a small solar system. A *value judgment* is a statement of opinion, such as the view that Albert Einstein was the greatest physicist in history.

When you have written down at least one example of each kind of "fact," consider this question: How would you prove each statement to someone else? Does the kind of "proof" depend on the kind of "fact"? If so, explain how.

8. Jumping to conclusions

It happens sometimes in our larger cities: A man staggers on a busy street and makes his way to the edge of the sidewalk. In the crowd his actions go largely unnoticed. He sits down and then slumps over. People who see him shudder and look quickly away. "Another drunk," they tell themselves. "What's this city coming to?" Thousands of people pass by.

In truth, the man has had a heart attack. The only observation apparent to most people is that the man is lying on the sidewalk. The assumption that the man is drunk is an *inference*. Jumping to conclusions is simply going too rapidly from observations (or reports) to inferences.

Here are five examples of our amazing ability to jump to conclusions. As you read each paragraph, cover the small type below it with your hand. What inference might *you* have made? What do you think is the truth?

a. A first-grade teacher noticed that Myron L scowled at her from the very first day. In fact, he frowned at almost everyone except a few friends who sat in his work-unit. He seemed to learn very slowly, even when the teacher drew diagrams on the board. Unable to keep up with his classmates, he grew anxious and irritable. He spent most of his time staring blankly at his desk and shaking his head. Just before Thanksgiving, the teacher reached a conclusion as to what should be done in Myron's case.

The inference: Myron is extremely unintelligent. He should be examined for the retarded class.

The truth: Myron needed glasses. (Luckily, the school nurse arrived for a routine eye check before the psychologist made an appearance.)

b. An art teacher gave an exhibition of her pupils' best work. It was held in the school gym at the end of the year. One morning before the first bell, she noticed a small second-grade girl standing in rapture before one of the paintings. She smiled to herself, for she thought privately that this was the best picture in the show. Between classes the little girl came back, and again during her lunch period. The same thing happened the next day, and the next. Finally the art teacher decided that the girl must have the painting. Since the girl's clothes indicated that her family was short of money, the teacher decided to pay for it herself. The student artist was happy to take $3.00. When the little girl arrived on the last day of the show, the art teacher rolled the painting up and gave it to the child. "Now," she told her, "you can take it home and hang it on your wall." The girl stood shocked a moment, then burst into tears and fled from the gym.

The inference: The girl was embarrassed by the unexpected gift.
The truth: The girl lived with her mother in the center of a large room rented by relatives. She literally did not have any wall to hang the picture on. (The art teacher discovered the truth when she went to the child's address after school to make another try.)

c. Unlike other teachers in the high school, Mr. M preferred to eat lunch alone at his desk. When asked about his habit, he always replied that he liked to take advantage of the rare period of peace and quiet on the third floor. One day a boy who happened to be on the floor during lunch period stopped in the corridor to glance through Mr. M's window. He saw the teacher unlock his coat closet and half fill a small glass from a bottle concealed in a paper bag. Locking the closet, the teacher carried the brown liquid to his desk and set it down behind the paper bag that held his lunch. The next day the boy brought two friends to witness the event. Soon rumors were flying through the school, and before long they had reached the principal's ears. The principal found an excuse to burst in on Mr. M ten minutes after the lunch period had started.

The inference: Mr. M was drinking on duty.
The truth: Mr. M suffered from arthritis and sipped a home-made remedy of vinegar, honey, and water with all his meals.

d. Shortly after her retirement, Miss P decided to take up amateur photography. She got some good advice and decided on the equipment she'd need. The camera would cost $49.95; the enlarger, $99.95. She was almost ready to buy these items when she happened to see an ad in a newspaper published in a city thirty miles away. She was overjoyed: the camera was advertised at $29.00, and the enlarger would cost only $69.00.

The inference: The store was offering tremendous bargains.
The truth: The store did not sell the camera without its case, which cost $20.00. Similarly, the enlarger could not be purchased without a $30.00 lens. Miss P drove sixty miles to save $1.90.

122   e. An elderly woman lived in a New York City apartment with an old dog as her only companion. The beloved dog grew ill and finally died. The end came on a Friday afternoon, and the woman was suddenly presented with a new problem. What did one do with the body of a twenty-five pound dog? She called up the A.S.P.C.A. (American Society for the Prevention of Cruelty to Animals). They would pick up the dog, she learned, but not until Monday. Did she then have to keep the dog in her apartment all weekend? No, she was told. If she could get the dog to the A.S.P.C.A. office before 5:00, they would be glad to take it. Immediately she changed her dress and put the dog's body in an old suitcase. She hurried downstairs, hoping that if she took a cab she could get to the A.S.P.C.A. before 5:00. Out on the sidewalk, she decided to leave the heavy suitcase on the street while she walked to a busy avenue half a block away to get a cab. Before she reached the corner, however, she turned around to see a teenage boy running hard in the opposite direction with the suitcase. She gasped as he disappeared a block away.

The inference: The boy would be surprised when he got to a safe place and discovered how wrong his inference had been.
The truth: He probably was!

Inferences can be right as well as wrong. In fact, inferences are right most of the time. Life would be impossible without the thousands of inferences we make every day. Still, it pays to remember that we *can* be wrong. It is all too easy to jump to incorrect conclusions. The inference made by the boy who stole the suitcase was about as wrong as it could be.

Search your own experience for an example of jumping to faulty conclusions. It can be a mistake of your own or one you have witnessed. But it should be a case in which the inference seemed reasonable at the time it was made. Explain the situation in a short paragraph, including all necessary details. Read it to the class. Let your classmates make the inference and—if possible—find the truth.

9. Our lasting inferences

An odd quality of inferences is their staying power. Some persons jump to conclusions on the basis of very little evidence. Then, no matter how much contradictory evidence they meet, they refuse to change their original inferences. For example, a man from Kentucky may have met three Vermonters long ago in the Army. He formed the conclusion that Vermonters are "great, great people." Since his discharge from the Army, he has met ten more people from Vermont. Seven of them have been quite ordinary people, and three have been scoundrels. But the man is still convinced that Vermonters are "great, great people." The three scoundrels, he says, are "exceptions to the rule" or "not *real* Vermonters."

It's not difficult to find this trait in other people. In ourselves, however, it's sometimes a hard task. Examine your own mental maps for an inference that should be changed. It should be a conclusion you "know" is wrong, but for

some reason refuse to change. Try to explain why you continue to hold it.
What does the opinion do for you? What would you really lose if you changed it?

10. Inferences in advertising

The power of inference is important to advertising. Look through a popular magazine. You might see a cigarette ad similar to this one: A well-dressed young couple is standing next to a long, black, chauffeur-driven car. Before them, a velvet lawn sweeps up to the front of a marble mansion. The man has just finished lighting the woman's cigarette and is now removing one from the pack for himself. The woman is inhaling blissfully, glancing up at the open door of the mansion they are about to enter.

What are the facts? An advertising agency has taken a picture of three paid models and a rented car. The owner of the mansion has probably been paid something too.

What are the inferences? The obvious one is that the truly beautiful people of our world smoke this brand of cigarette as a matter of habit. This is the inference the advertising agency wants us to make. But notice all the other inferences in the ad: That socially prominent people smoke and enjoy it. That it will be proper for the woman to enter the mansion holding a cigarette. That the man's maroon bow tie is "in" again this season. That the woman's rather flat heels are acceptable for social use. That men of the world use cigarette lighters, not matches. The list could go on and on.

Advertising is a powerful force in American life. Indirectly, ads for cigarettes sell everything from shoes to lawn fertilizer. Ads for lawn fertilizer sell everything from tuxedos to croquet sets. Ads teach us what to want, how to behave, and where to place our values. They are magical mental maps.

Find an ad that depends on the power of inference to sell its product. Explain the main inference—the one the advertising agency wants us to make. Now see if you can find five more inferences that have nothing to do with the product itself. How many more can you find? Write your observations on a piece of paper, clip it to the ad, and bring it to class.

Case Study:
The
Master Mechanic

Name *Thomas W.—*   Age *18*   Height *6'1"*

Weight *187* Hair *Brown*   Eyes *Blue-Green*

Health *Good; football injury to left knee*

I.Q. *112*   Average: frosh *82*   soph *87*   jr *89*   sr *90*

Activities *Motor Club; Film Group*

Sports *Football and basketball none in senior year.*

In the spring of his senior year at L——Technical High School, Tom W listed his name with the employment service run by the guidance department. During graduation week he received a notice to call R—— Motors for an interview. He lost no time in making an appointment. Not only was R—— Motors within walking distance of Tom's home, it was the kind of large garage he thought might offer real opportunities.

Mr. R's office was a small one right off the showroom. Tom entered to find Mr. R on the telephone. A man of about fifty, he had carefully arranged gray hair and a stern, heavily-lined face. His shirt seemed very white and clean for a man in the garage business. He waved a hand for Tom to sit down in the only vacant chair. In a minute he concluded his phone call and began the interview.

Mr. R: Okay, now. You're Tom W_____?

Tom: That's right, sir.

Mr. R: Don't "sir" me. It's a waste of time. I suppose you know why you're here.

Tom: Well, I wanted to see about that job.

Mr. R: You're hired.

Tom: *What?*

Mr. R: Can you start Monday?

Tom (confused): I don't . . .

Mr. R: Let me explain about the way I do business. I don't like to get all messed up in personalities. Mr. S_____ down at the school said you were the best boy he could send over. That's enough for me. You were hired before you walked in here.

Tom: I'm just a little . . .

Mr. R (Standing up): I don't hire men on the basis of their looks, their color, their political opinions, or anything else. I run a tight shop here. Every man has a job to do, and he either does it well or he doesn't do it well. It's as simple as that. There are two ways of running a business, like a business or like a social club. You start letting personalities influence things and you end up in bankruptcy court. Right?

Tom (standing up): I guess. . . . Sure.

Mr. R: Fact of the matter is, the shop foreman's brother-in-law wants this job. But that would be letting personalities get into the machinery here. Besides, all the facts are on your side. Don't worry—I know what I'm doing.

Tom: What about wages?

Mr. R: You'll get apprentice pay to start, and after that we'll see. We're not union here, but I pay good wages for good work. And I keep my men a long time. So— want a day to think it over?

Tom: It's down in the shop, right? Not up here on the grease racks and gas pumps?

Mr. R: The shop, right. Eight to four-thirty. Weekends off.

Tom: I think I'll take it.

Mr. R: Good. I have a feeling we're going to see eye-to-eye about things. Monday morning at eight then.

As Tom walked home, he found it hard to believe that he actually had the job. He had said almost nothing during the interview. Mr. R had seemed very businesslike, and he had also seemed fair. The only thing that worried Tom was

---

Marginal notes:

Has Mr. R jumped to a conclusion?

Two-valued orientation.

Don't personalities always "influence things"? Can you keep them out?

What "facts"?

the matter of the foreman's brother-in-law. Would the foreman be annoyed because a boy just out of school had won the job?

Tom met the foreman a little after eight the following Monday morning. Mr. R, busy as usual, had sent him down to the shop alone. Tom looked around and decided that the foreman must be the man in a white coat sorting job orders at a small desk.

Tom: Excuse me. I'm Tom W_____.

Foreman: Tom W_____? Oh, yeah, Mr. R_____ told me you'd be coming.

Tom: You know, I'm really glad to be here.

Foreman: What's your experience, kid? Just school?

Projection. It later came out that the foreman didn't like his brother-in-law and was happy *not* to have him in the shop.

Tom: They give a really good auto course at L_____. (Thinking: *He doesn't like me. He's sore because his brother-in-law didn't get the job.*)

Foreman: They do what they can, I guess.

Tom: I think they taught me a lot. And I got the Master Mechanic's Prize at graduation.

Foreman: Think you're a master mechanic?

Tom: No, of course not. That's just what they call the prize.

Allness. School (twenty years ago) is not school (today). Boy$_1$ is not boy$_2$.

Foreman: I was just kidding you. You see, I know all about that school. I went there myself twenty years ago. The boys they turn out can all read shop manuals and follow instructions, but they don't know any of the little tricks yet.

Tom: I know I've got a lot to learn.

Foreman: See that '72 Ford over there?

Tom: The green one?

Foreman: Right. The front wheel bearings need to be repacked. Think you can do it?

Tom: Sure. Got a bearing packer?

Foreman: No, we do it by hand. Use a floor jack. There's a full tool set there on the bench.

Inference. The foreman's failure to introduce Tom could have several causes.

Tom: Okay. (Thinking: *Why doesn't he introduce me to the rest of the mechanics? He's got them all poisoned against me, I bet.*)

In a short time, Tom removed the bearings from the left front wheel. He found a can of cleaning fluid and started to rinse off the old grease. A mechanic working nearby approached him.

Mechanic: That's not the right way.

Tom (looking up): Oh, hi. What do you mean, it's not the right way?

Mechanic: We don't rinse them off. We just push in some more grease and put them right back on the car.

Tom: *That's* the wrong way.

Mechanic: It's the right way!

Foreman (coming up): He's right, Tom. That cleaning stuff is for the trade schools. It doesn't matter, and we've got to save time around here.

Tom: Well, okay. (Thinking: *I'll do it his way, then. But it's still the wrong way.*)

Before long Tom had the bearings repacked and the front wheels back on the car. His next job was to take the cylinder heads off an old Chevrolet V-8 that was due for a valve job. Wanting to work fast, he bent over the motor and tried to ignore everything else that was happening in the big shop. Salesmen and customers wandered in and out. The foreman took a car out for a road test. Once Tom looked up to see the other mechanics sitting on boxes in a corner. It was their break time, he supposed. In a few minutes the foreman returned.

Foreman: Tom, you didn't take a break?

Tom: No.

Foreman: Why not?

Two-valued. Is there only either a "right" or a "wrong" way to do this job?

Tom: Well, no one told me. . . . (Suddenly) You know, this is about the most unfriendly place I ever walked into!

Foreman: Sit down a few minutes, Tom. Rest and cool off. (Lowering his voice) See, kid, it's like this. Before you came, the men were getting a night or two of overtime a week. Sometimes three, if they wanted it. Now with you here, they won't be getting all that overtime, for a while at least. They haven't got anything against you *personally.*

Tom: You'd never know it, but okay. (Sitting down to one side and thinking: *I don't believe him for a minute. He's got some plan cooked up to get rid of me. Then his brother-in-law can come in and take the job.*)

A misleading inference. The foreman has just told Tom the truth.

Mr. R (appearing suddenly): What are *you* doing?

Tom: Nothing. I . . . It's my break.

Mr. R: It's not break time.

Foreman (coming up): I told him to sit down a few minutes. He didn't take a break earlier.

Mr. R (to Tom): Break times are ten and two-thirty.

Tom (standing up): Good. Now at least I know.

Foreman (to Mr. R): Don't take it out on the kid. It's my fault.

Projection. How can Tom know the foreman's motives?

Tom (thinking as he returns to work: *Boy, what a slimy guy that foreman is. He gets me in trouble, then pretends to take my side like a big hero.*)

At lunch time two of the mechanics left for a diner across the street. The other men picked up their lunch boxes and went into a small room off the shop floor. Tom realized he'd left his lunch upstairs. He went to get it, and when he returned the door to the small room was standing half open. Tom entered to find the foreman and three mechanics seated around a card table. The foreman's back was to Tom. No one glanced up. Tom stood there a short minute, wondering what to do. There were no more chairs in the room. Should he look for one and bring it in? Suddenly he found himself walking back into the shop, determined to eat alone.

Tom munched his ham sandwich without tasting it. How long would this treatment go on? Till he quit? Perhaps he should quit right now, he thought. He could simply go upstairs and tell Mr. R he'd like to be paid for his morning's work. He thought of Mr. R's words: "Every man has a job to do, and he either does it well or he doesn't do it well. It's as simple as that." The trouble was, it wasn't as simple as that. Not by a long shot.

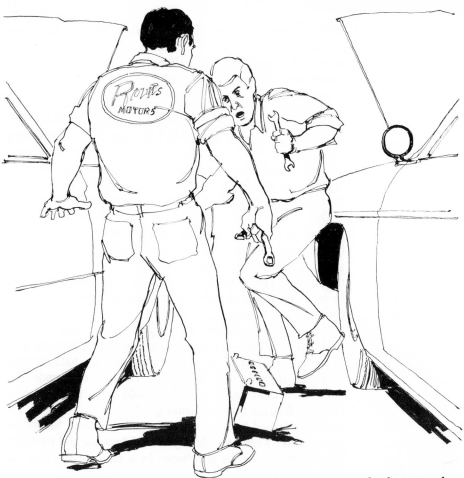

After lunch Tom found it hard to get back to work. He couldn't concentrate. He found himself dropping socket wrenches and forgetting where he'd put parts. An hour passed. One of the mechanics drove another car into the garage and parked it about eighteen inches from Tom's Chevrolet. The two men didn't have room to work. Suddenly there was a crash that shook the concrete under Tom's feet. He looked down to see a cracked battery not four inches from his toe.

Jumping to a conclusion.

Tom: You dropped that on purpose!

Mechanic: I did not!

Tom: You're telling me that was an accident?

Mechanic: It slipped off the battery carrier. See, I've still got the carrier here in my hand.

Tom (angry now): What does that prove?

Foreman (coming up): What's the trouble here?

Mechanic: He claims—

132 along without thinking much about their responsibilities. Given Mr. R's attitude toward his workers, could Tom's problems have been avoided by responsible action on lower levels? If so, how? Is it true that no matter what a person's job is, it always includes communication? Explain your point of view.

3. Here and now

Studies show that most people, most of the time, consider themselves to be in uneasy personal situations of some kind. These are usually situations that good communication might improve. In fact, the people involved know the importance of "talking things over." Their problem is not a failure to realize the importance of communication. It is a failure to know how to open or reopen the channels of communication. Pride, fear, an inferior position, projected fantasies, the memory of past disappointments—all these factors hold them back.

Chances are that you are now involved in such a situation yourself. It may have lasted for a few days or for a few years. It may involve classmates, friends, teachers, parents, or other persons. It may cause daily distress, or it may just nag at your mind now and then. The important thing is that you feel good communication could improve things.

Tom solved his problem simply by going to the "top man" and explaining his position as honestly as he could. Would this procedure work in your case? Probably not; different problems demand different solutions. Here are a few more you might consider:

1. Letting the situation reach the "boiling point" or deliberately provoking an incident. The words may be harsh when they finally come, but at least communication will be established.

2. Placing yourself in a position where communication is unavoidable.

3. Asking a mutual friend or any fair person to see if he can discover where the misunderstanding lies.

4. Acting in a manner that disproves the other party's incorrect opinions about you.

5. Discovering whether your own opinions have any basis in fact.

Choose some personal situation that you think stands a fair chance of improvement. Consider this situation in the light of the five solutions above, and try to think through other solutions of your own. For instance, you might have to apologize for a past mistake. Or you might have to find some undisputed area that you and the other party can share in common. Decide on a course of action, and then *do something*. For a possible future report, record your progress whenever appropriate, stressing not the problem itself but your efforts and their results.

4. Semantics on the job

Many work situations can lead to misunderstandings. This is particularly true for newly hired workers. The new person often steps into a complex network of personal relationships he knows little about. He is likely to jump to conclusions and to project wrong thoughts into other people's minds. These tendencies are especially dangerous when the new worker is nervous and inexperienced, or when his coming seems to make another worker's situation worse.

Not all new employes have these problems, however. Some employers foresee possible difficulties and use semantic techniques to make life easier for the new worker. In such situations, the workers involved are told exactly why a new person has been hired. They also know exactly what he is to do and when he is to begin. They have been encouraged to air any objections, and they know from experience that their suggestions will receive a fair hearing. When the newcomer arrives, he is introduced and made to feel welcome. Everything he needs to learn is clearly explained. His supervisor knows that it will save time in the long run to take a little extra time now: "There, have I made myself clear?" "Do you have any questions?" "If you have any problems, just come and see me." "We feel that communication is part of everybody's job here."

Perhaps you have had some experience in a work situation. If not, ask your friends or members of your family. Try to find an employment experience that was either very good or very bad. It should involve a new employe and, if possible, more than one other person. Describe this experience in detail. If it was a good one, what principles of communication made it so? Any in addition to the above? If bad, what were the misunderstandings that made things go wrong? What "semantic insurance" might have been taken against them?

When these reports are completed, you and your classmates should form into small groups for discussion. First consider the good situations. Make a list of all the techniques you can find to improve a new employe's morale and efficiency. Then turn to the bad experiences. When you have heard all in your group, choose the one report that seems to provide the best role-playing opportunities. For instance, suppose a prospective worker is called in for a job interview. She is asked a series of very personal questions she thinks are irrelevant. How does she react? Or later, on the job, how does she handle a disgruntled worker who tries to get her to join some revenge plan against the supervisor? Or suppose the new employe soon finds that the supervisor is claiming credit for work she herself has actually done. She decides to talk to someone about it. But to whom? And how does she begin?

When you have chosen your role-playing situation, select people to play all the parts except that of the new employe. These persons should understand the situation and their own parts thoroughly. Also make sure that one person in your group can act as narrator, explaining all the necessary details. Then bring the whole class together and put members of the other groups in the position of the new employe. This works best when two or three students are asked to leave the room, to be put on the same "spot" one after the other. The rest of the class can then discuss the reactions of different individuals to the same situation. Whose behavior was most successful? Why?

UNIT 6
levels of knowledge: two key understandings

From Electrons to Ideas: the Structural Differential

Like many subjects one can study, semantics has two distinct sides, the theoretical and the practical. The last chapter was devoted solely to the practical aspects. With the present chapter we return to theory.

—STOP. Did you notice anything wrong with the paragraph above? You should have. Chapter 8 stressed the dangers of either-or thinking. Look up at the paragraph again. Doesn't it imply that theory can be separated from practice? Is this possible? Does it make semantic sense to state that we can deal exclusively with *either* one *or* the other?

Theory and practice should not be separated. One can be stressed, of course, but the other is always there. This book attempts to involve both theory and practice in the study of semantics. And this chapter will present a theory of great practical value: the principle of abstraction.

Strange Voices and Five-Dollar Bills

Awareness of the process of abstraction is the key to semantic sanity. It will take some effort on your part. First, we need to pull together some of the knowledge we have gained so far. Try to do this for yourself by thinking about the following semantic misevaluations or mistakes. Each of the accounts is true, and each can be explained in semantic terms.

138

1. A man sat alone in his bleak room in a mental hospital. He (thought he) was conversing with Dean Martin. An attendant strolled in and gently tried to kid the man: "I've told you a thousand times that you're not hearing the voice of Dean Martin."

"Of course I am," snapped the man. "Don't you think that Dean Martin, of all people, has a *voice?*"

2. A young woman suffered badly from a form of hay fever. She was particularly allergic to roses. One day she entered a room and (thought she) saw a large vase of roses on a table. Immediately she started to sniff and sneeze. This was strange, for the objects in the vase were *paper roses.*

3. A little girl from the city visited a farm for the first time. She had come at just the right hour, the farmer announced. He took her out to the barn to see some baby chicks hatching from eggs under a mother hen. The little girl watched in silence a few minutes. "Those are not eggs," she told the farmer. "Eggs are what my mommy takes out of the 'frigerator."

4. Several years ago a man and his wife conducted a costly experiment to find who are more honest, men or women. They started with two hundred $5.00 bills. One hundred of these bills were placed in stamped, unsealed envelopes addressed to the husband. They were accompanied by a short note from an imaginary friend: "Thanks for lending me this last Saturday. I was in a jam, and you really helped me out." The other hundred bills, with similar notes, were also placed in envelopes but addressed to the wife. Then the couple visited a hundred gas stations. The man dropped his envelopes in men's rooms; the wife left hers "accidentally" in ladies' rooms. In the days that followed, many of the man's envelopes came back in the mail. Few of the wife's were returned. When the experiment was published in a national magazine, most readers concluded that men are more honest than women.

Pulling the Picture Together

We should already have enough semantic skill to explain these four cases. We understand now that the only world we know—the only world we can ever know—is the world that exists in our heads. This world is made up of *patterns of events* in the human nervous system. It is an *intensional* world of *mental maps* that represent—correctly or incorrectly—the actual *territories* around us. We can also call these maps *verbal maps* because many of them are provided for us by the words we use. (Anyone who still has doubts on this point might look at the phrase "man and his wife" in the paragraph above. What attitudes about marriage does the customary term *man and wife* reveal? How would the constant use of *woman and husband* change our mental maps of the typical marriage relationship?)

Using this framework, we can analyze the four cases quite simply. The insane man has a pattern of events in his nervous system that convinces him of Dean Martin's presence. He "sees" and "hears" the fa-

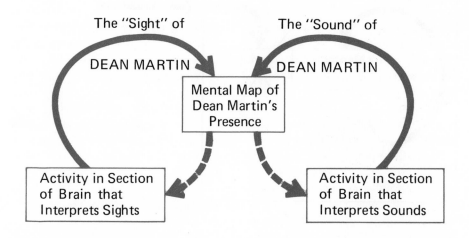

mous singer, even though Dean Martin is nowhere to be found in the immediate extensional world. His orientation is thoroughly intensional. Dean Martin "exists" only in the closed box of the man's own mind (see diagram above).

In the second case, we need to go outside the human nervous system. The un-sane young woman really does see some objects in her environment: paper roses. But she does not come into actual contact with the pollen to which she is allergic. Where does this "pollen" come from? Her mind:

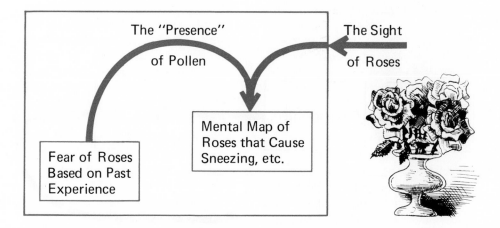

140

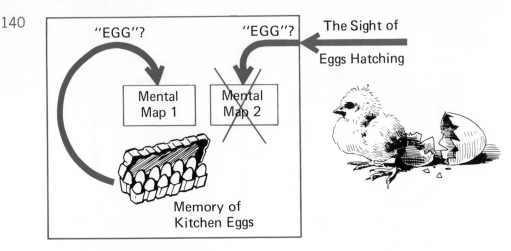

The little girl presents a similar case, except that her error is based less on fear and more on the definition she has given the word *eggs*. In her mother's kitchen she has learned that objects called *eggs* contain a sticky white substance and a yellow yolk. Now she is faced with a new mental map for the word *eggs*. For a moment she tries to decide which map is the correct one (see diagram above).

The last example is more complicated. Here the objects to be considered are far removed from the persons who form the mental maps. The objects are the persons who picked up lost letters in gas station rest rooms. The mental maps belong to persons who read an article describing the experiment. These maps are inferences based on reports of observations concerning unseen behavior:

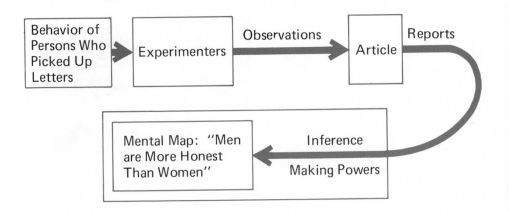

Notice that the farther an inference is removed from "reality" the less reliable it is likely to be. In this example, for instance, there is a huge distance between the "facts" and the inference. For this reason, the inference is questionable. First of all, an inference concerning all men and all women is based on the behavior of two hundred people, at most. Are *any* two hundred people an adequate sample of the human race? Also, how can we be sure that an equal number of men and women picked up the "lost" envelopes? Perhaps the men were more observant, more curious, or simply more willing to pick something up from a rest room floor. Moreover, it is very possible that the women had more need for the money. In many families, a secret $5.00 might please the wife more than the husband.

The Structural Differential

Each of the four examples above required a different diagram. Semantics would be a simpler subject if we could rely on a single device to show the many complicated relationships among human beings, words, and things. Fortunately, such a device exists. It is the invention of Alfred Korzybski, and it is called the STRUCTURAL DIFFERENTIAL.

Look at the photograph of the structural differential on this page. At first glance, it seems to be an artist's nightmare, a kind of "ugly-mobile." We see a confusion of strings, pegs, and geometric shapes filled with holes. What does the structural differential seem to illustrate about semantics? Anything?

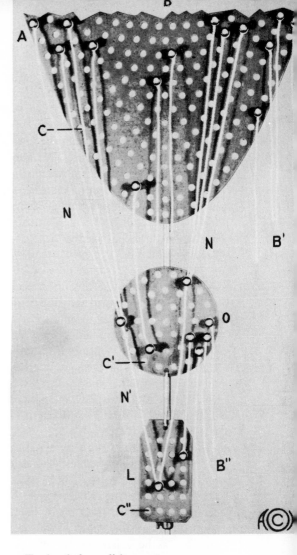

Each of the solid structures represents a separate kind of human "knowledge." Each stands for a different level of our awareness of "things." The large structure at the top (A) stands for the level of "atomic events," the level of "things as they really are," or "whatever is really going on there." The round circle (O) is the "object" level, the level on which we perceive "things" as they appear to be. The lowest structure (L) is the "label" level, the level on which we give names to the "things" that appear in our minds.

142   To simplify the explanation, let's take an actual case. Suppose we are looking at a large brown dog we've seen many times before. From previous chapters, we know that we cannot know *all* about this dog. We also know that we can think of the animal not as he appears to our eyes but as he exists in "reality." For instance, the color we call brown is a quality not of the dog but of the light reflected by his fur.

This dog that exists in "reality" is the A-level dog. On this most elementary of all levels, the dog is a pattern of trillions of atomic events. There are no colors, no noises, no smells—no human sensations of any sort. This is the level that underlies human perception and recognition. On the A level, our dog is "a mad dance of 'electrons,' " as Korzybski put it.

The structural differential puts these understandings about the dog into clear visual form. Look again at the large structure marked A (atomic events). The small holes (C) represent the *characteristics* of the dog as he exists on the level of atomic events. Notice too that the bottom of the structure is a smooth curve called a parabola. The ends of this curve could be extended out of the picture, off the page, and so on indefinitely. The edge marked B is broken to show that we should think of structure A as extending outward and upward forever. Thus broken line B indicates that in "reality" our dog has an infinite number of characteristics. To know *all* about the dog, we would need to know everything about the construction and function of each of his trillions of atoms. We would need complete understanding of his molecular construction, his cells, organs, etc. Such knowledge is beyond human powers. And even if we could know everything, what we learned one second might be untrue the next. (Remember the apple?)

The "object" dog, the animal as we actually see him growling or wagging his tail, is represented by the circle marked O. Again, the holes (C′) stand for characteristics. But this time the characteristics are not unlimited; they are bound by a firm circle. The C′ holes represent all the characteristics of the dog that we might learn by observation, such as the color brown, the odor, the exact length of the ears, the shape of the teeth. The strings (N) connect the characteristics we observe on the object level to the characteristics no one can observe on the level of atomic events. Notice that relatively few of the holes on the level of atomic events have strings attached to them. This means that most of the characteristics of the A-level dog are left out when we move to the next level. Some of these omitted characteristics are indicated by dangling strings (B′). In other words, from the trillions of atomic events on level A, we have *abstracted* a recognizable pattern we know as the dog.

In semantic usage, the verb "abstract" means *to move to a different level, leaving characteristics out.* The process is known as ABSTRACTION. We practice abstraction when we recognize the brown dog on the basis of just a few features. That is, of the infinite number of atomic events that make up the "real" dog, we require only a few simple characteristics for recognition. The rest of the extensional happenings that make up the dog are simply left out. The dog we see (O) has only a tiny fraction of the characteristics of the A-level dog.

So far, we have tried to imagine the dog as a pattern of atomic events, and we have noted how this "atomic" dog (A) differs from the dog we see (O). We have not yet given the poor dog a name. Let's do so now by calling him *Nozzie*.

Notice that the name *Nozzie* is not part of the dog we see on the object level. The same dog, after all, might have been named *Tom* or *Julian* or *Bernard*. The minute we use a name to refer to the dog we move to the label level (L). This means that we abstract again. The word *Nozzie* is not the same thing as the dog we perceive. *Nozzie* is merely a label we give to a dog we often see. In other words, with the term *Nozzie* we associate the characteristics (C″) found on our mental map of the dog.

The number of characteristics on the label level is smaller than the number on the object level. This is so because our mental maps commonly do not include all the features we might discover through observation. For instance, our mental map of *Nozzie* probably contains no information on the small scar on his right ear or the bend near the base of his tail. If we sat down alone and tried to list his characteristics, we would come up with only a partial list (N′). If later we were to examine the dog, we would notice other characteristics we had not previously associated with our label (B″).

Whenever we abstract, we leave characteristics out. (Thinking It Through 1, page 146.)

Abstraction Unlimited

Summarizing what has been said, we can think of our dog on at least three separate levels. First, we can conceive of him as a part of the colorless, silent world of atomic events. Second, we can see him as a "real" thing, a non-verbal object. Third, we can apply the label *Nozzie*, forming a mental map with the characteristics we associate with the name.

Our explanation of the structural differential has come a long way, from a "mad dance of 'electrons' " to a label in our heads. Even after reaching the L level, however, we are still on a relatively simple verbal level. After all, words are more than labels. After we label a thing (*Nozzie*), we can classify that label under another label (*dog*). We can also make a statement about the label, then another statement about the statement we have just made. In theory, there is no limit to how far we can go.

The picture of the structural differential on page 144 links our original label (L) with L_1, L_2, and L_3. This indicates that once we reach the simple label level (L), we can continue to abstract on other purely verbal levels. For instance, for L_1, we can make a statement about our dog: "Nozzie is a Labrador Retriever." Here again we abstract, for we must leave out characteristics. The general term *Labrador Re-*

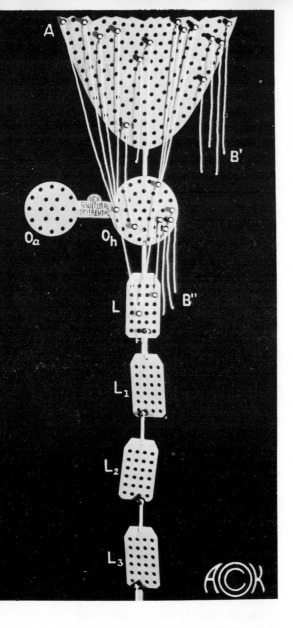

to introduce inferences and value judgments. After observing Nozzie wolf down his supper we might conclude, "Dogs eat quickly." Or, noticing his big, brown, sincere eyes, we might state, "Dogs are good animals." (What strings connect this last statement with "reality"? The sentence concerns not dogs but the speaker's feelings about dogs. We might do better if we changed it to read "I like dogs.")

Look at the photograph again. Notice that the picture is cut off below the L_3 symbol. The complete structural differential has a string of L structures, the last one marked L_n to indicate that the abstracting power of the human mind is unlimited. Notice too that there seem to be two "object" circles, O_h and O_a. From its position, we know what O_h represents, but what about O_a?

In developing the structural differential, Alfred Korzybski introduced the O_a circle to indicate the kind of "world" that animals inhabit. The symbol O_h stands for the "human" object, the "thing" as seen by human beings. The O_a circle represents the object as seen by animals. There are no strings attached to it, for to an animal, the object as seen is all there is. Period. No animal except man has the mental power to understand the difference between the level of atomic events and the object level. To another dog, our Nozzie is just what he appears to be as a non-verbal object, no more and no less. So there can be no strings running from the O_a circle up to the level of atomic events. Also, no animal but man can symbolize things with words $(L \ldots L_n)$. Only humans can string L symbols together until they lead

triever has fewer characteristics than the particular label *Nozzie.* Under *Labrador Retriever,* we can include only those features that Nozzie shares with other Labrador Retrievers. Similarly, for L_2 we might say, "Labrador Retrievers are dogs." Once again we have abstracted, since now we must remove all the "strings to reality" that Nozzie does not share with all dogs. On the L_3 level, we are far enough from Nozzie himself nowhere. (Thinking It Through 2–10, pages 148–153.)

Back to Paper Roses

The structural differential is a useful device. It helps us understand the important process of abstraction. It constantly reminds us that whenever we make *any* statement about *anything,* we are at least three levels removed from "reality." It also provides a method of visualizing a great variety of semantic misevaluations. Take, for instance, the four examples at the beginning of this chapter.

Consider the insane man and Dean Martin. Does Dean Martin exist for the man on the O level? Of course; the man hears the singer's voice and apparently witnesses his physical presence. Does he exist on the level of atomic events? No. The structural differential could be rearranged to show the true nature of the man's insanity. There would be no strings between the level of atomic events and the object level. What he sees as an object is an illusion created by his own mind.

What about the example of the young woman and the paper roses? In this case we do have something on the level of atomic events: the "reality" underlying the paper roses. We would have to run a few strings from level A to level O—but not very many. Similarly, a few strings would lead from level O to level L. The really important characteristics of the roses on the L level would be represented by pegs unattached to anything above them. These pegs would stand for the features of the "roses" that produce the pollen the young woman

fears. The "pollen" is a product of her mental label, not of the perceived object, not of the underlying "reality." The young woman's definition of *roses* includes their pollen-producing characteristics.

The example of the little girl and the eggs is somewhat similar. In this case, however, several strings should run from level A to level O. All the objects she has seen as eggs truly *are* eggs. Her trouble is that several of the strings that should extend on down to the L level stop at O. These include all the characteristics of object-level eggs that result in baby chicks. Her definition of L-level *eggs* omits these features. When she goes to a farm and suddenly encounters the new characteristics, she has a real problem. She can either change her definition of *eggs* to include the new characteristics, or she can decide that an object having the new features is a different kind of object. She chooses the latter course, and is wrong.

The last example, the honesty experiment, covers more of the structural differential. We know that the inference "Men are more honest than women" is on a very high level of abstraction. We also know that when we reach this distant level, many characteristics have been left out. In this case, some three billion people have been left out—those included on the high L level but not found on the object level. Also, since in this case we know the O level only by reports of observations of unseen behavior, we cannot be at all sure of its characteristics. Along the line a good many square pegs may have been shoved into round holes.

Reviewing the Key Points

---

1. Try to remember that you abstract continually, leaving characteristics out. Even when you see an object on the non-verbal O level, you have abstracted it from "reality."
2. Visualize the structural differential often to help you remember the level of atomic events, the object level, and the variety of label levels.
3. Distrust high-level inferences and value judgments.

Getting It Straight

A. Try to define the following without looking back at the text: *structural differential, level of atomic events, object level, label level, L*$_n$.

B. Read the sentences below. If a sentence *agrees* with what the book has said, put an A next to the number of the sentence on your paper. If a sentence *disagrees,* write a D. If a sentence *neither* agrees *nor* disagrees, mark it with an N.

1. Few of our mental maps are provided by our language.
2. The term *man and wife* must soon be replaced by *woman and husband.*
3. Alfred Korzybski's original structural differential is now in the Smithsonian Institute.
4. The level of atomic events should be thought of as having an infinite number of characteristics.
5. The object level should be thought of as having an infinite number of characteristics.
6. The first label level is usually an exact copy of the object level.
7. When we abstract, we move away from the level of atomic events.
8. When we abstract, we leave characteristics out.
9. Inferences and value judgments have no place on the structural differential.
10. Inferences on high abstraction levels tend to be unreliable.

C. Why do you think Alfred Korzybski named his device the *structural differential?*

THINKING IT THROUGH: THE STRUCTURE OF KNOWLEDGE

1. Diagramming one of your labels

Demonstrate your understanding of the structural differential by using it to diagram your knowledge of the label *sewing machine.* Include only the first three levels, A, O, and L. Start by listing all the characteristics that your mind associates with the label. If you know very little about sewing machines, you may be able to list only three or four, such as *needle, bobbin, pedal*. On the other hand, if you know how to use a sewing machine, you may be able to name many parts (and parts of parts). Also list characteristics that are not parts, such as the size and overall shape, the oily smell, and the hum. When your list is complete, draw an L-level structure at the bottom of a piece of paper and fill it with as many little circles as you have characteristics. What you now have is a representation of your mental map of the label *sewing machine*.

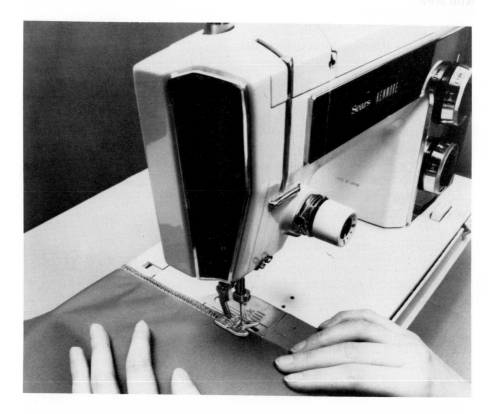

To draw the object level, you will have to go over your list again. How many of the items have you actually experienced by sight, sound, smell, or touch? This number of little holes in the L structure should be connected by "strings" or lines to holes in the large object-level circle. The rest of the holes on the label level should be left unconnected, since you have experienced these characteristics only as words, not as perceived objects or qualities. Some holes in the large object circle should also be left unconnected, since your object-level sewing machine will include some characteristics you know little about and have no labels for. For instance, a *presser foot* and a *tension adjustment dial* are prominent parts of a sewing machine that might not be part of your verbal map.

Finally, draw the A-level parabola. Connect it to the object circle with as many strings as you think necessary (at least as many as run from O to L). Compare your diagram with those of a few other members of the class. Do some comparative counting and cross checking. For *sewing machine,* whose intensional pattern of events seems to most closely correspond to the extensional pattern of events? Where and how was this person's knowledge gained? Do any two people in the class have exactly the same mental map of the term *sewing machine?* Why or why not?

2. Improving the structural differential

The purpose of the structural differential is to help people understand a number of patterns and relationships. First we have the relationship between atomic "reality" and the "things" we see. Next comes the relationship between these "things" and the labels we give them. Finally come the many relationships between labels on purely verbal levels. Do you think the structural differential accomplishes its purpose well? If not, what additions or simplifications would you suggest? For instance, a number of persons have been confused by having to look *down* the differential to reach *high* levels of abstraction. If you think you can correct this (or any other) flaw in the differential, give your ideas to the class for consideration.

3. Increasing semantic awareness

So far we have considered the structural differential mainly as a device for teaching and learning. But its main purpose is to increase semantic awareness. Alfred Korzybski recommended that the student of semantics keep a structural differential in open view where it could be seen often. He himself adopted this practice. He said that the sight of the differential continually reminded him of the principles it symbolized. Teachers of semantics often have a differential on view in their classrooms. The device seems to speak silently; it is a constant reminder.

The only way for you to test this practice is to have a structural differential of your own. You can make one in a short time with cardboard, pins, and pieces of string. The top parabola can be hung on a wall or attached to the top of a short stand. Perhaps you are lucky enough to have access to wood, plastic or leather and the necessary tools. If so, go to it!

The important thing is not the quality of the device but the quality of your thinking. A structural differential of glittering gold is useless if kept in a dark closet. Put your model in a place where you can't miss it. Think about it frequently. The students in one semantics class even made small differentials which they wore as lapel pins. These symbols increased semantic awareness and excited the curiosity and interest of other pupils in the school.

4. "Punctuating" the news

In explaining the principles of semantics, Alfred Korzybski often used the structural differential to indicate levels of abstraction. With regard to almost any object, he would first wave his hand at the large parabola, indicating that we should be aware of the hidden atomic events that underlie everything we perceive. Then he would move his finger from the original object to the O circle, and finally to his lips. The object level, he would later explain, is "unspeakable." It is the world as perceived, not the world as labeled. Only after he pointed to the L levels would he start talking about the object. Later, in discussing almost anything, he might walk over to his structural differential, point to the non-verbal levels, and place his finger on his lips. His listeners understood.

Try using the structural differential to "punctuate" a short talk of your own. A good way to do this is to find an interesting newspaper editorial that ranges from reliable observations and reports to inferences and value judgments of the highest order. As you read the editorial slowly aloud, use the "punctuation pauses" to point to corresponding levels on the differential. You might also pause after several key words and move your finger from the non-verbal levels to your lips. Your audience should understand that their understanding of the terms used may be far removed from whatever "reality" underlies them.

5. "Unspeakable" you

One of the ideas represented by the structural differential is easily born out by self-examination. On the object level, most people have fairly clear impressions of their mental, physical, and emotional characteristics. Yet most people also feel that many of these characteristics cannot be fully expressed in words. The more people search for words, the more they find that words do not represent what they inwardly feel to be "real." We often hear statements like these:

"Yes, I'm lonely . . . but not in the way 'lonely' usually means."

"He makes me so mad with that word! I'm not just 'pretty.' "

"I'm not really quick tempered—it's just that I *care* about things!"

"You can call me lazy, because you're my friend and you understand."

"I'm too smart to be smart."

Write down three adjectives that "describe" three of your major traits. Next to these words write their L-level definitions, the meanings most people (and the dictionary) would give them. Now examine yourself on the O level. Do you exactly fit the L-level labels? If not, try to explain how you—as a "real object"—differ.

6. Abstractions up and down

The old game "Twenty Questions" might well be called "Abstraction." One player thinks of a specific object and tells whether it's animal, vegetable, or

150   mineral. These are very abstract terms, since among them they include almost everything in existence. The other players then have twenty yes-no questions to guess the object. The idea is to guess it in as few questions as possible. Good players know that the game is won by proceeding to ever lower levels of abstraction, a step at a time.

The game might be played in reverse, starting at the lowest verbal level and proceeding toward higher abstractions. A player loses when he is forced to use that supreme abstraction, the word *thing.* He is set back a point when someone else can insert a term between the last word and his new one. Starting with our brown dog, for instance, the sequence might go like this: *Nozzie, Labrador Retriever, dog, mammal, vertebrate, animal, living thing, thing.* And from the word *thing,* of course, we might go back down to another object: *thing, manufactured object, printed matter, book, textbook, English text, semantics text, Making Sense* (as a title), *Making Sense* (this copy).

Starting with any object you wish, see if you can ascend through at least five levels of abstraction to the word *thing.* Then come back down through at least five levels to a different object. Try for as many levels as you can, and make the two objects at the ends as unlike each other as possible. You might diagram your series by linking two structural differentials together at their "tails."

7. Exploring on your own

The structural differential can be applied to human activity in a great many fields. Some writers of fiction, for instance, say that there are two basic ways of finding a story. The author can start on a high level of abstraction and work down, or he can start on a low level and work up. In the former case, he would start with his theme and ask himself a series of increasingly specific questions:

Theme: courage. What kind of courage? In what interesting situation would this courage be needed? What would happen if the character didn't find the courage? What should the character be like? What should his name be?

An author beginning on a low level of abstraction might start with a certain object-level character and work up:

What are my Uncle Fred's characteristics? Why do I find him interesting? What sort of situation would force him to be courageous for the first time in his life? If he found this courage, what would the theme of the story be?

Possibly both authors, working in opposite directions, might arrive at the same story.

Think about other fields that interest you. Can you apply the structural differential? If you have trouble, take any subject you know something about. What first interested you, a low-abstraction feature or a high-abstraction feature? Could another person have become interested in another way? Have you devoted too much of your attention to one end of the scale?

Or you might try remembering stories from books, movies, or TV. A number of stock situations are based on conflict between two ends of the abstraction scale. For example, the stereotyped old political boss (low level) signs up for an evening course in government. The young instructor (high level) gradually yields control of the class to the political pro. Conflict develops, and the class situation becomes a political situation. The instructor fights with theory, the old boss with time-tested practice. Does all this sound familiar?

When you have found your subject, write a short paper entitled "The Structural Differential and _____."

8. The beast in you

The relationship between O_h (the human object) and O_a (the animal object) is an interesting one. Animals cannot conceive of the atomic "reality" behind the "things" in their environment. Neither can they abstract to higher and higher verbal levels. To be sure, some animals can "learn" a small number of words. But to an animal, a word is not a symbol but a sign.

A sign is a signal that commands a certain action or announces the presence of a thing or a person. Dogs, horses, and some other animals can be taught to obey simple verbal commands. Dogs can learn a few names. The dog's labels, however, are not really on the human L level. An animal seems unable to separate its words from the objects they name. For example, suppose that a dog associates the name *Bob* with a boy next door who often plays with him. When the dog hears the label *Bob* he will start looking around for the object Bob. His master's words "Bob is not here" only make matters worse. For the dog, *Bob* cannot mean Bob as an *idea;* it always means Bob as an *object,* here and now.

Animals, then, cannot understand the complex world of human beings. The fascinating thing is that neither can humans understand the much simpler world of animals. We know that the only world that exists for any individual

152   is the intensional world, the "world as he sees it." This statement is also true
for animals. What does a flower look like to a hummingbird? What does a
grandstand look like to a racehorse? No human can ever really know. We can
only imagine.

Choose some animal and try to spend a short period inside its head. If you
can, find out something about the animal's perception. Does it see in color?
Does it see well at a distance? (A librarian or biology teacher may be able
to help you with books.) A dog's world, for instance, is something like a
black-and-white TV movie with the sound garbled. If you lived in a dog's
world, few things would have names, but almost everything would have a
distinctive smell. Your mind would have feelings and interests but no words
to use as tools of thought. Your whole past would be like your own "lost"
infancy, before you learned to name things and remember them. Your future
would not exist, and could not be planned for.

If possible, follow a real animal around and try to imagine the world it
inhabits. This is not easy; we humans seldom bother to remember that animals
live in a different world. You will need to develop a non-verbal awareness of
significant objects. Total success is impossible—but how far can you go? Discuss your experiment with the class. Do not fictionalize your experience in the
manner of modern authors who put human minds inside of animals.

9. The best in you

The little girl with her "eggs" and the young woman with her "roses" had
problems with definitions. Such problems often arise when we fail to base our
definitions (characteristics of the L level) on lower-level "reality." Alfred
Korzybski pointed out the trouble caused by misleading definitions of terms
like *marriage*. Before two people are married, their definition comes largely
from other L-level sources, such as the reports of other people, books and
magazines, radio and TV. It usually includes a marriage partner who is seen
as a high-level abstraction, with many characteristics (including flaws) left out.
Couples who form such L-level definitions are often disturbed when they do
get married. The object-level "reality" of marriage cannot possibly live up to
the label-level definition. The flaws that were once left out suddenly become
most apparent. When trouble develops, the parties behave very much like the
little girl who decided that eggs were not eggs. They declare that their marriage
is not marriage, and seek the divorce courts.

College is another term whose definition often causes trouble. Is college a
place where one inhales wisdom from the atmosphere of giant libraries and
ivied halls? Is college an endless round of fun and games? Young people who
form definitions like these often have to make serious semantic adjustments.

Choose one term that stands for something important in your future. "Define" it by writing down all the characteristics you can, starting with the most
significant. Now go through your list and attempt to mark each item with
a symbol from the structural differential. O stands for object-level experience.

L_1 to L_4 can stand for low-level abstractions you feel are firmly grounded in "reality." L_5 to L_8 can stand for high-level inferences and value judgments.

People with the best semantic adjustments have their verbal "strings" anchored firmly to the ground. Finding your own extensional anchors will bring out the best in you. What steps could you take, if any, to improve the definition of your important word? List several things you should do, and then, when circumstances permit—do them!

10. Completing the circle

This chapter includes two photographs of the structural differential. Neither of these pictures is a complete one. As finally developed by Alfred Korzybski, the structural differential included a string of L-level structures, the last labeled L_n. This L-level "tail" could be allowed to hang straight down. Or, to illustrate another point, it could go first down, then up, with the L_n structure pegged to the A-level parobola. Try to visualize this picture: a structural differential with nine connected L-level structures, the first attached to the O-level circle, the last to the A-level parabola. What do you think Alfred Korzybski was trying to illustrate by this arrangement of the differential?

Consideration of the following questions should help you:

1. How much do we really know about the atomic events represented by the A-level parabola?

2. How has most of this "knowledge" been gained? Through direct observation? Are atoms really like the miniature solar systems shown in some chemistry books?

3. Why might it be correct to say that the level of atomic events—*as we know it*—is an abstraction of a very high order?

Try to think your way through this complex but important problem. Then explain your new discoveries in a well-worded paragraph.

Chopping Up
the Verbal World:
Elementalism

The magician's art is among the world's oldest. With his voice his hands, and his eyes, he tricks us into looking at only one aspect of what he's doing. He diverts our attention from what is really happening. Then, with a snap of his fingers or a wave of his wand, *presto:* the missing card reappears, the rabbit comes out of the hat, the woman who has been sawed in half skips lightly off the stage.

The Magic of Language

In a way, we are all magicians. We all use words, and words by their very nature call attention to only a few aspects of all that is really hap-

pening. Other aspects go unnoticed because our words don't bring them to mind. Then, without a snap, wave, or *presto:* strange things begin to happen. We look at these events with concern. We sigh, groan, and shake our heads. We become magicians who have fooled even ourselves.

To understand how this happens, think once again of the structural differential. At the top, we remember, is a parabola standing for the atomic events that form the "reality" of the object we perceive. Let us label this object a *tree* (see diagram p. 155).

The structural differential helps us think of the word *tree* in a new way. But it does not tell us everything. We know, for instance, that a tree does not exist in isolation. For it to be

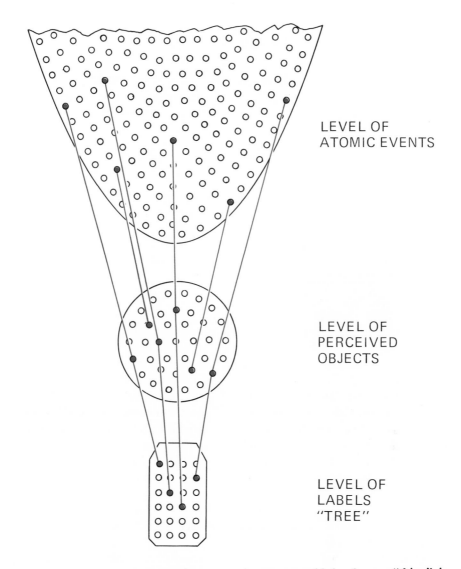

LEVEL OF
ATOMIC EVENTS

LEVEL OF
PERCEIVED
OBJECTS

LEVEL OF
LABELS
"TREE"

what we call a *tree,* it must continually interact with its environment. The roots of trees require water and certain minerals. Their leaves need sunlight and a balanced atmosphere. Without trees it would seldom rain, for most of the water vapor in the air comes from green leaves. Trees also produce the free oxygen the animal kingdom needs for survival. In truth,

the tree we think of as a "thing" is also an "action"; it is always *doing* something. It is a happening, an event, a process. It is *a process that is part of a larger process.*

Now we can easily see why the number of characteristics on the level of atomic events must be considered infinite. Suppose we started to count all the patterns of events in the en-

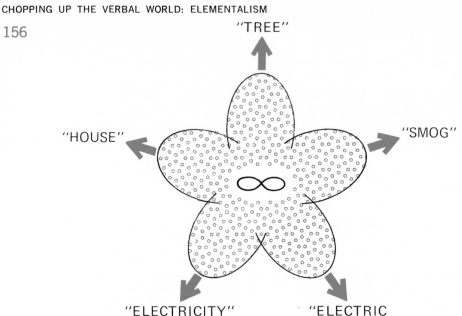

vironment that are necessary for our tree to exist. Where would we stop? We would find that everything seemed to be related to everything else. This understanding can be visualized by placing the parabolas of several structural differentials together in a circle. Notice that the areas of infinite characteristics overlap each other. Notice too the infinity symbol at the center (see diagram above).

This diagram indicates that the things we label with separate words are not really as separate as we commonly believe. Our words name different aspects of an infinitely large pattern of atomic events. When we make statements about these words, we call attention to only a small part of the pattern (see diagram below).

Notice that even more interrelationships are possible. For instance,

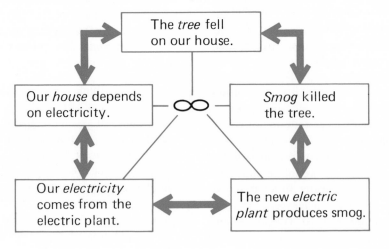

the house that depends on electricity is probably made of boards sawed from trees. Also, the electric plant may burn oil, formed underground long ago from prehistoric trees. In the world of atomic events, everything is related to everything else. Nothing exists in isolation, alone or apart.

Elementalism

Our tendency to let words make us think of things in isolation is called ELEMENTALISM. We are guilty of elementalism when we let the word *tree* make us forget that the "real" tree is a process within a larger process. In the intensional world of our minds, it is possible to separate the word *tree* from other words; in the extensional area, no separation is possible.

Elementalism is a constant danger to thought. Consider, for instance, the way we often think about school subjects. Some students view their schedule as though it really resembled the program card they got on opening day: a group of air-tight boxes with labels such as *geometry, English, world history*. These students seldom remember that all fields of human knowledge are related. They object when an English teacher pulls down a map: "This isn't social studies!" If a history teacher uses a poem to start a class, they ignore the proceedings until he returns to his proper subject matter. They shake their heads when a music teacher uses math to explain harmonics.

Whether we look outward or inward, we find the forces of elementalism at work. Looking outward, we may find ourselves in school, an institution designed to foster "learning." What we think of school often depends on what we think of "learning." We may spend six hours a day in school and do most of our homework. The rest of the time, we believe, we are free from the burden of "learning." But can "learning" really be separated from the rest of our experience? Isn't it true that most of our past "learning" has had nothing to do with school? We learn from play and from other leisure-time activities, often much more than we learn in school. In fact, there is little a person can do without "learning."

Looking farther afield, we find ourselves living in the United States —a free and independent nation, we like to think. But is *any* nation truly "independent"? The words *United States* can stand alone; the huge pattern of happenings the words stand for cannot. The economy of the United States is dependent on trade with many other countries. The value of the dollar is dependent on international money agreements. The peace we cherish is dependent on the sensible behavior of foreign countries. Like the tree already discussed, the United States is a process within a larger process. It is part of an interdependent world.

When we look inward, we find that the mind doubles back on itself. We feel ourselves thinking, and it seems logical to assume that something must "do" the thinking. We label this "thing" a *mind* and talk about it as though it were a separate object.

But is this true? Can the "mind"

158

ever be isolated from the "body"? Without the body, there would be no mind. And without the mind, what would the "body" be? Furthermore, the chemical balance of the body affects the mind, as anyone who has ever swallowed an aspirin tablet knows. The process also works in reverse: our mental condition influences our physical condition. Doctors who have studied the problem state that over half our diseases have no bodily cause. One man's overworked mind produces ulcers. Another man's anxiety makes his hair fall out. Yet both men go on thinking of the "mind" as a separate thing.

Elementalism is a fact of language. If we are to use words at all, its effects cannot entirely be escaped. But there are a few practices that will weaken its force. First, we can try to develop a continual awareness of the interrelationships on the level of atomic events. When seen often, the structural differential can remind us of these. The little separate L-level structures that form the "tail" indicate that while labels can be isolated, the A-level "reality" must be viewed as a whole.

Second, we can remember the use of one of the extensional devices introduced in Chapter 6, the *etc.* In our thinking especially, it is helpful to use terms like *mind, etc., learning, etc.,* and *United States, etc.* And finally, we can make frequent use of another extensional device that has not yet been mentioned, the hyphen. Terms like *mind-body, time-space,* and *leisure-learning* remind us of the interrelationships that lie behind our single words. (Thinking It Through, 1–5, pages 163–167.)

Elementalism, etc.

If we think of the dangers of language as *"elementalism, etc.,"* we cannot help being aware of other related pitfalls. Closely connected with elementalism is the human tendency to REIFY (REE-uh-fi). The word means to turn a "non-thing" into a "thing." We reify ideas and qualities when we think of them as "real" things, objects to see and touch.

For example, suppose we selected a student at random and asked him to list "five things he wanted by the age of forty." In a few minutes he might come up with such a list:

1. I want *happiness.*
2. I want *a modern house.*
3. I want *an appliance business of my own.*
4. I want *love and respect.*
5. I want *a wife and two children.*

Notice that all the italicized words and phrases fit into the same grammatical position in the sentence. They occupy the direct object location, one of the positions for "things." But although they share the same grammatical position, the italicized terms express different degrees of "thing-ness." Modern houses and appliance businesses are the kinds of "things" we can point to. *Wife* and *children* are secondary labels for people we can point to. We cannot, however, point to any "thing" called *happiness, love,* or *respect.* These are not the kinds of "things" we can go out and find simply by working hard. When we think of qualities, emotions, and attitudes as concrete things, we reify them.

Small children and primitive people have a low level of semantic awareness. They reify constantly. A two-year-old finds it hard to understand the spirit of giving at Christmas except through a concrete "thing"—Santa Claus. A three-year-old, when told he is traveling west in a car, may say, "I have never been to west. How far is it?" Similarly, primitive people commonly think of qualities such as hunger, internal disease, and war fever as "things" inside them. Disease is the business of the witch-doctor, whose function is to drive the demons out of the human body. War fever is the gift of a tribal god, who must be rewarded by the sacrifice of things in return.

We should not scoff at these examples, for "sophisticated" people also reify. As the primitive person reifies hunger, so we reify the mind. We also tend to regard the "pursuit of happiness" as the search for a "thing." We often think of happiness as a kind of product we can acquire with enough money or effort. In a very real sense, however, happiness is not a product but a by-product. The person who is busy with fulfilling work-play activities is likely to be happy. The person who has no serious goals other than happiness can never be happy. He is a victim of both elementalism and reification. (Thinking It Through 6–8, pages 167–168.)

Semantics and Grammar

For the sake of simplicity, most of the discussion so far has concerned single words. But we know that words are seldom used singly. Instead, we group words in grammatical patterns called sentences. These grammatical patterns need not correspond to the patterns of events in the extensional world. The "laws" of grammar are not necessarily the "laws" of science.

We usually put our sentences in subject-predicate form. This grammatical pattern leads us to think that the world is full of a number of things (subjects) that can, or cannot, perform actions (predicates). But, what we think of as the subject and as the predicate often cannot be separated on the level of atomic events. Consider the sentence, "The forest fire burned the tree." Grammatically, the subject noun is *fire* and the predicate verb is *burned*. In "reality," however, what is the difference? The fire is the burning, and the burning is the fire. On the atomic level, there are often no clear subjects and no clear predicates. Causes become effects and effects become causes. Everything is related to everything else. Nothings exists alone or apart.

Look at the five sentences below. First try to identify the grammatical subjects and predicates. Then think about the underlying patterns of events as they exist in the extensional world. Is it true that the subjects "do" the actions?

1. The burning tree fell to the ground.
2. The dam broke.
3. It snowed last night.
4. The teacher erased the board.
5. Mary failed English.

160 Sentence 4, probably, is a fairly exact copy of a pattern of events in the extensional world. It is clear that a subject-actor (*the teacher*) performed some action (*erased the board*). But look at sentence 1. Does it mirror "reality" quite as clearly as sentence 4? What did the tree itself do? The force of gravity pulled it to the ground, and gravity might be said to be the "extensional subject." This distortion is more easily seen in sentence 2. The dam did little *except* break; it was acted upon. The action was probably performed by the pressure of rising water behind it. What, then, is the "extensional subject"? And what is the subject in sentence 3? What does the pronoun *it* stand for? The weather? The sky? Snow? The sentence concerns a *process* that took place during the night. The snow is the snowing, as the snowing is the snow. The meaningless subject *it* is used only because we feel that English sentences must have both subjects and predicates.

Sentences 1, 2, and 3 are misleading, but it is sentences like 5 that really cause trouble. At least two semantic principles are involved. First, elementalism leads us to see Mary in isolation, apart and alone. Except for the fact that she failed English, we know nothing about the many interrelationships between Mary and her world. Perhaps Mary's mother made her look after six smaller children. Perhaps her father lost his job and upset the whole family. Perhaps her eye doctor gave her the wrong prescription. Not until we put Mary's whole picture together can we see her failing English as what it really is—a part of a much larger process.

Second, the subject-predicate form of the sentence makes us feel somehow that Mary is responsible for her failing grade. Since it is not good to fail, Mary, as the grammatical "doer," has done something bad. This may or may not be true. Mary herself might tell us, "Mrs. Smith failed me." She does not need semantic training to know that shifting her grammatical position shifts the responsibility as well.

No semanticist would seriously suggest that we stop using subjects and predicates. Neither should we try to explain all the interrelationships of every word in every sentence. We should, however, try to increase our awareness of the abstracting power of language. Most English sentences are on a high level of abstraction. They leave characteristics out. They are full of "hidden subjects" and "hidden predicates." Read the following sentences quickly; then read them again, searching "between the words" for the underlying meanings:

Coach Traynor celebrated his sixth consecutive winning season.

Senator Stewart has never lost an election.

Your banking business needs our banking business.

Mrs. Jones cooked an excellent steak.

I love you.

Chinese Boxes

An English sentence can be thought of as a grammatical pattern of words that makes a statement or asks a question. It can also be thought of as a set of Chinese boxes, with smaller sentences hidden inside larger ones (see diagram below).

When we hear or read a sentence, we are usually concerned with the statement made by the outer box. That is, it is the complete sentence that makes the assertion or asks the question. The other, smaller sentences are simply assumed to be true. Thus, a sentence gives us information in two ways, through assertions (the outer sentence) and through assumptions (the inner sentences). This is particularly noticeable in the case of questions:

"Didn't you see the flashing red light?"

"What useful ideas did you pick up in the semantics course?"

"Do you think it's good for you to smoke a pack a day?"

Questions like these are often difficult to answer because of the assumptions they contain. The first question assumes there was, in fact, a flashing red light at the time and place in question. Even if the person being questioned answers *no,* he must still agree with his questioner on the existence of a flashing red light. Similarly, the second sentence assumes that semantics contains some useful ideas. The third sentence contains the smaller sentence, "You smoke a pack a day."

Persons who want to control our thought and behavior often make clever use of this "Chinese box" quality of English sentences. Such persons hide their really important

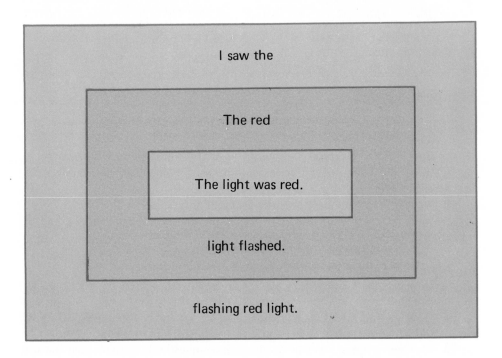

I saw the

The red

The light was red.

light flashed.

flashing red light.

Two smaller sentences are hidden within the sentence *I saw the flashing red light.*

meanings inside larger statements. They hope that in paying attention to the outer box, we will simply assume that everything in the smaller boxes is true. For instance, an automobile may be advertised as "the lowest-priced luxury car in America today." Although the sentence seems to be making an assertion about the price of the car, its important meaning lies in the term *luxury car.* In much the same way, the Declaration of Independence contains the famous phrase, "We hold these truths to be self-evident." The statement seems to concern the "self-evident" nature of the "truths." That the "truths" are actually true is simply assumed by our founding fathers. (Thinking It Through 10, page 170.)

Reviewing the Key Points

1. To avoid the effects of elementalism, try to be continually aware that although words can be isolated, things cannot. Use the *etc.* and the hyphen in your thinking.
2. Don't reify ideas, qualities, and emotions by thinking of them as concrete things.
3. Remember that the "laws" of grammar are not the "laws" of science. Grammatical subjects are not always "extensional subjects."
4. When you feel someone is trying to influence you, examine the assumptions hidden in his assertions. Sentences do not always mean what they seem to mean.

Getting It Straight

Try to answer the following questions without looking back at the chapter.

1. What is elementalism?
2. How can the structural differential be used to illustrate elementalism?
3. What two extensional devices can be used to combat elementalism in our thinking?
4. What is meant by the human tendency to reify?
5. What semantic danger is involved in the phrase, "the pursuit of happiness"?
6. How does "subject-predicate thinking" sometimes distort "reality"?
7. In what way are English sentences like Chinese boxes?
8. How can the Chinese-box quality of sentences be used to influence our thought?
9. What idea in this chapter is illustrated by the famous question, "Do you still beat your wife?"
10. In your opinion, which of the above questions contains the fewest assumptions? Explain.

THINKING IT THROUGH: ECOLOGY, ETC.

1. Become an art object

You read several times in this chapter that everything is related to everything else. If this is true, it must also be true that you are related to everything else—and every*one* else. Does this sound hard to believe? Think of a few of the ways you are related to a peasant in a secluded Chinese village:

1. Since both of you are human beings, you are probably remotely "related" in terms of common ancestry.

2. You are both affected by agreements reached between your two governments.

3. The number of persons forming "human links" between you and the Chinese is remarkably small, probably fewer than the number of students in your English class. For instance, your uncle might know a man—who knows a man—who has a good friend in Hong Kong—who has relatives in the peasant's province—who know a man—who knows the peasant.

4. If the nations of the world are economically linked together or interdependent, the peoples of the world are too. The clothes you are wearing may contain fibers produced in China. The oil for the peasant's lamp may come from an oil well drilled with a bit made in California.

5. You are both dependent on a world-wide ecological system that either of you can alter. (See *The ecological example,* page 166.)

As people are dependent on other people, so they are dependent on concrete things. It is not too much to say that you are related to a drop of water in the Pacific Ocean. That drop may contain harmful mercury which will pass from the water to a swordfish to the cells in your own body. It may evaporate and fall as rain on your house next month. Or it may stay in the ocean and provide the iodine needed by the seaweed that fertilizes some of the food you eat. *Everything is related to everything else.*

Most of the time, of course, we can forget about our relationships with individual Chinese peasants and distant drops of water. But we should not forget about the interrelationships among things and people that are close to us. These relationships form a pattern-process that often goes unnoticed because we are so involved. The force of elementalism makes us see things separately.

Try to think through a few of these relationships for yourself. You may want to start by writing down the names of three friends, three concrete things that are important to you, three interests (hobbies, etc.), and anything else that comes to mind. Decide on the importance of each item. Then search out the interrelationships. Think of the relationships among the different items as well as the links that connect them to you.

Now comes the challenge. Think of an art object that will show or symbolize the interrelationships in an interesting way. If you wish, start with a simple diagram and expand it to a collage, using symbols or pictures for the items and bits of string or colored yarn for the relationships. Or go three dimensional, constructing a mobile (moving sculpture) out of old coat hangers, string, and objects or pictures to represent the items. If you had to pick one small, accessible item to symbolize yourself, what would it be? A fork? A trumpet mouthpiece? A green leaf? A cardboard question mark?

Go to it. Think of this exercise as "re-creation."

2. English et cetera

The study of semantics seems to fit naturally into a course we might relabel *English et cetera.* For in truth, what is "English"? Some English classes study foreign literature in translation. Others study humanities and the arts. Still others study telephone manners, transformational grammar, propaganda analysis, film technique, the women's rights movement, etc. *"English" is related to everything else.*

Prove this statement to yourself by trying to list all the fields your study of "English" has led you to in the last year. If you take time to think, the length of the list should surprise you. You might start with the fields mentioned in this semantics book and then think back over other recent units. Don't forget about the content of novels, short stories, and essays. When you finish your list, compare it with those of other members of the class. Discuss these questions: What is "English" now? What should "English" be?

3. Triangulation, etc.

In doing the above exercise, did you come up with any relationships between "English" and math? There are several important ones. For example, the metaphors in poetry can often be expressed as mathematical relationships. If a poet writes, "The ship then plowed the stormy sea," we can see the comparison in the following form:

$$\frac{ship}{sea} = \frac{plow}{soil}$$

The equation is something like a statement of proportion: *ship* is to *sea* as *plow* is to *soil*. Notice that, as in math, we can transpose the terms:

$$\frac{1}{2} = \frac{6}{12} \qquad \frac{1}{2} \diagdown \frac{6}{12} \qquad \frac{1}{6} = \frac{2}{12}$$

$$\frac{ship}{sea} = \frac{plow}{soil} \qquad \frac{ship}{sea} \diagdown \frac{plow}{soil} \qquad \frac{ship}{plow} = \frac{sea}{soil}$$

Geometry, too, has its uses in "English." The "love triangle," for instance, is common in literature. In fact, the triangle can be useful in considering almost any story or novel. Good literature often contains complicated relationships. We can miss these complications unless we force ourselves to look for three-way patterns, not simply for two-way patterns. The practice of *triangulation* is a helpful one.

When you finish reading your next story or novel, start drawing triangles to explain its structure. You may want to begin by putting a character's name in the center of a triangle. Label the points with personal qualities, the names of other characters, places, or anything you think important. What is the relationship between each pair of points? With a little practice, you will find that you can draw triangles within triangles. You can indicate more relationships by using dotted lines, arrows, and angles of different sizes. The illustration on this page will suggest some possibilities, even if you have never read F. Scott Fitzgerald's *The Great Gatsby*.

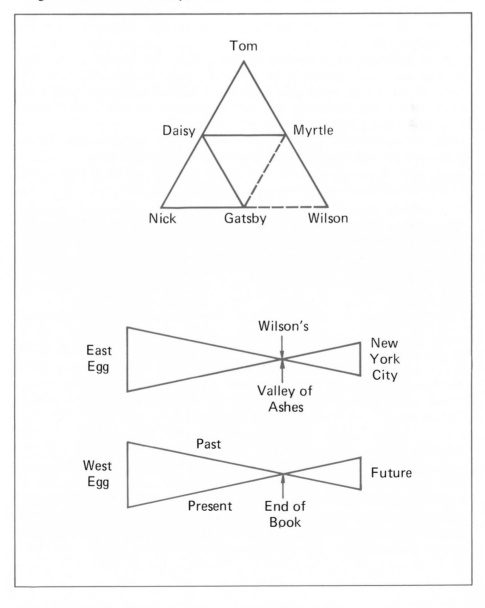

In recent years *ecology* has become a popular word—and for good reason! Ecology is the study of how living things are related to their environment (including, of course, other living things). Since human beings are living things, the subject can also be viewed as the study of man's natural life-support systems.

The importance of ecology is shown by its increasing place in the nation's schoolrooms. In many schools, however, ecology is studied only in biology and general science classes. But if everything is related to everything else, ecology must be related to English. Perhaps someone in your class listed ecology in exercise 2, *English et cetera.*

In the world outside the school, English and ecology overlap. The two are related in a number of ways. First, ecology—in one form or another—has long been an accepted subject of literature. John Steinbeck's *Grapes of Wrath,* a popular book for a generation now, can be called an ecological novel. It shows what happens when people upset the balance of nature. Steinbeck's view is that when man abuses the land, the land abuses man. New relationships must be established.

Second, the doctrines of the ecologist are strikingly similar to those of the semanticist. In *The Closing Circle* (Knopf, 1971), ecologist Barry Commoner makes these similarities clear. In the opening pages of the book, he proposes a "first law of ecology": "everything is connected to everything else." Does this sound familiar? Many of the examples Dr. Commoner uses in his book might well be illustrated with the structural differential. They show that the ecologist's main concern is to discover more about the interconnected world of atomic events that underlies our world of thought and labels. Whether we realize it or not, cars provide pollution as well as power and prestige. Crop fertilizers affect water supplies as well as corn yields. Paper companies produce dead fish as well as facial tissues. *Everything is related to everything else.*

Lastly, many persons concerned with ecology find that their hardest problems are not scientific but semantic. The purely scientific solutions are often at hand, but the semantic questions remain unanswered: How do we use words to get the message across? How do we wake people up to environmental dangers? These questions are certainly proper to an "English" class.

Most communities in the United States now find themselves in some sort of "environmental crisis." The details appear regularly in newspapers, with both conservationists and economic groups pleading their cases. Choose a current ecological issue that affects your community to use as the subject of a five-to-ten page paper. The paper should be entitled "A Semanticist Views＿＿＿＿." You, of course, will be the semanticist.

You cannot write this paper overnight. Time will be needed to collect past information and follow recent developments. Also, some of the material in the next few chapters of this book will be useful. As you gather your data, start to think about the issues from a semantic viewpoint. For instance, what are the essential interests of the parties involved? Should the current questions be the focal points of attention, or is there some better way of meeting the needs of all concerned? How do the parties use word magic and mumbo jumbo? How do the parties approach each other—like fighters in the ring, or like sensible human beings trying to solve mutual problems? What allness attitudes are involved? What about jumping to conclusions? Does the force of elementalism result in the omission of some important factors? What propaganda techniques are used to influence public opinion? Does the situation seem to justify their use? A quick glance through this book will suggest other important questions your paper might consider.

Your paper should be a semantic analysis of a continuing problem, not an answer to that problem. Your main task is to demonstrate your understanding of the verbal behavior involved in the controversy. Take sides only if you want to. You might end the paper by suggesting some semantic principles you believe could be helpfully practiced by all concerned.

5. Poetry, prose, and you

Here are two quotations from a famous American author. Relate them to each other, to this chapter, and then to your own life. (*Neat* is an old-fashioned word for cattle. A *chattel* is an article of property other than land.)

It is one of those fables which out of unknown antiquity convey an unlooked-for-wisdom, that the gods, in the beginning, divided Man into men, that he might be more helpful to himself; just as the hand was divided into fingers, the better to answer its end. . . . Man is not a farmer, or a professor, or an engineer, but he is all. Man is priest, and scholar, and statesman, and producer, and soldier. In the *divided* or social state these functions are parcelled out to individuals, each of whom aims to do his stint of the joint work, while each other performs his. . . . The state of society is one in which the members have suffered amputation from the trunk, and strut about so many walking monsters—a good finger, a neck, a stomach, an elbow, but never a man.

> The horseman serves his horse,
> The neatherd serves the neat,
> The merchant serves the purse,
> The eater serves his meat;
> 'Tis the day of the chattel,
> Web to weave, and corn to grind;
> Things are in the saddle,
> And ride mankind.
>
> —RAPLH WALDO EMERSON

6. "Things" that money can't buy

Happiness, popularity, love—all are goals that too many people tend to reify. Happiness should not be searched for as though it were a "thing." Popu-

168   larity just seems to come naturally to some people; those who struggle for popularity seldom achieve their aim. Love, too, is best viewed not as a "thing"
but as a condition or quality.

What is meant by the old expression, "falling in love with love"? How
does it illustrate the human tendency to reify? To what degree, and in what
circumstances, is it good to be "in love with love"? Give an example from
experience or observation.

7. The sum of $1 million

Another old saying goes, "Money can't buy happiness." Most people, of
course, have never had the chance to find out. When they hear the saying,
they are likely to reply "Yeah, but it sure helps!"

There is truth on both sides of this issue. Every person, no matter what
his interests, needs *some* money for the activities that will make him happy.
And beyond this, money often provides a feeling of security. But it remains
true that happiness isn't something one can attain simply by spending money.
This is why so many millionaires are responsible, hard-working people. They
have discovered that a life of leisure eventually becomes a life of boredom.

Suppose that a local bank held $1 million in your name. The sum would
be yours on your twenty-first birthday. What differences do you think the
money would make in your life, now and in the future? Make your answer
short—but serious.

With your class, discover how many answers are roughly similar to each of
the following:

1. I despise money as the root of all evil in a sick society. The $1 million
would make no difference because I would refuse it or give it away.

2. I would welcome the money to make my present career goal easier to
attain.

3. I would use the money to pursue a new career goal it would make possible.

4. I'd honestly try to enjoy myself. With over $50,000 a year from tax-free
city bonds, I'd be a fool to work or worry.

Where in this pattern does your response fit? Which answer makes the least
sense to you? Why? Which may show a tendency to reify happiness? Which
will result in the most happiness in twenty-five years? Discuss your answers to
these questions with your classmates.

8. Your emotional roller coaster

Rich or poor, everyone has his emotional ups and downs. On some happy
days the world seems to smile at us, and we smile back. On other days nothing
can make us smile. We drag ourselves out of the wrong side of the bed and
wear a glum face all day.

Some people who have studied the strange ways of happiness have been
amazed that it often has little to do with the "things" that should make us
happy. One researcher charted his emotions on a one-to-ten scale for 1500

consecutive days. With the aid of a computer, he found that his moods tended to follow a regular weekly pattern, with a high on Wednesday and a low on Sunday. Yet Wednesday was a busy work day, while Sunday was a day set aside for "happiness." Other investigations have shown that suicide rates in rich, productive countries tend to be much higher than rates in poor countries. Also, suicide rates seem to rise in the spring, the season traditionally associated with health and joy.

These odd facts are probably related to the reification of happiness. We *expect* something called happiness to come along with Sunday, springtime, and material possessions. If the longed-for bliss doesn't arrive, we wonder why. We feel that since the circumstances are right, something must be wrong with us. Strangely enough, we become more unhappy than we would otherwise be.

Keep track of your emotions for a period of time, using a simple chart with a one-to-five scale. Try to make your entries at a regular time late in the day.

Can you discover any patterns in your ups and downs? Do the events noted at the bottom of the chart have any connection with the "happiness line"? Does the chart reveal any information that might change your expectations or behavior? If so, express your thoughts in a few sentences.

November

	1	2	3	4	5	6	7	8	9	10	11	S	13	14
Wonderful day!			X										X	
Pretty good	X				X					X				
Okay		X				X			X					X
Tolerable				X				X			X			
Ugh!							X					X		
		Tom's party		Trip to Madison	Rain all day		TV blues			Relatives!!!	Argument with Helen			Home with cold

9. Grammar with a purpose

The extensional world is complex and interrelated. To talk about it at all, we must abstract, leaving characteristics out. Our words simplify and distort. Our sentences twist "reality" into grammatical patterns. Most people are only vaguely aware that the patterns of grammar are not the patterns of extensional events.

Skillful users of English, however, are quite aware of this fact. Such persons know how to use grammatical patterns to their advantage. One of their tricks is to change an active sentence (1) to a passive sentence (2), then drop the original subject (3):

1. The administration will raise taxes this year.
2. Taxes will be raised by the administration this year.
3. Taxes will be raised this year.

1. The student council requests all students to leave their lockers open for inspection.
2. All students are requested by the student council to leave their lockers open for inspection.
3. All students are requested to leave their lockers open for inspection.

1. Unless you make payment immediately, our agents will repossess the car.
2. Unless payment is made by you immediately, the car will be repossessed by our agents.
3. Unless payment is made immediately, the car will be repossessed.

No one likes to raise taxes, to order a locker inspection, or to repossess an automobile. No one likes to be thought of as an active doer of such actions. By the clever use of passive sentences, the doers can make themselves invisible. What we don't see in words somehow seems not to be there.

Keep your eyes and ears open for passive sentences that affect you. These are sentences in which the "extensional subject" either sneaks behind the word "by" or goes into hiding. They can usually be identified by the absence of the word *by*. Keep asking yourself, "By whom?" (Look again at the structure of the three sequences given.) If you wish, you can make a list of other grammatical devices used for the same purpose (such as, "It is requested that . . ."). Include as well other examples of the passive voice making a difference in meaning (compare "Jane graduated from Jackson High School" with "Jane was graduated from Jackson High School").

10. Advertising by assumption

The "Chinese-box" feature of English sentences is often used in advertising. The advertiser seems to concern himself with the statement made by the outer box, while in truth, much of his message is carried by the assumptions of the inner boxes. For instance, examine the conclusion of a rather typical bank ad:

Come to us to see about that extra cash for the great summer vacation you deserve.

On the surface, the sentence seems to ask the reader to select a certain bank for his vacation loan. But look at the inner sentence: "You deserve a great summer vacation." This questionable fact is simply assumed! Some readers might wonder why a person who has failed to earn the necessary money really merits an expensive vacation. More probably, however, the reader lets the assumption sneak through as the truth. Why quarrel with a compliment?

Think about some radio, TV, and magazine ads. Find a few sentences that contain clever assumptions put there purposefully by the advertiser. On a sheet of paper, try to diagram the sentences as Chinese boxes. Remember, a sentence can contain several assumptions, and an assumption can be made in a single word (". . . adds just the right touch to your *flashing* eyes"). Share your best discoveries with the class.

UNIT 7

looking outward, looking in: propaganda and personality

The Power of Propaganda

Propaganda—what does the word mean to you? Don't look it up in a dictionary; just think a minute. What about its denotation? Its connotation? What kinds of people do you associate with the term? What kinds of activities?

Propaganda is a good word with a bad reputation. Denotatively, it refers to any organized effort to influence public opinion. And since man is by nature an opinion-holding creature, man has always used propaganda. Primitive man had his chiefs, his witch doctors, his tribal priests. Modern man is beseiged by propaganda from hundreds of sources—governmental, political, religious, economic. The world seems a stage with everyone shouting at once.

Connotations Good and Bad

Today the word *propaganda* has unpleasant connotations for many people. The term suggests scheming dictators, lies, thought control, and the Big Brothers above us. The verb *propagandize* has a sinister ring to it. These connotations, however, are comparatively modern. Originally, *propaganda* was a Latin word, from the phrase *de propaganda fide,* "for the propagation of the faith." In 1622 Pope Gregory XV set up a committee of cardinals to supervise the Church's missionary work in foreign lands. He called the group the College of Propaganda. For many years the word *propaganda* traveled in good company. Then things

176 changed. With the rise of the modern nation-state, public opinion suddenly became important. Especially in wartime, governments had to rely on popular support. Wars, once the squabbles of kings fought by the kings' soldiers, became struggles between the people of different nations. Also, modern technology supplied the vital tools of the propagandist, such as the printing press, the radio, the public address system. One by one, the governments of the world established offices of propaganda. Communists and fascists strode the propaganda path to power. The most successful propagandist of modern times was probably Adolf Hitler's "minister of popular enlightenment," Paul Joseph Goebbels. "We have made the Reich by propaganda," Goebbels boasted at the height of Hitler's power.

How, then, should we use the word *propaganda* today? This is not an easy question. In general, semanticists agree that the meanings of words are found in people's heads, not in dictionaries. But the trouble with *propaganda* is that when we look in people's heads, we find different meanings. Some persons still use this word in its strict denotative sense only. Others use the term to refer not to *organized* persuasion in general but only to *unfair* persuasion. Still others avoid the term entirely. The propaganda arm of our government is called The United States Information Agency. Most large companies prefer the term *public relations* for their propaganda offices. Hundreds of pressure groups state that their purpose is to *educate* the public.

Amid all this confusion, the meaning we give the word *propaganda* is largely a matter of personal choice. The important thing is that we understand one another. And for this to be possible, we need to remember that *propaganda* is often used with no unpleasant connotations. The person who calls Dr. Goebbels a "good propagandist" does not necessarily keep a picture of Adolf Hitler on his bedside table. All the person probably means is that Goebbels used the techniques of propaganda effectively.

In discussing propaganda, we should try to separate the techniques themselves from the purposes for which they are used. Too often the word *propaganda* merely mirrors our likes and dislikes. It is always the other fellow's candidate who has to "resort to propaganda"—ours "rises above politics with a statesmanlike speech." In all probability, both candidates are using the techniques of persuasion to the maximum. What we really like or dislike are the candidates and their ideas, not the techniques they use.

No propaganda technique, *in itself,* is either right or wrong, good or bad, ethical or unethical. A technique is simply a tool, and tools can be used for what we consider good, or for what we consider bad. During World War II, for instance, the American people were subjected to a huge propaganda campaign against the Japanese and the Germans. Even at the time, people realized they were being influenced by lies and emotional appeals of the crudest order. Yet few voices were raised in protest. The essential rightness of the nation's cause justified even the most "unfair" propaganda.

For this reason, then, it is good to separate techniques from value judgments. Once we learn the techniques, we can identify them in different contexts. Only then are we ready to ask the important questions: "Is this technique effective *in this situation?*" "Is this technique justified *at this time, in this place, and for this cause?*"

Propaganda Techniques

Making sense out of modern America demands an awareness of propaganda techniques. In some countries, the citizen is expected to believe everything he hears—for he hears only the official party line. In our nation, however, the citizen is expected to judge everything he hears. And good judgment becomes steadily more difficult as propaganda grows more abundant and more clever.

In a country where free speech is the rule of the land, free inquiry into this speech must be the rule of the schools. Learning the techniques of propaganda is your responsibility. You probably know many of them already. Look over the list that follows, devoting most of your attention to the techniques that are new to you.

SOFT SOAP. Flattery often gets a propagandist somewhere fast. We find "soft soap," or insincere compliments, in many forms of propaganda, from advertising ("You as an intelligent investor will surely recognize the advantages of XYZ Mutual Fund") to political speeches ("You know, folks, I really enjoy campaigning here in Kentucky because you good people have always been able to spot a phony issue").

THE BIG LIE. "The great masses of the people," wrote Adolf Hitler, "will more easily fall victims to a great lie than to a small one." Why? Because if the lie is preposterous enough, people will assume that no sane person could tell it as a lie. A politician who makes a speech about six communists in the State Department is likely to be ignored. But if he announces that there are 254 communists in the State Department, people will listen. If he didn't really know, how could he make such a seemingly outlandish statement?

THE GLITTERING GENERALITY. Statements on a high level of abstraction often make up in sparkle what they lack in substance. "My aim is simple," says one politician, "to restore to the people of this country their birthright—the American way of life!" Many such generalities can be spoken by any speaker on any occasion. They often bring down the house, but they seldom bring down the abstractions.

TRANSFER. If a politician makes a speech standing under a large picture of Abraham Lincoln or Thomas Jefferson, his aim is obvious. He hopes the audience will transfer some of the famous President's appeal to himself. Similarly, a cigarette ad relies on transfer if it shows the product being enjoyed by attractive people in glamorous situations.

TESTIMONIAL. A testimonial is a recommendation by a well-known person. "Hello, I'm Marilyn Moviestar," says an image on our TV

Drawing by Kraus; Copr. © 1954 The New Yorker Magazine, Inc.

screen, and a few days later, we too are trying the small indigestion tablet she finds so effective. Political testimonials are also common.

QUOTING OUT OF CONTEXT. Testimonials can't be secured from persons who are no longer living. The best the propagandist can do is to skim their writings for usable statements. Thus William Shakespeare continues to comment on the conduct of life, and George Washington regularly denounces the United Nations as an "entangling alliance." These testimonials from the past are usually short statements removed from larger contexts. It is possible, of course, to quote living persons out of context—but they are alive to fight back.

See if you can match the following quotations with the names beneath.

More than one of the quotes can come from a single source. Answers are on page 183.

1. "If you call a tail a leg, how many legs has a dog? Five? No; calling a tail a leg doesn't *make* it a leg."

2. ". . . that this nation, under God, shall have a new birth of freedom, and that government of the people, by the people, for the people, shall not perish from the earth."

3. "Human nature will not change. In any future great national trial, compared with the men of this, we shall have as weak and as strong, as silly and as wise, as bad and as good."

4. "Labor is prior to, and independent of, capital. Capital is only the fruit of labor, and could never have existed if labor had not first existed."

5. "I am not, nor ever have been, in favor of bringing about in any way the social and political equality of the black and white races. While they do

remain together, there must be the position of superior and inferior, and I, as much as any other man, am in favor of having the superior position assigned to the white race."

Sources: Jefferson Davis, President of the Confederacy
Alfred Korzybski, author of *Science and Sanity*
Abraham Lincoln, 16th President of the United States
Karl Marx, founder of communism
Franklin Delano Roosevelt, 31st President of the United States

NAME CALLING. The smearing of one's opponents with negative labels is an old tradition in American politics. In some elections, it seems as though the political system were composed not of Republicans and Democrats but of "pinko professors," "extremists," "warmongers," "welfare freeloaders," "neo-fascists," "fat cats," "bleeding-heart liberals," and two sides of a "lunatic fringe."

PLAIN FOLKS. It pays to have the common touch. In advertising, it often pays handsomely. If a product is used and enjoyed by Mrs. Normal, it is bound to appeal to the average woman everywhere. Ads using the "plain folks" technique sometimes print short letters of praise from unknown people living in unknown places. Politicians eat corn in Kansas and bagels in Brooklyn.

FANCY FIGURES. Propagandists are well aware of the value people place in statistics. Numbers are impressive, if not convincing. Are corporate after-tax profits near $50 billion, an all-time high? Horrors! (Actually, corporate profits now take a much smaller percentage of national income than they have traditionally; wages have gone up more rapidly.) Does a certain brand of bread build strong bodies ten ways? Hurrah! (Actually, so does grass—as long as it contains traces of ten vitamins and minerals.)

CARD STACKING. The card sharp who stacks the deck can make any game come out his way. So can the propagandist who knows how to arrange facts and figures to prove his case. Also widely used is the stacked questionnaire:

Which would you prefer? (Circle one.)
1. Junior colleges to be administered locally by persons now in charge of high school administration.

2. Junior colleges to become a part of the State University system.
3. Junior colleges to be governed by a special board responsible only to the State Commission on Higher Education.

Regardless of which response is circled, one is forced to express the opinion that junior colleges should be supported at public expense. Suppose the person being questioned sincerely believes that public education should stop at the twelfth grade? How does he answer the questionnaire? What does he do when its results are used to prove that "nearly sixty per cent of the persons in this state believe that a junior college system should be part of the State University"?

BANDWAGON. This technique uses the human desire to do what everyone is doing. No one likes to be left out, especially when a certain product is "sweeping the country" or a certain candidate speaks of the "overwhelming motion of a massive, grassroots movement." Climb on the bandwagon, folks—don't you dare to be different!

REPETITION. Even when we say we "don't like" a commercial or a printed ad, our being exposed to it again and again has its effect. The propagandist who has money enough for constant repetition can fool nearly all the people nearly all the time. Buy brand names. Buy brand names. Buy brand names.

APPEAL TO FEAR AND PREJUDICE. Fear is a strong human emotion, perhaps the strongest. Deodorant ads are based on our fear of "offending." A politician may assure us that election of his opponent will lead to nu-

clear war or collapse of the economy. Appeals to prejudice are often indirect. A campaign for "law and order" can appeal to racial prejudice. The slogan "A man's home is his castle" can mean "Your lily-white neighborhoods will be safe under me."

TWO-VALUED ORIENTATION. Propagandists often take advantage of our tendency to think in two-valued patterns. All products except a certain "superior" one are by implication "inferior." There is no middle ground. In the same way, one political party is said to contain all the virtue, the other all the vice. Adolf Hitler knew this technique well: "As soon as by one's own propaganda even a glimpse of right on the other side is admitted, the cause for doubting one's own right is laid."

SELLING THE IMAGE. Studies have shown that many voters don't know what their candidates stand for. Nor do these voters particularly care. They put images before issues. They vote for the individual, not for the message. For this reason, a great deal of political propaganda is devoted to a candidate's image, not to this person's ideas. Make-up specialists and TV coaches are rapidly becoming as important as speechwriters. In the same way, "institutional" ads for large corporations advertise not a company's products but its good name.

THE COMMON ENEMY. Nothing unites people like a powerful enemy they fear in common. Where natural enemies do not exist, the skillful propagandist will often create them. To unify the German people behind him, Adolf Hitler created an internal enemy (the Jews) and an external enemy (the "selfish" nations that dared oppose his "reasonable" demands for more "living space"). In our era, anyone who could convince people that we are in imminent danger of an attack from outer space would probably unite the world.

PRESENTING INFERENCES AS FACTS. Before his assassination a few years ago, George Lincoln Rockwell, self-styled leader of the American Nazi Party, used to tour the country trying to create a common enemy. He warned of a take-over plot by Jews and blacks. His speeches were full of "facts" that were actually high-level inferences. For instance, in a bitter voice he would read the names of the presidents of the television networks, ABC, CBS, and NBC. At the time, all three of these men happened to be of Jewish descent. Then he would move on to the "fact" that "the Jews are now taking over the entire communications system of this country." As for the blacks, Rockwell appeared to feel truly sorry for them! According to him, they were merely the tools of sinister Jewish interests. "Everybody knows," Rockwell would say "that eighty-five per cent of the crime in this country is committed by Negroes." But to what kind of "crime" was Rockwell referring? Embezzlement and income-tax evasion? Certainly not. His "fact" applied only to street crime, and only to areas with large black populations. One might as well say that the French have dangerous criminal tendencies because most crime in Paris is committed by Frenchmen. For Rockwell

to apply his statistics to the nation as a whole was to move from fuzzy fact to idiotic inference.

WORD MAGIC. Words do more than convey their denotative meanings. They also convey opinions and emotions. The good verbal magician will select only those terms that suit his propagandistic purposes. For instance, the same political program may be denounced as "inflationary spending" or hailed as "a recognition of basic human rights." A politician can either "speechify" or "deliver an address." A campaign for "socialized medicine" may succeed if relabeled "cradle-to-grave care." One candidate's "slums" are another's "under-privileged areas."

"To hell with iridium! Find me a chemical that will rhyme with 'whiter' and 'brighter.'"

Drawing by Dana Fradon; Copr. © 1954 The New Yorker Magazine, Inc.

182 Reviewing the Key Points

1. Remember that the word *propaganda* does not necessarily carry negative connotations.
2. Evaluate propaganda techniques only in context. No technique is good or bad when viewed in isolation.
3. Keep the techniques themselves in mind: appeal to fear and prejudice, bandwagon, card stacking, the common enemy, fancy figures, glittering generalities, name calling, plain folks, presenting inferences as facts, quoting out of context, repetition, selling the image, soft soap, testimonial, transfer, two-valued orientation, word magic.

Getting It Straight

A. How familiar are you with the most widely used propaganda techniques? Try to identify the methods used in each of the following examples of political writing. You may find that in some instances two or more techniques are used together.

1. Ladies and gentlemen, watching my opponent's performance in office brings to mind Mark Twain's old remark that he couldn't understand why politicians were so bad in this country, when they were the best that money could buy.

2. At this point, let me read a letter I received from a little ten-year-old girl down in southeast Texas. . . .

3. Ladies and gentlemen, it's always a privilege to address an audience capable of understanding the realities of the American political situation today.

4. We should never forget what that great American Dwight David Eisenhower told us about the "military-industrial complex."

5. And, my fellow citizens, the economic royalists who now govern this country will soon go the way of the dinosaur.

6. Now the fact of the matter is that the spenders we've been sending to Congress have now pushed the national debt up over $2,000 for every man, woman, and child in the United States.

7. I predict not only victory, I predict the greatest landslide in the history of American politics!

8. First we had the New Deal; then we had the Fair Deal, then we had the Misdeal, and now they expect us to vote for the Raw Deal!

9. Surely every thinking person in this country knows that the Republican party has always been the tool of big business.

10. Let's hear that cheer again! . . . And again! . . . And again!

B. Copy the propaganda techniques on a card for easy reference. Then, for a day or two, keep your eyes and ears open for examples. See if you can find examples of at least ten techniques without really looking for them. Jot down a few words about each, and be prepared to discuss them with the class.

If you have to search out examples, study TV commercials, magazine ads, and editorials and letters in newspapers.

The list of techniques in this chapter is by no means complete. You may be able to discover some new ones for yourself. Also, remember that the techniques often overlap and that two or more can be used at the same time. You should be able to come up with more than one label for a few of your examples.

QUOTATIONS QUIZ, PAGE 178. All the statements are attributed to Abraham Lincoln. Beware of quotations removed from context!

THINKING IT THROUGH: SPOTTING THE TECHNIQUES

Here are six newspaper editorials for you to analyze. An editorial is a statement containing a newspaper's opinion on a certain subject and the reasons for that opinion. As such, it is an instrument of propaganda. Its purpose is to influence public thinking on an important issue.

After reading each editorial, try to identify the propaganda techniques used. How effectively are they employed? How effective is the editorial as a whole? In your opinion, are any techniques overused or not justified by the circumstances?

STAY IN SCHOOL

Somehow we've failed the youth of America. In spite of a massive stay-in-school campaign, the nation still has about a million dropouts a year.

This is nearly a million too many.

Education is the backbone of the American system. Liberals and conservatives alike consider it a force for good. The scientists and statesmen of tomorrow are the students of today. Youth who stay in school know that education is the key to the present, the door to the future. In the struggle for survival, education is all. H. G. Wells' words have never been more true: "Human history becomes more and more a race between education and catastrophe."

The practical results of education are known to all. Potential dropouts might well consider these estimated lifetime income figures from the U.S. Bureau of the Census:

Less than eight years of grade school	$189,000
Eight years of grade school	247,000
One to three years of high school	284,000

Four years of high school	341,000
One to three years of college	394,000
Four years of college	508,000
Five or more years of college	587,000

And the general public might well consider the employment picture. Job shortages exist, but they are for school-trained technicians. In plain English, there are just not enough jobs for dropouts. In many cities the unemployment rate for dropouts tops 33%. If the rosy economic predictions for next year do not pan out, we can expect hundreds of thousands of dropouts to be thronging our streets, unable to find work but able to find trouble. Most of these kids are the children of minority groups who deserve a better break.

You're probably not a dropout. You're reading this newspaper, which shows that you have more than functional literacy. You don't read like a fifth grader, and you don't think like one. So it's your job to talk to those kids you know. Tell them to stay in school, to stick with the crowd.

It's your responsibility.

Dropouts or Dropins?

We've suspected for some time that something was phony with the whole dropout campaign. We've had a hunch that someone down at the Board of Education was telling it like it isn't. For instance, take those charts that show the kid how much more money he is likely to make if he stays in school so many more years. The trouble with the figures is that they ignore all the differences among kids except the number of years they stay in school. They ignore the fact that the dropout is often a different kind of person. In school he is likely to be less cooperative, less motivated, less determined, and less successful. In life he is likely to be less cooperative, less motivated, less determined, and less successful. It is these factors, not simply the years he spends in school, that account for the differences in incomes.

We've suspected these things for a long time, and now we have proof. The University of Michigan's Institute for Social Research agrees with us. In a four-year study of 2,213 youths through high school and into employment, the Institute found that dropping out made little or no difference. The dropouts were more likely to have failed a class and to come from broken homes. They scored low on tests of self-esteem and had a high delinquency rate. But the mere fact of dropping out changed nothing. Indeed, after the dropouts quit school, their scores on self-esteem tests went up. Those who found jobs also had higher incomes the year after they would have graduated than did comparable kids who stayed at their desks.

The Board of Education should stop its anti-dropout campaign without delay. First, it's based on misleading and shameful statistics that the Board should promptly hide. Also, the campaign is giving dropouts a bad name. If the Board is supposed to serve all the youth of the city, how can it justify labeling nearly a quarter of them "dropouts"? Admittedly, kids who quit school are often mixed-up, frustrated, even angry at the system. But they need understanding and help, not insulting labels. They're "dropouts" only from the Board's point of view. For society as a whole, they're "dropins."

So let's change "dropouts" to "dropins." Let's forget the charts, the phony propaganda, the Board's particular brand of baloney. Let's forget about the high school diploma and hire people on the basis of merit alone. No kid is a statistic. No kid is an average. No kid is a "dropout" until death.

PATRIOTISM

"O say can you see, what's in it for me. . . ."

Our new national anthem? Perhaps, but we hope not. This change was jokingly suggested by Thomas Whelan when he was mayor of Jersey City. He was speaking to a group of local businessmen he thought weren't doing enough for the community.

The only trouble is that Whelan is now in jail, convicted of abusing his office to line his own pockets. Apparently he knew what was in it for him. And so do an increasing number of "patriotic" Americans. Patriotism is rapidly becoming the grunt of the private pigs at the public trough.

Patriotism isn't a matter of what one says—it's a matter of what one does. We like those famous words of President John F. Kennedy: "Ask not what your country can do for you; ask what you can do for your country." As late as 1961, one could stand up in public and state proudly that it's the doers who get things done. In our era Kennedy's words would cause embarrassment. For who are the doers today?

The millions of long-haired youth who sit around ripping apart the country we fought so hard to defend?

The millions of non-working freeloaders who demand as a right the tax dollars of others?

The millions of loafers on government payrolls who do less and less work as they scream for more and more money?

The millions upon millions of citizens who continue to vote for the liberal hoaxes of the last twenty years?

No, no, no, and no again. Today's doers, we suspect, are very much like the average reader of this newspaper. They work hard, often at jobs they don't like. They pay their taxes, which they never like. They hold the old American belief that the key to success is how hard one works, not how loud one shouts. They know that Lincoln was right when he said the government should not do for people what they can do for themselves.

These, then, are the doers. They are the patriots of modern America. They are one of the camps into which the country is now dividing. And they welcome this division because they know that in the long run their side will win. The opposition can do nothing but talk.

We know where we stand—and we stand proudly. In the final analysis it's either us or them. The doers or the non-doers. The patriots or the traitors.

Where do you stand?

THE POLITICS OF DISASTER

A smog-free New York will be strangely quiet, with only an occasional vehicle to stir up the dust on its weedy streets. Here and there families will be guarding their beans and cabbages, planted in the rubble of fallen buildings. Whole areas will be deserted, given over to rats and human scavengers. A few work crews will be chipping away at bricks, trying to uncover the city's one resource—the steel skeletons in its buildings. The year: 2075.

The result of an atomic holocaust? The picture could be, but it's not. The picture is the inevitable result of expansion at current rates. Economic expansion. Technological expansion. Pollution. Population. Products that produce disaster.

We'd like to dismiss this vision as the work of a science-fiction writer. Unhappily, we cannot. The prediction comes from the computers of the Massachusetts Institute of Technology. Expert Dennis Meadows has proven beyond doubt that population and production cannot continue to grow on a planet with limited space and limited resources. Sooner than we think (about the year 2020?) the system will start to break down. Population and pollution will surpass natural resources and food supplies. Says Meadows: "All growth projections end in collapse."

We'd also like to accept the view of those who say Meadows has stacked the cards he fed into his computer. But a similar conclusion reached by a British team has now won the approval of 33 prominent English scientists. Here at home, Meadow's work has been paralleled by work at the University of Kentucky and the University of California.

To avoid catastrophe, we will have to stop growth. Right here, and right now. We will have to unite against our common enemy—expansion. Yet on the political scene we find Democrats competing with Republicans on plans for Super Growth. Politically speaking, neither party could survive an attempt to slow down the economy. Neither party could afford to offend the special interest groups—the top 2% of all families who own 33% of the wealth of this nation.

The logical answer, of course, is the New Politics. Are you with us? You owe it to your grandchildren.

ANTI-GRAFFITI

Have you noticed? The flood of graffiti that has swept westward from New York and Philadelphia has now reached our gates. Defacing the city with marking pencils and cans of spray paint threatens to be the fad this summer.

Unless we do something about it. And fast.

188

Psychologists tell us that graffiti writers are ignored and frustrated children seeking identity and expression. We'd rather label a punk a punk and permissiveness as permissiveness. Young hoods with no respect for property do not deserve respect from the owners of that property. If we let them deface City Hall this summer, next year they'll blow it up. That's the way of vandals. Now is the time for the great majority of sensible citizens to adopt a program—and stick to it.

But what program? Fortunately we've got the examples of other cities not to follow. In Philadelphia, some of your Federal tax dollars went into something called the Graffiti Alternative Workshop. Your money bought cans of paint for known graffiti artists and provided surfaces for them to desecrate. The idea was that the kids would leave the rest of the city alone. Been to Philadelphia lately? Coddling these gleeful sprayers doesn't work.

The issue is simple. We can either give in to graffiti or let the punks give in to us. To win the battle, the City Council should pass the following program without delay:

Permit—even require—police and school personnel to frisk kids thought to be concealing graffiti instruments.

Prohibit anyone under legal age from carrying a marking pencil or can of spray paint. The parents should be fined from $100 to $500 or sent to jail.

If the epidemic continues, make the whole transit system off-limits to youth. Kids who have to walk two miles to school aren't going to think their graffiti-minded friends are quite so clever.

THE TERM PAPER SCANDAL

News from our larger colleges is that the term paper business continues to boom. In some cities the sale of term papers has even filtered down into high schools. Rates are high: $3.85 a page for original work and half that for a copy of one of thousands of papers on file. Profits are astronomical: over $100,000 last year for one nationwide firm with offices near 14 university centers. It's a million dollar business, and growing fast.

Where do the papers come from? Most of the originals, it seems, are pounded out by graduate students and young instructors. The used papers come from fraternity-house files, thefts on distant campuses, and students willing to take 25¢ a page for work graded "A" or "B." The papers are sold quite legally in outlets near major campuses.

Academic authorities, understandably, are growing disturbed. They have raised a hue and cry for laws that would end the practice. We disagree.

Today's student has no respect for meaningless and repressive legislation. Outlawing the sale of papers would simply drive the business underground. Also, just what is a "term paper," legally speaking? Couldn't the papers be sold in a note or outline form, to be rewritten by the student? "We're not selling term papers as such," one young businessman told a Boston court. "We're selling research, in the same way that a research company operates in the business world. What the buyer does with our work, that's his affair."

Furthermore, letting the term paper business flourish might in the long run do the student some good. Today's student is a cipher, a statistic, a computerized number. The hours he could spend learning, he spends sitting in huge lecture halls listening to professors who seem to know everything but his name. When he turns in a paper, it's read by an unseen and anonymous "graduate assistant." Such a commercial system deserves a commercial paper.

There are two kinds of education: the impersonal hypocrisy we now have and the dynamic involvement in learning that all students want. Yet Professor Big-wig still seems oblivious to the fact that the tide is turning. The professor who gets a commercial paper has asked for it. Surely a professor who really knows his students can tell whether or not their papers are honest. Mark Hopkins would not have been fooled.

Ourselves and Others: Programming the Blushing Computer

The mind of man has long been a mystery. Although we can examine a *brain* in a laboratory—a *mind,* we feel, is something else again. But what *kind* of "something else."

People have always thought about the source of thought. Primitive man often supposed the mind to be somewhere in the chest, the home of the many inner forces that directed his life. Later the mind was identified with purely spiritual matter, pictured by artists as radiant light. Still later the mind was imagined as a kind of machine. Even today we use the expression "wheels turning" to refer to thought.

In our era the mind is often compared to a computer. We talk knowingly of the ten billion electrical con-

nections in the tiny computer we carry between our ears. We speak of "input" (our experiences) and "output" (our responses). We act in certain ways and observe the "feedback." We think of ourselves as being "programmed" by persons who want us to react in certain ways. Occasionally we stop to examine the "programs" (mental maps) by which we live. The comparison of the mind and the computer is a good one— as far as it goes.

One trouble with the comparison is that a computer does not blush. Its operations are free of feelings, empty of emotions. No computer would let the pressure of a clock on the wall ruin its performance on a test. No computer would let embarrassment or envy lead it to pop off in strange ways. If we are to think of ourselves as computers, then, we must imagine ourselves to be blushing computers. And we would do well to stress the word *blushing,* approaching ourselves as feeling individuals who also think, not as thinking individuals who also feel.

The Semantics of Self-Adjustment

From previous chapters, we should already know how the science of semantics views the individual. In a word, the *individual* is just that—he or she is unique. Although he may share certain labels with other individuals (*store manager, Baptist, father,* etc.), he is different from every other person ever born. The world he knows is not exactly the same world anyone else knows. It is a world that exists in his head alone.

In a practical sense, this idea of the uniqueness of the individual seems to have two results. On one hand, each person's individuality should be recognized. He is entitled to be respected as a unique being. He himself should not try the impossible—to become a copy of someone else. And on the other hand, he should realize that what entitles him to respect are his private mental maps. He should remember that these maps may not be shared by others, and may not even be good copies of "reality."

Among our most important maps are the mental pictures we have of ourselves. Every individual knows himself in the same way he knows anything else, through the mental maps in his head. In other words, he carries what psychologists call a SELF-IMAGE. To discover your self-image you might first close your eyes and try to visualize your physical appearance. Then you might write a hundred or more sentences starting with "I am. . . ."

Like other mental maps, self-images can be distorted or downright incorrect. Many people think of themselves only in terms of their "bathroom mirror" image, forgetting that others see them from all angles —laughing, eating, and arguing with friends. Furthermore, many of the labels we apply to ourselves are high-level inferences or contain value judgments. *Pretty* and *plain, handsome* and *homely, courageous* and *cowardly, artistic* and *untalented—* all these are labels that may or may not fit the labeler. A student with a high I.Q. may not consider himself *smart* if he's intelligent enough to understand his own limitations. A teacher who thinks of himself as wise and witty may strike some students as a foolish bore. Who is to say?

Well-adjusted persons tend to have fairly accurate self-images that they accept easily. They've taken a personal accounting, and they've been honest. They know the harm that labels can do. A student who makes the honor roll isn't necessarily *highly intelligent;* a person who once stole a dollar isn't necessarily a *thief.* One lie does not make a *liar.* Labels that are too favorable cause trouble when we meet with facts that disprove them. Labels that condemn us unrealistically depress us and hold us back. They put us in a cage of

192 our own imagining. (Thinking It Through 3, page 198.)

The Self-Fulfilling Prophecy

When we apply labels to our self-image, we do two things. First, we describe, accurately or inaccurately,

our personal qualities at the present time. Second, often without knowing it, we predict what we will be like in time to come. When we use words like *lazy, musical,* and *nervous,* we usually mean that we have these qualities by nature, and therefore will have them in the future.

The labels we apply to our self-images tend to have unusually good glue. They stick with a vengeance. In fact, even when inaccurate, they often affect our behavior. We tend to become what our self-images say we are. Thus the person who thinks of himself as *lazy* is likely to act in a slothful fashion and really become lazy. The individual who labels himself *musical* will probably give music enough attention to become even more musical. The *nervous* person, expecting himself to be jittery, will grow nervous about his nervousness and end up a bundle of anxieties.

A SELF-FULFILLING PROPHECY is a term or statement that becomes true in the future simply because we believe it to be true today. As we label, so do we grow—or fail to grow. *Awkward, low I.Q., inferiority complex, unattractive*—words like these pack tremendous destructive power. Consider only the last one. Everyone knows an "unattractive" girl who obviously has applied the label to herself. It shows in her eyes, in her manner, and even in the way she talks. Worry about the label makes her less attractive than she naturally is. On the other hand, everyone also knows an equally "unattractive" girl who doesn't seem to let the label bother her. She's obviously aware that she's not Miss America, but she can joke about it. In fact, other people rarely think of her as being "unattractive." They see her as the *whole* person she really is. The individual who wants to get his life in order would do well to start with his labels. (Thinking It Through 2, 4 and 5, pages 198–199.)

Coping with Other People

Look again at the four words on the line above. Do you see any semantic weakness in them? Did you at first glance? They state, in effect, that other people have to be "coped" with. They imply that getting along with others is the same as "coping" with them—a view that could easily turn out to be a self-fulfilling prophecy. If we think of our interpersonal activities as a process of "coping," we will probably find that other people have to be "coped" with as long as we live. As we label, so do we behave.

Knowledge of the self-fulfilling nature of labels is important for our personal mental health. It is also important for understanding our relationships with other people. As our own labels affect our behavior, so too do the labels that others apply to us. For example, the children in one large city school were given an intelligence test to predict how well they should do during the year. The men who conducted the experiment gave the teachers the names of all children who scored in the top twenty per cent. These children, the teachers were told, should "spurt ahead" in their studies. Actually, the twenty per cent were picked at random; their selection had *absolutely nothing*

to do with their scores on the test. Yet the amazing thing was that each of the children listed did make far more than an average advance. Since only the teachers had been given the "confidential" test results, the tremendous advances could only have been caused by the teachers' expectations. The teachers had labeled the listed children *smart;* therefore they turned out to "be" smart. A test given a year later showed that the progress of the listed children was still well ahead of that of the children who had not been listed.

In public affairs, the self-fulfilling prophecy is often deliberately used to influence people's behavior. Does a politician appear ridiculous when he predicts certain victory on the eve of an election that all polls say he's bound to lose? Perhaps, but he's only trying to offset the self-fulfilling prophecy of the polls themselves. And how often does a party in power use terms like *recession* or *depression?* The officials know that even if we are in a recession, use of the term will only make things worse. If people accept the label *recession,* they will grow worried. They will save their money instead of spending it. This in turn will cause further economic weakness, perhaps a depression. Knowing the danger of the label *recession,* officials instead speak of a "rolling readjustment" or a "planned slowdown of a superheated economy." They assure the public that "prosperity is just around the corner" or speak of "looking across the valley to the coming economic upsurge." As we label, so do we believe.

Because self-fulfilling prophecies

194 are so important, let's relabel this section and start again:

Getting Along with Others

Some of our verbal communication doesn't really seem to convey "meaning" in the usual sense. It is largely noise for the sake of noise. In a way it is much like the "speech" of animals. For instance, parrots and some other birds are capable of PSITTACISM (SIT-uh-siz-um), the production of meaningless speech sounds to fit the occasion. Similarly, humans often spout such phrases as "Hi there, how are you?" and "Nice day, isn't it?" Noises like these reassure us that we are recognized and considered friendly, but the words themselves carry little real meaning. At other times, human speech resembles the howling of gibbons, tailless apes found in Southeast Asia. Tribes of gibbons settle disputes by screaming at each other from nearby trees. The group that shrieks the loudest wins the battle.

Most of the time, however, words do carry real meaning. In addition to being aware of self-fulfilling prophecies, how can we use our knowledge of semantics to get along well with others?

1. *Treat semantic handicaps like physical handicaps.* It's a sad human fact that while we treat the physically handicapped with consideration, we often treat the semantically handicapped with scorn, ridicule, and rudeness. The person on wooden crutches gets to go through the doorway first; the person on verbal crutches often gets slammed to the floor. This is especially true when we consider racial prejudice. We know from previous chapters that prejudice is, to a great extent, a semantic disability. From our study of the structural differential, we know that the person who unfairly calls us "bad names" is really talking about himself. Yet how often do we respond to such a person in a way that might help him? Not very often. Responses such as returning his insults or beating him up only make him more bitterly prejudiced. Whether spoken or not, "I'm sorry that you feel that way" is a better response.

2. *Beware of misunderstandings based on images.* Every person on earth has a self-image. He sees himself in a certain way. And perhaps unfortunately, he usually assumes that others see him that way too. He may not know that he presents quite another image to other people. For example, a girl who thinks of herself as "properly modest" may not understand why the class play committee won't give her the big part she wants. She doesn't understand that in the minds of the committee members, she is not "properly modest" but "pitifully timid." They don't want a leading player who might fall apart on opening night. An argument develops, and the parties appeal to a faculty advisor who thinks of himself as "fair." The committee members, however, think of him as one who always avoids trouble by siding with the majority. He does, and suddenly the girl takes the whole affair personally. She is hysterical for an hour and sullen for weeks. "They don't like me," she tells herself, instead of "Since my image of myself is ap-

parently not that of others, what can I do about it?"

3. *Remember that our allness attitudes provoke allness attitudes in others.* No one likes a person whose attitude implies that he knows everything. His "I-can't-possibly-be-wrong" manner leads people to look for instances in which he is wrong. He puts others on the defensive with his elaborate attempts to prove everything. Don't be afraid to be undecided, to suggest, to let others find part of the proof. Even in those rare cases when you honestly feel one hundred per cent right, watch the attitude behind your words. Allness has ruined many a good cause. Controlling allness attitudes may help you win friends and influence people, as Ben Franklin discovered:

I made it a rule to forbear [do without] all direct contradiction to the sentiments of others, and all positive assertion of my own. I even forbid myself the use of every word or expression in the language that imported a fixed opinion, such as *certainly, undoubtedly,* etc., and I adopted, instead of them, *I conceive, I apprehend,* or *I imagine* a thing to be so or so, or *it so appears to me at present.*

When another asserted something that I thought an error, I denied myself the pleasure of contradicting him abruptly and of showing immediately some absurdity in his proposition; and in answering, I began by observing that in certain cases or circumstances his opinion would be right, but in the present case there *appeared* or *seemed* to me some difference, etc. I soon found the advantage of this change in my manner; the conversations I engaged in went on more pleasantly. The modest way in which I proposed my opinions

procured them a readier reception and less contradiction; I had less mortification [humiliation] when I was found to be in the wrong, and I more easily prevailed with others to give up their mistakes and join with me when I happened to be in the right.

4. *Try not to project too much.* Particularly in unfamiliar situations, we are often tempted to project the worst into other people. This kind of projection is sometimes practiced by students who change schools. In most instances, the newcomer never liked the idea of moving, and the new school strikes him as decidedly inferior to the old. Most of all, he doesn't like the students, who seem clannish, not overly polite, and even indifferent to his presence. Soon his "I-don't-like-you" attitude transforms itself into a "You-don't-like-me" belief. Then, having projected his hostile feelings into others, he goes on to find "proof." Friendly remarks are treated with suspicion. Harmless jokes become cause for a day's brooding. Without knowing quite why, the new student finds himself surrounded by hostility. He doesn't understand that his is a typical case of projection. Like many people who complain about the hostile feelings of others, he should look at his own deep feelings first.

5. *Learn to listen.* Much of our listening is done for two selfish purposes: to pick up clues that will start us talking and to find fault with the words of others. How frequently do we make a sincere effort to understand exactly what someone is trying to say? Not often at all. The good listener knows that this effort is vital to good communication. He listens in-

tently and he even asks questions. In an argument he knows that the reasons people disagree with him are essential to his own case. As a citizen, he listens to many points of view, even those with which he may disagree violently. For him, "knowing" means knowing *many* sides.

6. *Focus on the issues, not on the person.* An argument or discussion that drifts into personal insult seldom comes to any conclusion. "You're stupid." "What an idiotic idea!" "Don't be a moron." These expressions get us nowhere. The next time you feel tempted to say one of them, try this one instead: "Why do you think (feel) that way?" Keep asking it until the person either convinces you or exposes his own ignorance. And in reverse, the next time you feel personally abused, politely remind your opponent that the original issue wasn't your intelligence, vision, sympathy, skull density, or whatever. Get him back on the track, and the conversation might get somewhere.

7. *Above all, keep your sense of humor.* The student of semantics tries to be continually aware of the way words affect his life. That is, when he acts verbally, he also witnesses himself as an actor. And when the actor in him takes a fall on the slippery stage of words, the semanticist in him can afford to laugh. Semantics is too serious a subject to be taken too seriously. (Thinking It Through 6–12, pages 200–204.)

Reviewing the Key Points

1. Examine your self-image, stressing those parts that are both positive and realistic.
2. Remember that the labels you apply to your self-image can easily become self-fulfilling prophecies. Watch negative labels particularly.
3. To improve your relations with other people, guard against image misunderstandings, allness attitudes, and unnecessary projection. Treat semantic handicaps with sympathy and avoid personal insult. Learn to listen to others and to laugh at your own mistakes.

Getting It Straight

Read the sentences below. If a sentence *agrees* with what the book has said, put an A next to the number of the sentence on your paper. If a sentence *disagrees,* write a D. If a sentence *neither* agrees *nor* disagrees, mark it with an N.

1. The human brain is like a computer in all respects.
2. Every human being is unique.
3. Well-adjusted persons usually accept their self-images easily.
4. The labels we apply to our self-images can become self-fulfilling prophecies.
5. The principle of the self-fulfilling prophecy should not be applied to interpersonal relationships.
6. The so-called speech of parrots is an example of psittacism.
7. The semantic handicaps of others should always be treated sternly.
8. Allness attitudes are helpful only when we are sure we are right.
9. In general, women are better listeners than men.
10. The semantic viewpoint gives us a boring approach to all verbal situations.

THINKING IT THROUGH: YOUR SEMANTIC COOL

1. Semantic reactions again

This chapter began with a comparison between the human mind and a computer. As we know, it is a faulty comparison. Even though we can (and must) use the word *mind,* no real mind exists in isolation. A computer, no matter how complex, always reacts like a programmed electronic device. When a human mind reacts, however, there are accompanying emotional and physical

198   reactions. Back in Chapter 7, we used the term *semantic reaction* to refer to this total response of the whole organism.

It is the semantic reaction—the response of the organism as a whole—that makes devices like the lie detector possible. The polygraph, or lie detector, measures slight changes in the electrical conductivity of the skin, heart rate, blood pressure, and respiration. In other words, it identifies a certain kind of "mental" activity (telling a lie) by recording the emotional and physical responses that accompany it.

Actually, we don't have to tell a lie to have measurable semantic reactions. The needle on a polygraph swings back and forth even when the subject is given a list of fifty common nouns to read slowly. Every person, it seems, has unusually strong semantic reactions to certain words. These words differ from person to person because our mental associations differ.

You can illustrate this principle by a simple word-association game. Sit in a circle and choose one person as timer. Anyone can start the game with a simple common noun. The person to his left then has three seconds to say a word that he associates with the first. If challenged, he must explain the association or lose a point. Persons who fail to beat the three-second limit also lose a point. The game usually produces some interesting associations and a surprising number of words that seem to block the thought processes of certain individuals.

2. The power of autosuggestion

About fifty years ago, the country was swept by a self-help fad known as autosuggestion. As taught by Emile Coué, the practice involved repeating to oneself at regular intervals, "Day by day, in every way, I am getting better and better."

What powerful principle of propaganda does this technique utilize? How would you explain autosuggestion in terms of the self-image? Do you think it would work for you?

3. Questioning your self-image

No one can put his complete self-image down on paper. We don't know ourselves that well, and no matter what our verbal powers, there would always be something left out. Still, everyone should be able to cover a page with short sentences beginning, "I am_____." Do this now—quickly, simply, and without too much thought. When you finish, mentally try turning the first two words of each sentence around and adding a question mark: "Am I_____?" Think particularly about the negative qualities. How true are they, really? For instance, *are* you a nail-biter? Did you bite your fingernails as a two-year-old? Can you see yourself biting away at seventy? Do you bite your nails twenty-four hours a day? Do you have a secret urge to bite your toenails? Once a Mohican, always a Mohican—but a *nail-biter?* No. The word *is* tricks us often, remember?

4. Your cover-ups

One reason our self-images are so often misjudged by others is that we sometimes act in ways that seem just the opposite of what our own images would indicate. For instance, a person who acts in an unusually cheerful fashion may actually picture himself as desperately sad. His smiles, jokes, and hearty laughs are just a cover-up. Perhaps he has even practiced good cheer for so many years that it seems to come naturally. He no longer knows which is the true self-image, the laughter or the tears.

Most people have some cover-ups in their surface behavior. Some young people go out and get in trouble because they regard their self-images as too straight and narrow. Some get high marks because they're secretly worried about their brain power. Some go out for athletics because they think of themselves as awkward.

What about your cover-ups? It's probably best not to discuss them, and certainly best not to try any big changes without professional help. For most people, cover-ups are a necessary part of growth. They're a means of getting it all together. But we should realize we have them, and we should be concerned if they're causing undue strain or deceiving others unfairly. In truth, most of what we cover up is perfectly normal and not worth the effort.

5. The Cinderella effect

If it's true that we tend to become what our self-images say we are, why don't we simply choose an ideal self-image and really try to believe in it? With enough belief, couldn't a person become a witty TV personality, a fearless race driver, a business leader, or anything he wanted? After all, we sometimes read of people who seem to have done just this. Some veteran politicians have actually "become" the public figures they once imagined themselves to be. Reporters who interview these politicians are amazed that they seem to be walking stereotypes; the individual has somehow vanished. Also, old-time movie stars were often given new names, new images, new wardrobes, new everything— almost overnight. They changed, didn't they?

Perhaps. But were the changes for the best? In everyday life, the stereotyped politician often strikes people as stuffy and somehow inhuman. The names of too many old-time movie queens are linked to temper tantrums, alcoholism, divorce, and even suicide. The magic pumpkin usually gives us a bum ride.

People can change, but not on the stroke of midnight and not in the direction of unrealistic self-images. Change is slow and starts with careful examination of our unrealistic negative labels. The person who keeps telling himself "I am dumb" is only going to hold himself back. The person who says "My intelligence is surely enough to get me through life well" can devote his energy to the positive labels that will get him ahead.

Nearly everyone can think of one unrealistic negative label he should drop and one positive label he should stress. Try to find these two labels for your-

200   self. You have a right to silence on these matters, but you can discuss your success in general terms with the class.

6. As others see us

The self-images of other people sometimes vary greatly from what we expect them to be. The following self-portraits were written by five very different individuals at the age of about thirty. After reading them, choose the one that you think will come nearest to your own self-image at that age. Then write down the names of at least ten people in your class and choose the portraits you think they would pick for themselves at thirty.

Question: "Has the life you've chosen made you happy?"

1. Sure, I'm happy. I've chosen my own values and let the world go its own sweet way. I'd like to do more with my talent, but somehow if you get too good you turn professional and then you join the rat race forever. The split-level house and the new car and the two sweet children and the ever-bigger paycheck—these were my parents' stupid dreams. The children I'd like, I guess, but I wouldn't want to settle down and live in one place and stop meeting the really interesting people in this so-called country. Why cop out on LIFE?

2. Does it matter whether *I'm* happy? With a third of the world underfed and a third of the nation in virtual poverty? Maybe what makes me happy is to make others happy. I spend four or five nights a week working for organizations that do some good in this world. During the day, my job's just a job—who wants to make a lot of money if it means exploiting other people? If I have any disappointment, it's my family. I wish they'd stop their "suffering" and try to understand me.

3. I'm happy because I'm pulling my share in this great nation. The energy of America is the sum total of the initiative and hard work of its citizens. And I'm doing my part. At the Company I started in Sales, and I don't mind admitting that I clawed a few backs to get into Management, where I am now. Neither do I mind admitting that I like my new house and my car and my weekend Wander-bus. These things make my wonderful family happy, and I'm not at all embarrassed by my success. It's only because people like me can buy these things that other people have jobs making them.

4. Here at the Homestead how could we fail to be happy? Peace, good friends, satisfying work, healthful food—all the ingredients of happiness are here. My family loves the outdoor life, and last year our farm co-op even made a little money for the first time. No one here would go back to the city, even though we sometimes missed its excitement at first. More and more we feel like the pioneers. We're showing the way, and millions will follow us into a new kind of American life.

5. What does the question mean—"the life you've chosen"? Who really chooses his life? I always just got along and tried to adjust, and I guess now I always will. In school I just tried to get by, and later when I got a job it was the same thing. You get married, and pretty soon you're trying to get along with that too. You adjust and then you readjust and life goes by fast. I don't mean I'm unhappy, I just mean I'm like most people who do what life tells them to do and sometimes try to have a little fun.

In class, read your list of names and numbers. Do all the persons you named agree with the portraits you've chosen for them? Where differences occur, discuss them in detail. What features of surface behavior led you to misjudge a classmate's self-image? Try to be honest, especially when it comes your turn to be misunderstood.

7. Shifting your point of view

When we think about ourselves, we naturally assume what grammarians call the *first person* point of view. In writing, we use the words *I, me,* and *myself*. When dealing with ourselves, this point of view comes more easily than does use of the third person—*he* (*she*), *him* (*her*), and *himself* (*herself*).

It's hard, and sometimes uncomfortable, to get outside the first person when thinking about ourselves. Writing about oneself in the third person is not easy. Yet when we do think of ourselves as *he* or *she,* we sometimes see ourselves in a new light. We are suddenly made aware that other people may not view us as we view ourselves.

Try this experiment. Suppose you are applying for admission to a special school. Your teacher is sent an evaluation form. The last item reads: "Describe the applicant in from one to two hundred words. Try to include both strong and weak points, as well as any other information that should come to our attention."

Remember, you are to write the description as you think your teacher would write it. Be honest, even if this means smothering yourself in embarrassing praise. Later your teacher may wish to tell you how your evaluation differs from the one he or she would have written.

8. Exchange your identity

Many party games are based on our ignorance of the self-images of others. You may have played the game in which, after one or two people are asked to leave the room, the rest of the players agree to assume the identity of someone else. This mystery identity can be that of one of the players or of someone not present. It can even vary from player to player, such as when each person pretends to be the individual on his right or his left. Then the questioners are called in and told: "We're all nuts here. We have a serious identity problem. You are to ask us questions until you find out who we are." These games are fun because they give us experience in role playing and constantly surprise us with our ignorance of other people.

For practice, your teacher might wish to have one student pair at random the names of everyone in your class and then record each pair on two slips of paper. If so, you will then be given a piece of paper with two names, your own and another person's. This person, in turn, will receive a similar slip of paper. The two of you will exchange identities. You are each to act and to answer questions as if you were the other person. You should *continue with usual class activities* until all identities have been guessed. Do not ask questions that wouldn't have been asked if the game were not being played.

Some identities will probably be guessed immediately; others may take several days. During this time, try to keep your "double" in the corner of your eye. Later, when you are "yourself" again, discuss with him or her the actions and answers you thought inappropriate. How does your own self-image differ from his or her idea of it?

9. Selling your image

Politicians running for high office often employ professional "image makers" to help them get elected. These professionals first make studies to determine the present public image of the candidate. How does the person appear in the mind of the average voter? The professionals then make attempts to correct negative aspects of the image. Do studies show that the candidate is considered too snobbish? Very well, a series of TV spots will show the person humbly exchanging opinions with a group of ordinary people. Is the candidate thought to be too ignorant of economic realities? Okay, news pictures will show the individual in serious discussion with a group of famous economists.

Suppose you are running for the highest office in your school. Try to forget your qualifications and even your desires. What harmful points do you see in your present public image? How might these negative points be corrected? Suppose you had half a year to create the best possible public image. What specific things would you need to say and do? Explain in detail an "image campaign" that might work realistically.

10. What do you care?

It's easy to talk of treating semantic handicaps like physical handicaps. But how much do we really care? How often have you ever gone out of your way to help someone with a semantic disability?

Perhaps you've tried to act in a way that would show someone that his prejudiced map was a poor copy of the territory. Perhaps you've been patient with someone who had an allness attitude, asking sincere questions that led him to discover his own ignorance. Perhaps you've managed to settle an argument by suggesting a compromise between two *either-or* positions.

Think back over your recent experiences in semantic awareness. Can you think of a situation in which you honestly believe you helped someone? If not, think back a little further. Think back to the period before you saw this book—after all, semantic awareness is largely a matter of common sense. In your whole life, did you never try to help another person because you thought that he was not in touch with "reality," that his "map" did not represent the "territory"?

In a written report of at least two pages, describe a situation in which you really tried to help someone. If you think it necessary, change names, dates, locations, etc. Report your experience in detail, using semantic terms when-

204   ever possible. What was the person's problem? How was he out of touch with "reality"? What did you try to accomplish, and how did you try to do it? How successful were you? How would your efforts differ if the problem arose today?

11. Learn to listen to learn

How good a listener are you? For a whole day, try to sound off as little as possible. Instead of talking, try to listen as much as you can. If you must talk with someone, try to ask him a question. Let *him* do all the talking. Really try to get inside the minds of other people. You may make informal and meaningless small talk. You may also answer the questions of others, and even make a few positive statements if you think people are discovering your secret purpose.

Were you able to go through a whole day in this fashion? If so, was it an easy day for you? If the answer to either of these questions is *no,* better try again. Many semantically trained persons can act this way comfortably. No one learns much when his mouth is open.

12. Oh, those group discussions!

Many students dislike formal group discussions—and for good reason. The advantages of group discussion are often lost because the persons concerned have never really thought about how they should behave in groups. Everyone goes ahead and does his own thing—even if it's simply coming down with lockjaw whenever a teacher calls for group discussion. No one expects anything to happen, and nothing does happen—the self-fulfilling prophecy again.

But group discussion can get somewhere if you keep a few principles in mind. First, the members of the group should know each other's qualifications. How competent is each member to discuss the proposed material? Suppose, for instance, that a group is to discuss the opening chapters of the novel *Moby Dick*. This discussion should start with a quick check to see how many students have read the assigned pages. Many so-called discussions fail because the persons involved have nothing to discuss. Knowing this beforehand can prevent a waste of time.

Second, the members of the group should themselves agree on the question to be discussed. "Chapters 1 to 6, *Moby Dick*" is not a question but a topic. Until a real *question* is asked, the group will probably get nowhere. A good portion of the period might be spent finding real questions: "Is Ishmael (the narrator) quite as depressed and uninspired as he says he is?" "What questions has the author tried to raise in the reader's mind?" "What background facts do we need to know in order to continue reading this novel with understanding?" The group that discusses its objectives first has a better chance of reaching them.

Third, the leader (if there be one) should think of himself as a traffic director. He should not use his leadership role to impose his views on the group. Under certain conditions, of course, he can contribute his knowledge and opinions. But his main responsibilities are to sum up occasionally and to keep the discussion both in order and on track.

Last, each participant must put the group interest before his own interest. The purpose of group discussion is to exchange facts and opinions in an effort to move toward a temporary or tentative answer to some problem recognized by the group. This purpose can easily be defeated by some of the types we all know:

THE BULL—Blinded by allness attitudes, it charges ahead with a loud bellow intended more to scare than to convince.

THE HYENA—This trickster's interest in amusement leaves little time for constructive contributions.

THE OX—Patient and steady, it quietly goes along with the majority and even seems to enjoy the burdens they give it.

THE COWBIRD—Its eggs go into the nests of others, who are expected to do all the work—often brilliant but irresponsible.

THE NIGHTINGALE—Singing for the sake of singing, it can go on for hours, even when nobody's listening.

THE MOUSE—The bright, beady eyes assure us of interest, but we seldom hear anything from this timid creature.

THE MOLE—Quiet as the mouse, except that it seems to be dreaming of a dark hole in the ground where it can get away from everybody and everything.

Becoming a good group member takes practice. For a few weeks your teacher may wish to limit all group discussion to half the class. This can be done by placing the chairs in two concentric circles, or simply by dividing the room in half. Each student in one group should be paired with a friend in the other. When it is your group's turn to discuss, your friend in the other group should observe your behavior as a group member. You and your friend should write observations on paper, discuss them frequently, and really try to help each other. Do not involve the whole class in your discussions with your friend.

At the end of the experiment, you should write a report on your strengths and weaknesses as a group member. Your friend should be allowed to add his or her comments before the report is handed in. Remember, don't criticize yourself or your friend too severely. Don't expect perfection in a short time. Look instead for movement, however slow, in the right direction.

UNIT 8

critical thinking:
some thoughts
about thought

Almost Alike: Metaphor and Analogy

Some things are alike. Others are unlike. Wherever we look, we find similarities and differences. So far, our survey of semantics has stressed differences. We know that although two words can be similar, the things the words stand for are often quite different. Communist$_1$ is not Communist$_2$. Movies (1930) are not movies (today). We also know that a word is never the same as the thing it stands for. The word is *not* the thing. The intensional world is *not* the extensional world. The map is *not* the territory.

Similarities and Differences

Notice, however, that even in exploring differences we were forced to use similarities. Think about the term *intensional world* in the first paragraph. Actually, there is no "world" in our heads. Semanticists use the term *intensional world* to suggest a similarity between what goes on in our nervous systems and what goes on in the world of atomic events. Likewise, when we say "the map is not the territory," we are assuming at least two similarities. One is the correspondence between the information on a real map and the information stored in our heads. Another is the resemblance between a geographic territory and the atomic events that make up "reality." In truth, learning to make sense involves the study of similarities as well as differences.

Most human mental activity pro-

210 ceeds in terms of similarities and differences. For instance, suppose we were to go to a seaside resort for the first time. There we might see, at first glance, a number of objects called *boats*—a single word that calls attention to similarities. At second glance we might notice some differences among the boats. Some would be rowboats, some sailboats, some yachts. In a week we would probably know more words to denote similarities and differences, such as *sloop, ketch, yawl.* We might learn that a dory is similar to a rowboat in that it is also moved by oars, but different in its nearly rounded bottom and tapered stern. The more we came to learn about boats, the more similarities and differences we would know.

This principle is true of almost any subject. A geologist knows similarities and differences among rocks. A biologist studies similarities and differences among living things. In nearly all areas, *knowing* means knowing similarities and differences. When we say we "know" a certain word, we usually mean we can define it by stating similarities and differences. For example, *to lope* means "to run" (similarity) "easily and loosely" (difference). If asked to define *elephant,* we'd probably start with the obvious similarity ("animal") and then go on to some of the words that denote differences ("largest," "trunk," "tusks," etc.).

The Magic of Metaphor

"A metaphor," millions of American students might tell us, "is a com-

parison that doesn't use *like* or *as.*" This definition has its weaknesses. True, a metaphor is a comparison; it does deal with similarities. But a metaphor is not just any comparison without *like* or *as.* When we say that a sloop and a ketch are both sailboats, we are making a comparison but not a metaphor. A sloop and a ketch are, in fact, very much like each other. When we compare them, we are calling attention to many similarities between two like things. Using the structural differential, if we started with the two labels and moved toward the object level, we'd arrive at two objects that were very much the same.

A metaphor involves the comparison of two things that are essentially unlike. A metaphor is a comparison made by the mind, not by noticing true similarities in the extensional world. When we say, for instance, "The house was a sheet of flames," we are comparing the appearance of a burning house to the appearance of a bed sheet. In the world of "reality," of course, there are few similarities between these two patterns of events. So it is with other metaphors: "The man had a *hardened* soul." "The administration declared *war* on poverty." "The Lord is my *shepherd.*" Metaphor making is a mental act.

Some talented people tend to think, speak, and write in metaphors. Sometimes they become famous poets, writers, or speakers. More often they simply use their talent in everyday situations. We know, for instance, that it was William Shakespeare who termed England "a *precious stone* set in the *silver* sea." But what forgotten metaphor-maker first came up with the word *limey* for an English citizen? (Long ago, British sailors used to eat limes to prevent scurvy.) What angry motorist first used *bottleneck* as a metaphor? Who first announced he was *torn* between two courses of action? Today we can *unearth* metaphors *sprinkled* throughout our *tongue,* whether they be *hidden, dead,* or *threadbare.*

Some of the following sentences come from the pens of famous writers; others you might hear almost any time. Examine them for metaphors. You may find more than one metaphor in a sentence, and even metaphors within metaphors. With the structural differential in mind, try to relate each item in each comparison to its underlying "reality."

1. "My dad flipped when he found the battery was dead."
2. "There's a divinity that shapes our ends, rough-hew them how we will."
3. "The brilliant scientist was hardly a live wire socially."
4. "A mighty fortress is our God."
5. "When want comes in at the door, love flies out the window."
6. "They moved from their old pigsty to a regular palace."
7. "You shall not crucify mankind upon a cross of gold."
8. "Groping for an answer, he wished he were dead."
9. "As if you could kill time without injuring eternity."
10. "Go fly a kite!"

Metaphors do not deal directly with the world of atomic events. In fact, they often deny in "reality" what they affirm on the level of labels. Even so, no semanticist would seriously suggest that we avoid using metaphors. It would be highly impractical to do so. Metaphors are part of language, the flashing wings of words. They add sparkle to our speech and dash to our thought.

Indirectly, metaphors serve another function as well. They often reveal what is on our minds. Obviously, metaphors do not come from the moon. They come from human experience, and they indicate what aspects of that experience most concern people. For thousands of years, people lived relatively uncomplicated lives, concerned largely with farming, hunting, and simple house-

212 hold routines. Not surprisingly, our older metaphors reveal these concerns. We talk about putting the cart before the horse, having a bird in hand, and teaching old dogs new tricks. Even as late as Abraham Lincoln's time fresh metaphors often concerned animals and farming. During the War Between the States, Lincoln, a master of metaphor, told the voters that it wasn't wise to change horses in the middle of a stream.

Many of today's metaphors reveal our devotion to science and technology, as well as an obsession with war. When we have a problem, we first consider its *elements,* then we *attack* it. *Arming* ourselves with knowledge, we study *strategy* and *tactics* for dealing with future problems. If we're lucky we'll find a *catalyst* (KAT-uh-list) who will make things happen. On the international scene, leaders watch public *reaction* as they *fight* to restore the *balance* of power. At home, the nation has declared *war* on poverty and crime. *Revolution* is in the air. Propaganda *campaigns* try to win the *battle* for men's minds.

Are all these "war words" really necessary? Some people think not. They believe that habitual use of the terms keeps our minds on war instead of peace. What do you think? A simple psalmist once started his verse, "The Lord is my *shepherd."* What metaphor might he use today?

"Attacking" Analogies

If we think about it, we will see that metaphors are of two kinds. The first kind we can call SIMPLE COMPARISONS. For instance, "The house was a sheet of flames" simply compares the appearance of a burning house to the appearance of an unfolded (and perhaps flapping) sheet. No other comparisons are involved. We are not invited to compare, say, the people that may have fled the house to the bedbugs that may have fled the sheet. Similarly, "The sky was an inverted blue bowl" asks us to compare only two things, the sky and the inside of a blue bowl. When the poet writes, "She was a phantom of delight," he is making simple comparison between a girl or woman and a charming spook or ghost.

The second kind of metaphor is more complex. Take the old saying, "You can't teach an old dog new tricks." Here we are not asked to compare only two things. We are asked to compare two comparisons. The first is the comparison between a dog and the tricks he might learn. The second is the comparison between a man and the skills he might learn:

$$\frac{dog}{tricks} = \frac{man}{skills}$$

A complex metaphor need not be a long one. Take the everyday term, *dead battery:*

$$\frac{battery}{electricity} = \frac{man}{life} \text{ or}$$

$$\frac{battery}{no\ electricity} = \frac{man}{death}$$

This kind of complex metaphor, when all the items are expressed as words, is called an ANALOGY. An analogy is a statement that the relationship between two items is in some way similar to the relationship between two other items:

$$\frac{writer}{book} = \frac{carpenter}{house}$$

$$\frac{spring}{fall} = \frac{youth}{old\ age}$$

An analogy can be written in a number of ways. We can use a complete sentence or a mathematical formula. We can also use the symbols (:) and (::), meaning *is to* and *as.*

writer : book :: carpenter : house
writer is to *book* as *carpenter* is to *house*
spring : fall :: youth : old age
spring is to *fall* as *youth* is to *old age*

Analogies are often found on standardized tests. We find analogies on college entrance exams, on tests for special schools, and on military tests. This is not surprising, since analogies can be used to test vocabulary, knowledge, reasoning ability, and the power to grasp many kinds of relationships. Some authorities believe that an analogy test is the best single indicator of a person's ability.

Before testing your own skill, let's review some of the more common types of analogies found on tests:

1. Part is to whole as part is to whole
   (Or whole is to part as whole is to part. All analogies can be reversed.)
   head : body :: peak : mountain
   flake : snow :: drop : rain
2. Part is to part as part is to part
   head : tail :: bow : stern
   car body : tires :: clothes : shoes
3. Word is to synonym as word is to synonym
   range : stove :: car : automobile
   sympathetic : compassionate ::
   large : big
4. Word is to antonym as word is to antonym
   smile : frown :: health : sickness
   gigantic : tiny :: proper : profligate
5. Grammatical form is to grammatical form . . .
   play : playing :: sleep : sleeping
   he : him :: who : whom
6. Worker is to tool . . .
   doctor : stethoscope :: carpenter : hammer

plumber : wrench :: typist :
typewriter
7. Worker is to product . . .
baker : cake :: milliner : hat
bee : honey :: cow : milk
8. New is to old . . .
car : wagon :: airplane : train
astronaut : pioneer :: moon :
frontier
9. Cause is to effect . . .
sun : heat :: car : pollution
work : money :: food : health
10. Noun is to quality . . .
bread : soft :: steel : hard
friend : love :: enemy : hate
11. Object is to composition . . .
tree : wood :: bottle : glass
shoe : leather :: book : paper
12. Object is to location . . .
polar bear : North Pole ::
penguin : South Pole
teacher : school :: farmer : farm
13. Symbol is to thing symbolized . . .
flag : country :: cross :
Christianity
dollar sign : money :: skull and
crossbones : poison
14. Actor is to action . . .
baby : cry :: adult : talk
dog : bark :: bird : sing

15. Singular is to plural (or many) . . .
man : men :: ox : oxen
tree : forest :: building : city
16. Number is to number . . .
1 : 10 :: 10 : 100
many : few :: few : none
17. Individual is to individual . . .
Shakespeare : O. Henry ::
Beethoven : Burt Bacharach
nephew : niece :: uncle : aunt
18. Character is to character . . .
Romeo : Juliet :: Archie : Edith
Tom Sawyer : Huckleberry
Finn :: Ishmael : Queequeg
19. Classification is to example . . .
tree : willow :: vegetable : bean
color : red :: taste : sour
20. Container is to "thing
contained" . . .
tank : gasoline :: paper bag :
groceries
Fort Knox : gold :: pod : pea

This list does not exhaust all the possibilities. The human mind can manage hundreds of different kinds of relationships, some so subtle that they're hard to put into words. *A plant is to a line as a man is to a plane.* Think about that one!

Reviewing the Key Points

1. Remember that similarities are of many different kinds. Ask yourself often, *"How* are these two items similar?"
2. Don't confuse metaphors with true similarities. A metaphor usually compares items that are unlike each other in the extensional world.
3. Learn to think in terms of analogies. Recognize the common types of analogies when you encounter them.

Getting It Straight

A. In your own words, explain why it is that not all comparisons are metaphors. Use the structural differential in your explanation if you wish. Also explain the difference between a simple comparison and an analogy.

B. On paper, write metaphors that fulfill the following conditions. The first one has been done for you.

1. Express a mental act in terms of a physical act.
   ("His tense mind leaped forward before the starting gun.")
2. Express an emotion in terms of music.
3. Express a political victory in terms of sports.
4. Express the behavior of a crowd in terms of wild animals.
5. Express a person's character in terms of a tree.
6. Express a person's life in terms of a river.
7. Express ignorance in terms of darkness.
8. Express a job you detest in terms of punishment for some crime.
9. Express a book you like in terms of a journey.
10. Express something about your behavior in terms of actors and acting.

C. Look back over the list of twenty types of analogies on pages 213 to 214. On your paper, write an original analogy that would serve as another example of each type. Use the form

:   ::   :   .

THINKING IT THROUGH: WORKING WITH ANALOGIES

Give yourself about an hour to complete the following analogy test. Before you start, number a sheet of paper 1 to 100. As you work through each analogy, *be sure to look at all possible choices and pick the best one.*

Analogies can be written in a number of ways. This test will give you practice in dealing with three of them. Items 1 to 33 and 34 to 66 are written in the two forms introduced in the chapter. Items 67 to 100 are written in the "long form" frequently found in analogy tests:

MOUSE : CHEESE ::
a. mole : ground
b. cheese : butter
c. man : vegetable
d. child : candy
e. car : gasoline

Choice *d,* of course, is the best one. The only reasonable alternative is *c,* but traditionally men do not love vegetables as mice love cheese and children candy. Analogies in the "long form" take more time to do, but the form itself should give you no trouble.

When you finish, check your responses with the answers on page 240. Don't worry about your mark or the time it took to finish the test. Look back over the test and see whether you can discover the reasons for your mistakes. If

216   you have trouble with any of the items, discuss your uncertainties with your teacher.

1. TRAFFIC : CAR :: CROWD : a) person b) noise c) truck d) danger e) children

2. HOUSE : SHINGLES :: MAN : a) hand b) heart c) head d) hiccups e) hair

3. QUESTION: ANSWER :: PROBLEM : a) puzzle b) solution c) help d) mathematics e) success

4. GLASS : DIAMOND :: BRASS : a) bronze b) jewelry c) gold d) silver e) plumbing

5. RAIN : HAIL :: WATER : a) vapor b) pond c) ice d) sky e) winter

6. BEAVER : DAM :: ROBIN : a) nest b) egg c) worm d) song e) air

7. TRIPLETS : TWINS :: TRICYCLE : a) wagon b) carriage c) bicycle d) unicycle e) triangle

8. SIDEWALK : FOOT :: STREET : a) path b) car c) traffic d) wheel e) cement

9. SOLDIER : ARMY :: SAILOR : a) ship b) port c) sea d) navy e) uniform

10. PLUS : MINUS :: PROFIT : a) business b) sale c) bankruptcy d) gain e) loss

11. COT : BED :: COTTAGE : a) building b) door c) cheese d) room e) house

12. HAND : PENCIL :: MOUTH : a) breathing b) lip c) talking d) pipe e) teeth

13. RIVER : TROUT :: JUNGLE : a) man b) malaria c) monkeys d) plants e) heat

14. FUEL OIL : FURNACE :: ELECTRICITY : a) battery b) air conditioner c) spark d) house e) wire

15. PURSUE : CHASE :: COMMAND : a) order b) obey c) ignore d) shout e) army

16. INFINITY : ZERO :: EVERYONE : a) someone b) several c) everybody d) few e) no one

17. HORSE : FARMER :: RABBIT : a) clover b) fox c) bunny d) magician e) cage

18. TELEVISION : NEWSPAPER :: PICTURE : a) frame b) diagram c) film d) advertising e) print

19. LIGHTENING : THUNDER :: SIGHT : a) sound b) pleasure c) vibration d) insight e) flash

20. LIPSTICK : FACE :: NAIL POLISH : a) beauty b) fingernail c) cuticle d) brush e) hand

21. OWL : WISDOM :: ANT : a) colony b) speed c) initiative d) size e) work

22. YEAR : DECADE :: DECADE : a) era b) century c) millennium d) ten e) month

23. STATE : COUNTY :: COUNTY : a) town b) country c) election d) block e) neighborhood

24. INCITE : RIOT :: IGNITE : a) match b) roar c) fire d) fear e) rock

25. GOAT : BROWSE :: COW : a) eat b) chew c) swallow d) graze e) drink

26. REPLY : ANSWER :: SUMMIT : a) bottom b) top c) rear d) beginning e) important

27. I : OURSELVES :: YOU : a) yourself b) your own self c) yourselves d) themsleves e) theirselves

28. BEAR : FLY :: FISH : a) swim b) eat c) walk d) see e) learn

29. UNITED NATIONS : CHINA :: UNITED STATES : a) Iowa b) South Carolina c) California d) Texas e) Florida

30. SQUARE : TRIANGLE :: PENTAGON : a) pyramid b) cone c) octagon d) rectangle e) line

31. TASTE : ACRID :: SMELL : a) nose b) sweet c) mild d) sharp e) aroma

32. BLUSH : EMBARRASSMENT :: LAUGH : a) amusement b) joke c) cruelty d) relaxation e) cry

33. WORLD WAR I : WILSON :: WORLD WAR II : a) Eisenhower b) Marshall c) Roosevelt d) Johnson e) Nixon

34. $\dfrac{\text{RING}}{\text{MARRIAGE}} = \dfrac{\text{TASSEL}}{\quad}$ a) divorce b) corn c) graduation d) college e) fertility

35. $\dfrac{\text{MOUSE}}{\text{RAT}} = \dfrac{\text{CRAB}}{\quad}$ a) claw b) sea c) invertebrate d) lobster e) whale

36. $\dfrac{\text{SEARCH}}{\text{FIND}} = \dfrac{\text{STRIVE}}{\quad}$ a) forget b) starve c) lose d) fail e) succeed

37. $\dfrac{\text{JOY}}{\text{SMILE}} = \dfrac{\quad}{\text{FROWN}}$ a) sadness b) smile c) illness d) bad debts e) face

218

38. $\dfrac{\text{BEGINNING}}{\text{END}} = \dfrac{\text{BOW}}{\quad}$

a) shoe b) courtesy c) stern d) knot e) play

39. $\dfrac{\text{STORY}}{\text{TALE}} = \dfrac{\quad}{\text{MOVIE}}$

a) book b) film c) plot d) photography e) suspense

40. $\dfrac{\quad}{\text{EARTH}} = \dfrac{\text{EARTH}}{\text{SUN}}$

a) moon b) Saturn c) Mars d) milky way e) comet

41. $\dfrac{\text{GENERAL MOTORS}}{\text{FORD MOTOR CO.}} = \dfrac{\text{CADILLAC}}{\quad}$

a) Ford b) Mercury c) Imperial d) Continental e) Volkswagon

42. $\dfrac{\text{COLD}}{\text{BOILING}} = \dfrac{\text{HEAT}}{\quad}$

a) thawing b) freezing c) thermometer d) ice e) burning

43. $\dfrac{\quad}{\text{CATERPILLAR}} = \dfrac{\text{FROG}}{\text{TADPOLE}}$

a) bird b) cocoon c) leaf d) egg e) moth

44. $\dfrac{\quad}{\text{SEAMANSHIP}} = \dfrac{\text{HORSE}}{\text{HORSEMANSHIP}}$

a) sea b) boat c) sail d) navigation e) port

45. $\dfrac{\text{SHOVEL}}{\text{BULLDOZER}} = \dfrac{\text{ARROW}}{\quad}$

a) bow b) target c) war d) bullet e) skill

46. $\dfrac{\text{NAIL}}{\text{HOUSE}} = \dfrac{\text{LETTER}}{\quad}$

a) number b) syllable c) word d) sentence e) book

47. $\dfrac{\quad}{\text{ARTIST}} = \dfrac{\text{SERMON}}{\text{PREACHER}}$

a) painting b) paints c) sculptor d) gallery e) easel

48. $\dfrac{\text{SWARM}}{\quad} = \dfrac{\text{HERD}}{\text{COW}}$

a) goose b) goat c) bee d) gazelle e) guru

49. $\dfrac{\text{THREE-QUARTERS}}{\text{ONE-HALF}} = \dfrac{\quad}{\text{SIXTEEN}}$

a) eight b) twelve c) twenty d) twenty-four e) twenty-eight

50. $\dfrac{\text{SWORD}}{\quad} = \dfrac{\text{QUILL}}{\text{BALLPOINT}}$

a) handshake b) knife c) cut d) gun e) fight

51. $\dfrac{\text{VEAL}}{\quad} = \dfrac{\text{BROILER}}{\text{FOWL}}$

a) beef b) pork c) mutton d) lamb e) venison

52. $\dfrac{\text{FORGET}}{\text{REMEMBER}} = \dfrac{\text{OMIT}}{\quad}$

a) remove b) overlook c) paraphrase d) include e) condense

53. $\dfrac{\text{SCHOOL}}{\quad} = \dfrac{\text{HOSPITAL}}{\text{SICKNESS}}$

a) knowledge b) teachers c) pupils d) cooperation e) ignorance

54. $\dfrac{\text{COMEDY}}{\text{TRAGEDY}} = \dfrac{\text{LAUGH}}{\quad}$

a) look b) cry c) drama d) murder e) momentum

55. $\dfrac{\text{FUTURE}}{\text{PAST}} = \dfrac{\text{ANTICIPATION}}{\quad}$

a) present b) fun c) enjoyment d) expectation e) recollection

56. $\dfrac{\text{TEETH}}{\text{BRUSH}} = \dfrac{\text{HAIR}}{\quad}$

a) ribbon b) comb c) tonic d) wig e) lanolin

57. $\dfrac{\text{EGG BEATER}}{\quad} = \dfrac{\text{FAN}}{\text{AIR}}$

a) bowl b) cake c) kitchen d) hand e) batter

58. $\dfrac{\text{SINCE}}{\text{BECAUSE}} = \dfrac{\quad}{\text{ALSO}}$

a) moreover b) consequently c) although d) whatever e) for instance

59. $\dfrac{\text{AIR}}{\quad} = \dfrac{\text{SEA}}{\text{SALT}}$

a) space b) bird c) oxygen d) nitrogen e) carbon dioxide

60. $\dfrac{\text{CREDIBLE}}{\quad} = \dfrac{\text{FLAMMABLE}}{\text{INFLAMMABLE}}$

a) untrustworthy b) incredible c) believable d) creditable e) debatable

61. $\dfrac{\text{CONNECTICUT}}{\text{HARTFORD}} = \dfrac{\text{OHIO}}{\quad}$

a) Cleveland b) Cincinnati c) Columbus d) Chillicothe e) Canton

62. $\dfrac{\text{SUBJECT}}{\text{PREDICATE}} = \dfrac{\text{ACTOR}}{\quad}$

a) make-up b) action c) script d) stage e) actress

63. $\dfrac{\text{TOUCHDOWN}}{\text{FOOTBALL}} = \dfrac{\quad}{\text{BASEBALL}}$

a) inning b) base c) run d) slide e) short stop

64. $\dfrac{\text{JUMPER}}{\text{SKIRT}} = \dfrac{\quad}{\text{TROUSERS}}$

a) runner b) cuff c) belt d) suit e) overalls

65. $\dfrac{\text{LAND}}{\text{ISTHMUS}} = \dfrac{\text{SEA}}{\quad}$

a) ocean b) coast c) inlet d) canal e) peninsula

66. $\dfrac{\text{IF}}{\text{THEN}} = \dfrac{\text{NOT ONLY}}{\quad}$

a) so b) and c) etc. d) to e) but also

67. SECOND : MINUTE ::
   a) week : month
   b) month : year
   c) year : decade
   d) day : week
   e) minute : hour

68. MINIATURE : SMALL ::
   a) happy : birthday
   b) huge : short
   c) colossal : large
   d) mountain : hill
   e) space : time

69. PENNY : DIME ::
   a) dime : nickel
   b) dime : quarter
   c) dime : fifty-cent piece
   d) dime : dollar
   e) nickel : silver

70. BEAUTY : ATTRACTION ::
   a) ugliness : repulsion
   b) terror : despair
   c) sorrow : grief
   d) fear : anger
   e) power : corruption

71. SNOOZE : SLEEP ::
   a) nibble : eat
   b) watch : wait
   c) listen : hear
   d) speak : talk
   e) gallop : trot

72. PEANUT BUTTER : BREAD SLICE ::
   a) over : under
   b) bottom : top
   c) outside : inside
   d) between : among
   e) by : through

73. DIET : REDUCE ::
   a) overeat : happiness
   b) smoke : cancer
   c) cease : desist
   d) budget : save
   e) food : calories

74. PEA : BEAN ::
   a) pork : beans
   b) lemon : orange
   c) rice : potato
   d) clam : chowder
   e) carrot : potato

75. INFLATION : MONEY ::
   a) goods : services
   b) stoutness : food
   c) death : eating
   d) poverty : employment
   e) politician : voter

76. MONKEY : APE ::
   a) worm : snake
   b) rhinoceros : elephant
   c) bird : bee
   d) tail : tree
   e) vertebrate : invertebrate

77. THIN : SKINNY ::
   a) nervous : nervy
   b) ill : sick
   c) stingy : economical
   d) intelligent : brainy
   e) pen : pencil

78. PETROLEUM : POWER ::
    a) iron : steel
    b) coal : heat
    c) diamonds : forever
    d) copper : electricity
    e) earth : soil

79. ACRE : LAND ::
    a) sextant : sea
    b) pint : quart
    c) fence : field
    d) hour : time
    e) town : township

80. KNOWLEDGE : WISDOM ::
    a) vitamins : minerals
    b) insight : sight
    c) fact : fancy
    d) skill : art
    e) white : black

81. DICTIONARY : ENCYCLOPEDIA ::
    a) sense : sound
    b) order : disorder
    c) connotation : denotation
    d) curiosity : ambition
    e) words : topics

82. COMPOSER : SYMPHONY ::
    a) conductor : orchestra
    b) carpenter : house
    c) mechanic : wrench
    d) sculptor : statue
    e) printer : book

83. FOOT : STEP ::
    a) eye : ear
    b) hand : mouth
    c) mouth : bite
    d) thing : idea
    e) stride : stumble

84. SCHOOL : GRADUATES ::
    a) hospital : sickness
    b) prison : rehabilitation
    c) factory : products
    d) army : soldiers
    e) church : ceremonies

85. LISTEN : HEAR ::
    a) run : move
    b) taste : swallow
    c) doubt : belief
    d) look : see
    e) find : search

86. COMPASS : CIRCLE ::
    a) ruler : line
    b) yardstick : foot
    c) arrow : direction
    d) tape measure : inseam
    e) speedometer : speed

87. THERMOMETER : TEMPERATURE ::
    a) illness : fever
    b) stethoscope : doctor
    c) x-rays : bones
    d) scale : weight
    e) glasses : vision

88. GOLD : NUGGET ::
   a) rock : stone
   b) gasoline : kerosene
   c) silver : fork
   d) water : pail
   e) wood : chip

89. CLOTH : SEAMSTRESS ::
   a) fox : hunter
   b) baby : babysitter
   c) wood : cabinet maker
   d) laws : judge
   e) chalk : teacher

90. BLACK : MARKET ::
   a) red : light
   b) green : vegetables
   c) blue : ribbon
   d) white : lie
   e) green : light

91. MISTAKE : EMBARRASSMENT ::
   a) clarity : confusion
   b) achievement : pride
   c) glory : grief
   d) routine : elation
   e) success : sadness

92. DAISY : ORCHID ::
   a) flower : fragrance
   b) hamburger : frankfurter
   c) muslin : satin
   d) chrome : steel
   e) pottery : plate

93. ISLAND : CONTINENT ::
   a) lake : ocean
   b) gulf : sea
   c) mountain : prairie
   d) continent : isthmus
   e) peninsula : land

94. CAT : MOUSE ::
   a) evil : virtue
   b) intelligence : stupidity
   c) person : marionette
   d) God : man
   e) predator : prey

95. BLUEPRINT : HOUSE ::
   a) seed : plant
   b) photograph : painting
   c) pattern : dress
   d) teacher : education
   e) cookbook : casserole

96. MOTOR : ENGINE ::
   a) girl : boy
   b) boy : girl
   c) person : woman
   d) man : woman
   e) non-humans : humans

97. HORSEPOWER : TRUCK ::
   a) candlepower : electricity
   b) candlepower : candle
   c) candlepower : watts
   d) candlepower : lamp
   e) candlepower : light bulb

98. PYRAMID : TRIANGLE ::
   a) box : cube
   b) cube : rectangle
   c) rectangle : angle
   d) angle : line
   e) line : point

99. RED : STOP ::
   a) green : jealousy
   b) blue : sadness
   c) black : grief
   d) yellow : caution
   e) white : innocence

100. LIGHT : DARK ::
   a) concave : convex
   b) silence : sound
   c) heat : cold
   d) evil : virtue
   e) poetry : prose

Thinking Straight— and Even Straighter

Words warp thought. The lens of language focuses our perception and often distorts our ideas. We might say that although words make thinking possible, they frequently make *straight* thinking impossible. For thinking straight is easier talked about than done. We need to be aware of the changing territories that underlie our mental maps. We need to remember several semantic traps: the either-or fallacy, subject-predicate thinking, elementalism, etc.

Words also win arguments. How often, in a dispute with someone, have you felt that although you had all the facts, your opponent had all the words? You knew that something was wrong with his reasoning,

but you didn't know quite what. This chapter will ask you to place yourself in a series of imaginary situations. As you read each of them, see whether you can tell what's wrong with the other person's reasoning. Then read the explanation that follows.

Your purpose in reading this chapter should be to learn to recognize certain kinds of faulty reasoning. Don't worry too much about the Latin terms used for some of the errors of argument. They are used here only because, over many, many years, they have come to be identified with certain forms of argument. Their purpose is neither to confuse you nor to help you confuse others.

How Not to Say "No"

At the intermission in a school dance, you find yourself outside with a boy you like but don't know well. He offers you a little yellow pill, which you decline.

He: Why not?
You: Sorry. I guess I'm just not a pill-popper.
He: That's not a reason. That's just stubbornness.
You: Well, I just don't know exactly what would happen.
He: All that's going to happen is that you're going to feel great tonight.
You: But I don't feel bad now.
He: Look—you just have to swallow one time and you're going to feel even better. It's as simple as that.
You: Well. . . .

Assuming that a cause has only one important effect can be called STRAIGHT-LINE THINKING. It is "thinking straight" at its worst. In the example above, the boy concentrates only on the effect of the pill during the next few hours. What about the effect the next day? What about the effect on your self-image? What about the effect on your thinking the next time you're offered an unfamiliar pill? The boy's faulty cause-to-effect reasoning is not quite as "simple" as it seems to be.

We can seldom know all the significant effects of a single cause. For this reason, some straight-line thinking is unavoidable. Still, bad examples are much too easy to find. For instance, one school purchased a number of expensive "teaching machines." Experiments had shown that students using these machines learned more in less time than they did in the average classroom. In the minds of the school authorities, the machines were seen as a cause and increased learning was seen as an effect. In practice, the machines proved to have another effect. Once the novelty wore off they began to bore the students. They quickly lost their advantage over the typical classroom tools. Today the machines gather dust in the boiler room. Straight-line thinking had cost the school a lot of unnecessary money.

The Miracle Cure

You have stopped to visit your grandmother during a vacation trip. You are surprised to find that her arthritis is much improved. You are even more surprised at the reason she gives.

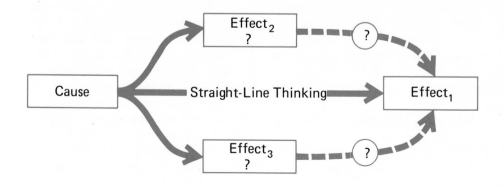

She: I suppose you've noticed this thick copper bracelet I'm wearing.

You: Yes, I did see it.

She: Well, it's cured my arthritis, almost completely.

You: Really?

She: The doctors don't believe in it yet. But it's been proven, all across the country. A copper bracelet cures arthritis.

You: That's amazing, but I just don't really see how . . .

She: Then just look at me! I put this bracelet on six months ago. I felt much better in two weeks, and I haven't had a really bad spell since.

You: I know, but . . .

Your grandmother, of course, has no real proof that the bracelet has cured her arthritis. She knows only that she started feeling better *after* she put it on. In her reasoning, however, the word *after* has become *because* she put it on. This fallacy is usually called POST HOC ERGO PROPTER HOC (after the fact, therefore because of the fact).

Examples are common. Suppose Mr. A votes for Mr. Z to be President of the United States. Mr. Z wins, and the country prospers for a year. Mr. A reasons that things are going well because of Mr. Z's election. He doesn't know that the rising business cycle would have brought prosperity no matter who had become President. Again, *after* has become *because. Post hoc ergo propter hoc.*

A Modest Proposal

Your father, a dairy farmer, blames his continually rising costs on "ex-orbitant" settlements won by labor unions. Not a union man himself, he feels that labor is to blame for many of the country's problems. He often states that labor unions put their own selfish interests above the national interest. Because you have grown up in his household, you tend to agree with him. Now you are arguing the question with a girl whose father is a local union official. The argument drags on and on. Finally she turns to you in irritation.

She: Really, I don't see how you can support such a weird idea.

You: Weird. Why?

She: Don't you know that Adolf Hitler made the labor unions put the national interest above their own interests?

You: Well, I didn't know that but . . .

She: Of course! Hitler said that the purpose of organized labor was to glorify the state. How can you stand there and argue like a Nazi?

This form of argument is known as ARGUMENTUM AD HOMINEM (argument to the man). What your opponent has done, of course, is to attack an *idea* by denouncing a *man* connected with it. She has tried to discredit your views by associating them with one of the most detestible men in recent history. But what is the logical connection? The original argument concerned the role of labor unions in modern-day America, not their role in Germany (1935). Your ideas, right or wrong, should be considered on their own merits. They would be the same ideas even if Adolf Hitler had never existed.

Not long ago *argumentum ad hominem* brought grief to an English teacher who served as publications advisor. She discovered at the last minute that the yearbook committee had neglected to select a motto. To satisfy the printer's demands, she hurriedly picked up a book of quotations and found something good: "From each according to his abilities, to each according to his needs." The teacher didn't know—and didn't notice—that the quote came from the founder of communism, Karl Marx. When the yearbook appeared, with the year's motto prominently featured, the teacher was fired. No one, apparently, attacked the motto itself. It was simply assumed that because it came from Karl Marx, it had to be contemptible and un-American.

Take Your Stand

You are trying to dispute the views of someone who is very alarmed by the population problem. He is sure that unless something is done, and quickly, starvation for millions is just around the corner.

He: I just can't understand your point of view.

You: I admit there's a population problem, but I think you're being an alarmist about it.

He: Me an alarmist? I think you're being incredibly cruel.

You: Cruel?

He: Yes. Don't you realize that in another four generations every person on earth will have only one square yard of land to stand on?

What do you say to such a person? You tell him that it's illogical to engage in ARGUMENT FROM ABSURD EXTREMES. Obviously no one can imagine a functioning world in which everyone is given one square yard of ground. The picture is an absurdity. Even though your opponent's basic

view may be correct, it isn't correct for him to carry your side of the argument to the point of ridicule.

Almost any reasonable opinion can be carried to the point of absurdity. If we argue for more pollution controls, our opponent will inform us that our measures will result in "the economy grinding to a complete standstill." If we argue for stricter gun controls, we will be told that "the criminals will keep their guns and take over the country." Persons who carry our moderate opinions to preposterous lengths should be asked to prove that their absurdities are possible.

Just a Matter of Semantics?

Once again you find yourself (a boy) drifting into what has become a weekly argument with your father. A successful plumbing contractor, he has long planned to send you through college to a master's degree in business administration. You have other ideas: a college degree in art and a master's in education.

He: Well, I just don't see where all this art and education is going to get you.

You: What do you mean, "going to get" me?

He: Don't you want some goal in life?

You: Sure, I want to teach art.

He: That's a goal? I thought I was raising my son to be a man!

At this point, you would probably shake your head and leave the room. The trouble is that your father has defined *goal* and *man* his way, not yours. He is engaging in ARGUMENT FROM DEFINITION.

228   We often argue from definition without realizing it. This type of dispute is seldom settled, since it really concerns words, not what the words stand for. For example, not long ago a group of scientists busied themselves for a time with the question of whether man is instinctively aggressive. "Yes," said one group of specialists, "man is aggressive by instinct." Another group, examining the same facts, reached the opposite conclusion: "No, aggression is not a human instinct." The argument continued until it was realized by all that the issue was a VERBAL QUESTION. The answer depended not on the evidence but on the definition of *instinct*. As a non-semanticist might say, it was "just a matter of semantics."

Needed: A Verbal Defense

Like most young men, you're worried about someday having to serve in the Army. The issue is doubly troublesome for you because you honestly believe you're becoming a pacifist. You think war—any war—is a senseless waste of human life and energy. Now you're discussing the question with a friend who believes that no individual should have the right to decide the question of war for himself.

He: I think your attitude is pure selfishness.

You: Selfishness? No, it's just the opposite. I'm putting *humanity* first.

He.   All right, suppose you were married and had a couple of kids. War breaks out with China. Would you go?

You: No, I would not.

He: Now suppose a lot of people are like you. They won't fight. China invades the country. A couple of Chinese soldiers walk into your house. One grabs your wife and the other starts smashing your kids in the head. Wouldn't you fight to defend your family?

You: Of course I would.

He: So what's the difference? National defense is just collective family defense.

Your friend is obviously a skilled debater. He's carried your argument close to an absurd extreme. He's also used a FALSE ANALOGY. That is, he's tried to suggest that because two things are alike in some respects, they are alike in all respects:

$$\frac{you}{family} = \frac{armed\ forces}{country}$$

An analogy is a statement that two relationships are alike in some respects, not in every way imaginable. Analogies should be used to clarify and explain, never to prove. That man is related to the ape does not mean that apes should study semantics. That a man should defend his family in an emergency does not mean that he should shoot at Orientals in far-off rice paddies. He may think it proper to do so, but we can hope he has better reasons. (Thinking It Through 1, page 232.)

A Familiar Mental Pattern

You are sitting in a school assembly a few days before student council elections. Four eager candidates for president have been alloted seven minutes each for speeches. One candidate, a girl you don't know personally, impresses

you. She spends half her time explaining why the council needs a "real activist" as president. Then she gives her qualifications as a "real activist." She finishes: "I think you all know that this year only a real activist should be president. My experience proves that I am a real activist. Therefore, I feel that I am the best qualified candidate, and I sincerely seek your support. Thank you very much."

The girl's conclusion sounds impressive, you think. But why? One reason, probably, is that the candidate has arranged her material in the form of a syllogism (SIL-uh-jiz-um). That it is a FAULTY SYLLOGISM goes unnoticed, the syllogistic form is so impressive!

A syllogism is a time-honored form of argument with two premises or statements and a conclusion. Here is an ancient example:

Major premise: All men are mortal.
Minor premise: Socrates is a man.

Conclusion: Therefore, Socrates is mortal.

Syllogisms are common in our everyday thinking:

Major premise: If it's raining outside, I should wear a raincoat.
Minor premise: It's raining outside.
Conclusion: Therefore, I should wear a raincoat.

In fact, the syllogism is so common that its very form affects our thinking. When we hear a syllogism, we are convinced by the shape of the argument as well as by its substance:

Major premise: A real activist should be president.
Minor premise: I am a real activist.
Conclusion: Therefore, I should be president.

Look at this syllogism closely. Notice that even though we might accept both premises as true, the conclusion does not follow logically. It is therefore a faulty syllogism. There could be another "real activist" available who would make an even better president. Replacing the terms with others makes this clear:

Major premise: A woman should someday be President of the United States.
Minor premise: I am a woman.
Conclusion: Therefore, I should someday be President of the United States.

Unfortunately, the formula *premise + premise = conclusion* seems as impressed on our minds as is $2 + 2 = 4$. Beware the faulty syllogism! (Thinking It Through 2, page 232.)

You're Wrong and I'm Right

As a native and resident of California, you are understandably proud of your state. Not long ago a new girl moved in a couple of doors down the street. Her family came from Florida, and she seems to detest California. She likes to argue, and she is always managing to prove that Florida is bigger or better in some way. One day she drops the remark that Florida has the longest coastline of any state.

You: It does not. California does.
She: You're so wrong it's funny.
You: I can prove it. There's an old encyclopedia upstairs. You take the "F" and I'll take the "C."
You (later): Found it yet?
She: Florida has 1350 miles of coastline.
You (with a groan): California has 840.
She: Looks like I win again.

Has she won, really? She has proved that you are wrong, that California does not have the longest coastline of any state. But has she proved herself right? Certainly not. In fact, Alaska's coastline is much longer than Florida's. Both of you were wrong. She has claimed victory only by trapping you in a FAULTY CONTRADICTION.

In a true contradiction, if one statement is right, the other must be wrong (and vice versa):

Statement 1: The far side of the moon is made of green cheese.
Statement 2: The far side of the moon is not made of green cheese.

Logically, both these statements cannot be right. Neither can both be wrong. If either is right, the other must be wrong. In an argument, one could win by proving the other side to be false.

A faulty contradiction is an argument in which both sides could possibly be false:

Statement 1: The far side of the moon is made of green cheese.
Statement 2: The far side of the moon is made of moldy pastrami.

Green cheese or moldy pastrami? In an argument, we could not prove that one statement is right simply because the other is wrong. Yet more often than we realize, this is the form of our arguments. They are faulty contradictions. We cannot prove that Florida has the longest coastline by showing that California does not. We cannot prove that democracy is the best form of government by pointing to the evils of communism. We cannot prove that our religion is the true faith by pointing out apparent weaknesses in certain other religions. (Thinking It Through 6, page 238.)

Reviewing the Key Points

> 1. Don't let faulty reasoning affect your own thought, and don't let others use it to win arguments.
> 2. Be alert to the common traps:
>
> | | |
> |---|---|
> | straight-line thinking | argument from definition |
> | *post hoc ergo propter hoc* | false analogy |
> | *argumentum ad hominem* | faulty syllogism |
> | argument from absurd extremes | faulty contradiction |

Getting It Straight

A. Look back over the chapter and note the types of faulty thinking that appear in small capitals. Copy the terms on a sheet of paper and think about each carefully. If you don't know what a term means, reread the portion of the chapter devoted to it. Then, without looking back, try to match the terms with the following definitions:

1. An argument that attacks a person associated with an idea rather than the idea itself.
2. A comparison that uses true similarities in an attempt to prove similarities that have no basis in fact.
3. A question that really involves not the evidence at hand but the meaning given a word (or words).
4. A form of argument that carries the opposing viewpoint to a ridiculous length.
5. A form of argument with two premises and a conclusion that does not follow logically.
6. The fallacy that because X precedes Y, X causes Y.
7. A form of argument that relies on the special meanings given to certain words.
8. A form of reasoning that fails to consider all possible effects of a single cause.
9. An argument in which both sides could possibly be wrong.

B. Which type of faulty reasoning would you associate with each of the following? List your answers on your paper.

1. "Don't listen to anything she says: she's going to a shrink."
2. " 'When I use a word,' Humpty-Dumpty said, 'it means just what I choose it to mean—neither more nor less.' " (Lewis Carroll)
3. "Well it hasn't happened since, has it?"
4. "An elderly lady friend of mine [had] gone down and down to the point where medicines no longer had any helpful effect on her, and I told her I could cure her in a week. I said she must give up smoking and drinking and eating and swearing, and by the end of the week she'd be on her feet. Why, she said, she couldn't give up smoking and drinking and

swearing because she'd never done any of those things. So there it was: she'd neglected her habits. She was a sinking ship with no freight to throw overboard. I guess one or two little bad habits would have saved her." (Mark Twain)

5. "But you have to agree with me now! I've just knocked your whole argument full of holes."

THINKING IT THROUGH: REASONING ABOUT REASON

1. Prove yourself innocent

One kind of false analogy is that which results in GUILT BY ASSOCIATION. Suppose Mr. A is frequently seen in the company of Mr. B. They often go to the racetrack together and sometimes visit a German restaurant afterwards. Then one day Mr. A is caught with a small box of pure heroin in the trunk of his car. The arrest gets wide publicity. In the public mind, Mr. A is judged guilty. Mr. B is judged guilty too—because of his association with Mr. A.

Obviously, Mr. A and Mr. B are similar in some respects. They enjoy going to the races, and perhaps they share an interest in German food. But to brand Mr. B a criminal simply because of Mr. A's arrest is to make a false analogy.

Have you ever been accused of wrongdoing simply because of your associations? Most people have, at one time or another. Perhaps you were accused of smoking because you happened to be in a smoke-filled room when the Assistant Principal walked in. Guilt by association is not easy to take. If it has ever caused you to suffer, write out the situation briefly on paper. In your opinion, was there any escape from the situation? Discuss the probable results of different kinds of efforts you might have tried to make to demonstrate your innocence. Then read your paper to the class.

2. Finding hidden premises

Sometimes it's hard to remember that syllogisms are common in our everyday thought. After all, most people don't walk around saying to themselves: "Premise 1: . . . Premise 2: . . . Conclusion: . . ." But they do engage in syllogistic thinking. Consider the following conversation:

Joe: I'll bet your uncle's got lots of money.
Moe: Why?
Joe: Well, he drives a big Cadillac and always wears new clothes.

A little thought will reveal the syllogism in Joe's mind:

Premise 1: All men who drive big Cadillacs and wear new clothes have lots of money.

Premise 2: Moe's uncle drives a big Cadillac and wears new clothes.
Conclusion: Therefore, Moe's uncle has lots of money.

One reason we fail to recognize the syllogisms in our thought is that Premise 1 often goes unstated. Premise 1 is usually a broad, general truth that we assume to be true in all particulars. Since universal statements often have exceptions, Premise 1 can easily be wrong, leading to a faulty conclusion:

Premise 1: All fat people eat too much.
Premise 2: Mildred is fat.
Conclusion: Therefore, Mildred eats too much.

It is possible, of course, that Mildred suffers from a glandular imbalance and eats very little. It is also possible that Moe's uncle is deeply in debt for his car and his clothes. In each case it was Premise 1, the general truth, that was wrong.

For a day or so, try to reconstruct the syllogisms behind the remarks you hear. Even the most casual statements often proceed from syllogistic thought: "Mr. Jones will be a grouch today." "It'll rain for sure this afternoon." Try to discover five, preferably ten, syllogisms. Write them out formally with two premises and a conclusion. Then look carefully at all the first premises. Can you find even one that is true without exception? If possible, ask the persons who made the remarks if they would consider their hidden premises to be universally correct statements. If you find any first premises you think are always true, discuss them in class. Does everyone agree? Many of our faulty conclusions come from premises that are both hidden and unsound.

3. Diagramming your syllogisms

The conclusion of a syllogism can be wrong for two reasons. First, as shown above, one (or both) of the premises can be incorrect (although a true conclusion can occasionally proceed from faulty premises). Second, the conclusion can fail to follow logically from the premises:

Premise 1: All dogs have four feet.
Premise 2: My cat has four feet.
Conclusion: Therefore, my cat is a dog.

Another example:

Premise 1: Only rich men own yachts.
Premise 2: My uncle is a rich man.
Conclusion: Therefore, my uncle owns a yacht.

In trying to discover whether a conclusion follows logically from certain premises, you might find it helpful to diagram the syllogism. A helpful model for such a diagram is one based on this syllogism:

Premise 1: All A's are B's.
Premise 2: All B's are C's.
Conclusion: Therefore, all A's are C's.

234   If we consider A's, B's, and C's as dots enclosed within circles labeled with these letters, we can diagram the syllogism step by step:

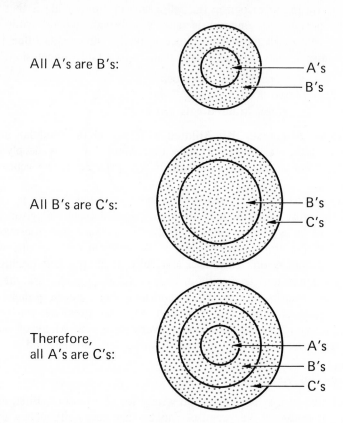

All A's are B's:

All B's are C's:

Therefore,
all A's are C's:

Using this technique for the syllogism about "all dogs" and "my cat," we get the diagram shown below. Notice that the "cat" circle is not inside the "dogs" circle. The syllogism does not prove that a cat is a dog.

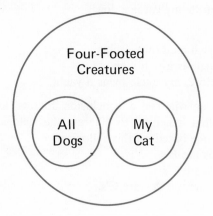

The syllogism about rich men owning yachts fools us because the terms in the first premise are not in their normal order. If "only rich men own yachts," then "all yacht owners are rich men." Starting the syllogism with this last statement, we get the diagram shown below.

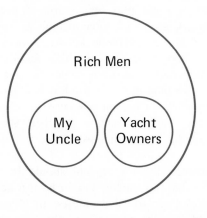

If you did exercise 2 above, you probably encountered at least two syllogisms that puzzled you. Were they logical or not? Clarify these syllogisms by putting them in diagram form. If you haven't met any questionable syllogisms of your own, try diagramming the following:

Premise 1: All alcoholics like a good drink.
Premise 2: Some politicians like a good drink.
Conclusion: Therefore, some politicians are alcoholics.

Premise 1: All Puerto Ricans are United States citizens.
Premise 2: Some New Yorkers are Puerto Ricans.
Conclusion: Therefore, some New Yorkers are United States citizens.

4. Sense and non-sense

This is a book on semantics and critical thinking. It is not a text on formal logic. If it were, you would probably be asked to memorize the time-honored "Laws of Thought":

Law of Identity: If anything is A, it is A.
Law of Contradiction: Nothing can be both A and not A.
Law of the Excluded Middle: A thing must be either A or not A.

In other words, the law of identity might state that if anything is a truck, it is a truck. The law of contradiction would then state that nothing in the world can be both a truck and a non-truck. The law of the excluded middle would state that each thing in the world has to be either a truck or a non-truck.

For about two thousand years, these laws have been used as guides to straight thinking. The modern semanticist, however, has his doubts. In his view, the laws seem to work best when we are dealing with imaginary A's, B's, and C's.

That is, as laws of *thought* they seem nearly infallible. In this sense, they are like the laws of mathematics and geometry: "2 + 2 = 4"; or "a triangle is a stable figure; a square is not a stable figure."

The trouble with the laws of both thought and mathematics is that they are a kind of map language. They often break down when applied to real territories. Two quarts of sugar plus two quarts of water do not equal four quarts of sugar water. A group of three people is not more stable than a group of four. And as almost everyone knows, American factories turn out thousands of vehicles every year that combine features of cars and trucks. Are they trucks or non-trucks? In some states, a panel truck or small van with a back seat and more than one side window is classified as a truck for tax purposes, but as a non-truck for use on special roads closed to trucks. In some states marshmallows are candy (taxable); in others they are non-candy (not taxable). The things of the extensional world are not the imaginary A's, B's, and C's of our minds.

The semanticist believes that the student should be aware of the laws of thought. He also thinks that the student should have a healthy distrust of them. Trucks and marshmallows are trivial examples. In identifying what they are— or are not—the laws of thought give way to the laws of the state. But other examples are not so trivial. For instance, no legislature has ever determined what a *friend* should be. According to the laws of thought:

Identity: A friend is a friend.

Contradiction: No one can be both a friend and not a friend.

Excluded Middle: Everyone must be either a friend or not a friend.

This kind of thinking can do more harm than good. Consider first the law of identity. The expression "a friend is a friend" (as in, "well after all, a friend is a friend") packs a meaning not even suggested by "A is A." Now think about the statement produced by the law of contradiction. In your experience, is it correct? Don't you know people you classify as friends for certain purposes and as non-friends for others? And as for the law of the excluded middle, don't you know people who go around classifying everyone they know as friends or non-friends? We know too well what such people are like!

Choose two of the following terms to place in the formulas of the laws of thought. In a paragraph for each term, explain how strict use of the laws could have disastrous results in these cases.

ally	talent(ed)	honest(y)
enemy	sin(ful)	black

(Note: the laws of thought are associated with the Greek philosopher Aristotle. Alfred Korzybski believed that most traditional thinking reflected what he called an *aristotelian system.* To describe his own modern, scientific system, Korzybski chose the term *non-aristotelian,* or *non-a.* You may encounter the term in other books on semantics.)

5. Going around in circles

If you can think back to yourself as a four-year-old, you can probably remember conversations like this one:

Question: Daddy, why doesn't that lawnmower work?
Answer: Because it's broken.

Question: Why is it broken?
Answer: Because it doesn't run.

Question: Why doesn't it run?
Answer: Because the motor won't start.

Question: Why won't it start?
Answer: Because it's broken. . . . Etc.

Nowadays, probably, you move in different circles:

Question: Dad, can I take the car over to Joe's tonight?
Answer: No, not tonight.

Question: Well, when *can* I take the car out?
Answer: When you're old enough.

Question: When will I be old enough?
Answer: When you can take the car out. . . . Etc.

Answering in this way is sometimes called BEGGING THE QUESTION. We beg the question when we use as evidence for a conclusion some necessary part of the conclusion itself. To state, in effect, "you're not old enough because you're not old enough" is to beg the question. The reason given simply restates the conclusion. Consider another example:

Ann: Senator X has his faults, but he's a truthful politician.
Jan: How do you know?
Ann: He said in his last speech that he never told a lie in thirty years of politics.

Ann is begging the question. She is using as evidence the very conclusion she is trying to defend. In order to believe what Senator X *says* about his truthfulness, we first have to believe that he is, in fact, truthful.

Begging the question is common in all walks of life. No doubt you remember being told never to start a book report with the threadbare sentence, "I liked this book because it is interesting." The sentence is a poor one because it begs the question. Obviously, a person "likes" something he finds "interesting." This is what *interesting* means. With little loss of meaning, the sentence might be rewritten, "I liked this book because I liked this book." The conclusion itself is being used as evidence.

Instances of begging the question often sound ridiculous when we pause to think about them. ("I don't like rhubarb because it tastes so awful!") For the next few days, alert yourself to examples of begging the question. Listen particularly for the word *because.* In most cases, what follows should really be a *cause,* not simply a restatement of an effect or a conclusion. Listen also for answers that aren't really answers, that just restate the question or conclusion. Try to find at least one humorous or ridiculous example of begging the question. Write it down to share with the class.

6. Role playing

Identifying types of faulty reasoning is one thing. Learning to deal with them is quite another. Practice the skill by placing yourself in each of the following five situations. Your first task will be to recognize the flaw in the other person's thinking. Then you must decide what response to make. If you said this or that, what would the other person probably say? You might choose to continue the argument, using your opponent's fallacies against him. Or you might choose to try to stop the argument temporarily. This would allow you to analyze your opponent's thinking for him—with labels and diagrams, if you think proper.

Continue the situations by role playing in class. If your teacher has assigned you the part' labeled "other" beforehand, take time to work up your emotions and perhaps to do some research.

1. As a talented artist, you are asked to be on the decorating committee for a big school dance. You try to decline since you don't plan to attend the dance yourself. (In fact, you have never been to a school dance.) You can't see why you should do the work necessary for someone else's fun. Now you meet the chairman of the decorating committee in the hall.

Other: Look, we just can't let all your talent go to waste.
You: Thanks, but there *are* other people, you know.
Other: I'm not talking about other people. I'm talking about you.
You: Sorry, but my answer's still—
Other: Now that's a very poor attitude!
You: Why?
Other: We've got a whole gym to decorate. Suppose everyone had your attitude. Suppose everyone said *no!*
You: (?)

2. A good friend of yours worships modern jazz. You can take it or leave it. Actually, you would rather leave it when it comes to the latest jazz group, "The Lepers."

Other: Hey, I just bought the latest Lepers record. How about coming over to the house for the first listen?
You: Honestly, it just doesn't do anything for me.
Other: It's great. Don't you know that?
You: Why is it great?
Other: It's great because it's the best thing to come along in five years, that's all.
You: (?)

3. You're home alone one afternoon when the doorbell rings. It's a man selling a burglar alarm device. You tell him that you're not the head of the house, that you have little money, and that frankly, you're not interested. But he persists. Finally you see that he won't leave until your refusal approaches rudeness.

You: Look, I told you I'm not going to buy it.
Other: Well, I think if you understood—
You: Nine ninety-five for that little piece of junk?
Other: Little, yes. But the Burgalert is not junk!
You: Prove it.
Other: It's good protection because it keeps the robbers outside where they belong.
You: That's just begging the question.
Other: Huh?
You: I said prove it.
Other: Well, our tests show that over ninety per cent of homes protected by this little marvel have not been entered unlawfully since the device was installed.
You: (?)

4. One of your friends is a conservative hard-liner on most social issues. One day she announces that she has a solution for the drug problem in the United States. You listen with interest, expecting the death penalty at the very least. Her cure surprises you.

Other: Drugs are a problem only because we've made them a problem by making them illegal and scarce.
You: You mean—
Other: Sure. Remove all restrictions. Let drugs circulate as freely as mothballs or peanuts. Who ever heard of a peanut problem?
You: But I don't see—
Other: Don't you think that if bread were outlawed we'd have a big bread problem?
You: But with drugs, the problem would remain, wouldn't it?
Other: With more housing, how could we have a housing problem? With more employment, how could we have an employment problem?
You: (?)

5. Your father, a star debater in his school years, has long urged you to join the Debating Club. The idea just doesn't appeal to you. For one thing, you're always busy appearing in school plays. For another, although you like to argue interesting topics with friends, you can't see yourself standing up on a stage and debating formal resolutions according to formal rules. Now, early in the school year, your father brings up the subject again:

Other: What about the debating team this year?
You: No, I don't think so.
Other: It sure did a lot for me. I know how to arrange my facts and present them so that my side wins. And I still don't lose many arguments.
You: That's one of the troubles, Dad. All this fuss over sides and points and winning. In semantics class we learned that discussion has it all over debate.
Other: Huh?

240 You: Yes. Debates are two sided, so they encourage two-valued orientations. In a debate you attack or defend; you don't cooperate. You deal with solutions that are already found, not with finding new solutions. Your aim is to influence people, not to invite them to participate. And as for truth—

Other: No, that's all bunk.

You: Why?

Other: Because you just don't have the winning spirit it takes to get up on a stage and use words as weapons—that's why!

You: (?)

Answers to analogy test on page 216:

1. a	21. e	41. d	61. c	81. e
2. e	22. b	42. b	62. b	82. d
3. b	23. a	43. e	63. c	83. c
4. c	24. c	44. b	64. e	84. c
5. c	25. d	45. d	65. d	85. d
6. a	26. b	46. e	66. e	86. a
7. c	27. c	47. a	67. e	87. d
8. d	28. c	48. c	68. d	88. e
9. d	29. c	49. d	69. d	89. c
10. e	30. d	50. d	70. a	90. d
11. e	31. d	51. a	71. a	91. b
12. d	32. a	52. d	72. a	92. c
13. c	33. c	53. e	73. d	93. a
14. b	34. c	54. b	74. b	94. e
15. a	35. d	55. e	75. b	95. c
16. e	36. e	56. b	76. b	96. c
17. d	37. a	57. e	77. d	97. d
18. e	38. c	58. a	78. b	98. b
19. a	39. b	59. e	79. d	99. d
20. e	40. a	60. c	80. d	100. c

The Last Word: Semantics and a Sane Future

This survey of semantics and critical thinking has been but a brief look at the field. The rest is up to you. If the book has given you some useful insights into the way people think, talk, and behave, make use of them. Semantics is a subject to be used, not to be tested on today and forgotten tomorrow.

Needless to say, you shouldn't pretend that because you've read one book, you're prepared for all the problems of life—even for all the verbal problems. No single book can do this. No one theory is going to make much of a difference. No one idea is going to change the world. People who say that words by themselves have power are talking nonsense.

*Books, theories, ideas, words—*these terms are from the language of maps, not of territories. They point up the fact that a little semantic learning can be a dangerous thing. The danger is that we can easily tumble into a tempting mental trap of our own making. We can become so attracted to semantics as a subject of study that we forget about semantics as a way of life. We can forget that theory and practice go together. It's not enough to take comfort in the belief that the world would be a better place if only everyone were a semanticist. Of course it would! To say that people who really understood each other would get along better is begging the question at its worst. Strangely, the study of semantics sometimes results in the creation of an unattainable dream world.

The place to start is with *your* world. This is the only world you know, the only world you can know. The future of this world is the future of you. If you want to make it a better place, think about becoming a semanticist. Why not? Semanticists are simply people from all walks of life who have a common interest in language, thought and behavior. They are rich and poor, young and old, urban and rural, liberal and conservative. They are engineers, teachers, businessmen, students, doctors, lawyers, and perhaps even Indian chiefs. Few of them are considered "professors of semantics" or "professional semanticists." The term is not a title as much as it is a quality.

Courses in semantics are now offered by many colleges. Groups of people interested in semantics meet regularly in cities throughout the country. Two non-profit organizations serve as headquarters for semantic inquiry and education. Each issues an excellent periodical and distributes catalogs of books on semantics and related subjects. These organizations are:

Institute of General Semantics
Lakeville, Conn. 06039

International Society for General Semantics
P.O. Box 2469
San Francisco, Calif. 94126

One final word: On the cover of this book, and on several of the inside pages, is a picture of an egg. It's not an ordinary photograph, for only half the egg can be seen clearly. You have probably wondered about it: "Why an *egg?*" "Why the lights and shadows?" "What does it mean?"

Well, what *does* it mean? If you know, you're a semanticist right now. Welcome.

Finding the Significant Terms

abstraction, 142
agreements, 114
allness attitudes, 72
analogy, 212
argument from
    absurd extremes, 227
    definition, 227
argumentum ad hominem, 226
Aristotelian system, 236
autosuggestion, 198

"bandwagon" technique, 180
begging the question, 237
"big lie" technique, 177

"card stacking" technique, 179
classifying, 53
"common enemy" technique, 180
concrete poetry, 98
connotation, 56
contexts, 48

dating, 75
denotation, 56

"ear-mindedness," 7
ecology, 166
"either-or" thinking, 110
elementalism, 157
"etc.," 74
euphemism, 58
extensional
    devices, 73
    orientation, 19
"eye-mindedness," 8

false analogy, 228
faulty
    contradiction, 230
    syllogism, 229

general semantics, 18
glittering generalities, 177
gobbledegook, 8
grammarian, 45
guilt by association, 232

indexing, 76
inferences, 114, 181
Institute of General Semantics, 242
intensional orientation, 19
International Society for
    General Semantics, 242

jumping to conclusions, 120

Korzybski, Alfred, 17

laws of thought, 235

lexicographer, 45

magic words, 57
maps and territories, 19
meanings of words, 48
metaphor, 210
multi-valued orientation, 111
mumbo jumbo, 10

name calling, 179
non-Aristotelian system, 236
non-verbal communication, 93

observations, 114
operational definition, 16

perception, 29
"plain folks" technique, 179
post hoc ergo propter hoc, 226
projection, 33
propaganda, 176
propaganda techniques, 177
psittacism, 194

quotes, 74

reification, 158
reports, 114

Science and Sanity, 18
self-adjustment, 191
self-fulfilling prophecy, 192
self-image, 191
selling the image, 180
semantic reactions, 100
semantics, 15
sign, 3
"soft soap" technique, 177
space signals, 96
stereotyped thinking, 76
straight-line thinking, 225
structural differential, 141
syllogism, 229
symbol, 3

testimonial, 177
time signals, 97
transfer, 177
triangulation, 164
two-valued orientation, 110

unconscious communication, 94

value judgments, 115
verbal
    barking, 9
    pollution, 4
    questions, 228

word magic, 57, 181

243

Acknowledgments

We thank the following authors and companies for their permission to use copyrighted material:

JULIAN BACH LITERARY AGENCY, INC.—for cartoon "Eat" by Saul Steinberg, copyright © 1960 by Saul Steinberg. Reprinted by permission of Julian Bach Literary Agency, Inc.

FABER AND FABER LIMITED—for Canadian rights to reprint "The Animals" by Edwin Muir from *Collected Poems 1921–1958*.

FOLLETT PUBLISHING COMPANY—for "Re" by Vito Hannibal Acconci, from *The Young American Poets* edited by Paul Carroll. Copyright © 1968 by Follett Publishing Company, division of Follett Corporation. Reprinted by permission.

HARPER & ROW PUBLISHERS, INC.—for material from p. 54 in *Handling Barriers in Communication* by Irving J. Lee and Laura L. Lee. Copyright © 1956, 1957 by Laura L. Lee. By permission of Harper and Row Publishers, Inc.

HOLT, RINEHART AND WINSTON, INC.—for excerpt from *Social Psychology* by Otto Klineberg, © 1940.

HORIZON PRESS,—For permission to reprint photos (pages 51–52) by Harry Lebelson from *Images of Our Time,* copyright 1971, by permission of the publisher, Horizon Press, New York.

THE ALFRED KORZYBSKI ESTATE—for permission to reproduce two pictures of the Structural Differential from pages 388 and 393 of *Science and Sanity: An Introduction to Non-aristotelian Systems and General Semantics* by Alfred Korzybski, published by International Non-aristotelian Library Publishing Company, distributed by Institute of General Semantics, Lakeville, Conn., 1st ed. 1933, 4th ed. 1958.

MC GRAW-HILL BOOK COMPANY—For drawing "Dog$_1$ is not Dog$_2$" (page 77) by Ted Key. From *How to Develop Your Thinking Ability* by Kenneth S. Keyes, Jr. Copyright 1950. Used with permission of McGraw-Hill Book Company.

WILLIAM MORRIS AGENCY, INC.—for a selection entitled "A Mother's Vigilance" from "The Five Warring Tribes of South Africa" by James A. Michener, published in *The New York Times Magazine* of January 23, 1972. Reprinted by permission of William Morris Agency, Inc., on behalf of author. Copyright © 1972 by Marjay Productions, Inc.

NEW DIRECTIONS PUBLISHING CORPORATION—for "How to Be An Army" from *Collected Poems* by Kenneth Patchen. Copyright 1943 by Kenneth Patchen. Reprinted by permission of New Directions Publishing Corporation.

OXFORD UNIVERSITY PRESS—for "The Animals" from *Collected Poems* by Edwin Muir. Copyright © 1960 by Willa Muir. Reprinted by permission of Oxford University Press, Inc.

PARENTS' MAGAZINE PRESS—for excerpt from *Danger—Men Talking!* by Stuart Chase, copyright © 1969 by Stuart Chase. Reprinted by permission of Parents' Magazine Press.

THE SATURDAY REVIEW—For drawing "Deer Crossing" by Ed Fisher (page 50) Copyright © 1955 by The Saturday Review Associates, Inc. First appeared in *Saturday Review,* October 8, 1955. Used with Permission.—for drawing "Moby Dick" by Ed Fisher (page 58). Copyright © 1954 by The Saturday Review Associates, Inc. First appeared in Saturday Review, November 6, 1954. Used with permission.

SOMETHING ELSE PRESS—for "Apfel" by Reinhard Dohl, "Silencio" by Gomringer, "Rendering" by Bremer, from *An Anthology of Concrete Poetry,* Emmett Williams,